LA RAZA COSMÉTICA

Critical Issues in Indigenous Studies

NATASHA VARNER

LA RAZA COSMÉTICA

BEAUTY, IDENTITY, AND SETTLER COLONIALISM

IN POSTREVOLUTIONARY MEXICO

THE UNIVERSITY OF
ARIZONA PRESS

TUCSON

The University of Arizona Press
www.uapress.arizona.edu

ISBN-13: 978-0-8165-4207-9 (hardcover)
ISBN-13: 978-0-8165-3715-0 (paperback)

Cover design by Leigh McDonald
Cover art by Jesús Heguera
Typeset by Leigh McDonald in Adobe Jensen Pro [10.5/14] and Brandon Grotesque [display].

Publication of this book is made possible in part by the proceeds of a permanent endowment created with the assistance of a Challenge Grant from the National Endowment for the Humanities, a federal agency.

Library of Congress Cataloging-in-Publication Data
Names: Varner, Natasha, 1981– author.
Title: La Raza Cosmética : Beauty, Identity, and Settler Colonialism in Postrevolutionary Mexico / Natasha Varner.
Description: Tucson : The University of Arizona Press, 2020. | Series: Critical issues in indigenous studies | Includes bibliographical references and index.
Identifiers: LCCN 2020011823 | ISBN 9780816542079 (hardcover) | ISBN 9780816537150 (paperback)
Subjects: LCSH: Indian women—Mexico—Social conditions—20th century. | Women in popular culture—Mexico—History—20th century. | Visual metaphor. | Mexico—Race relations—History—20th century.
Classification: LCC F1219.3.W6 V37 2020 | DDC 305.48/897072—dc23
LC record available at https://lccn.loc.gov/2020011823

CONTENTS

List of Illustrations   vii

Acknowledgments   ix

Introduction   3

1. *La reina de la raza*: The Making of the *India Bonita*   24

2. La Flor más Bella del Ejido: Springtime Maidens, Invented Tradition,
and Making a "Modern" Mexico City   49

3. *Cine folclórico*: From Racial Fantasy to Cinematic Spectacle   77

4. Virgén Xochimilco: Pure Women and Waters in Mexico City's
Suburban South   99

5. Doña Luz Jiménez: "The Most Painted Woman in All of Mexico"   122

Conclusion   146

Notes   153

Bibliography   175

Index   181

ILLUSTRATIONS

1.   India Bonita contestant Gudelia Castillo   29

2.   María Bibiana Uribe and María Conesa appear on stage
     together at El Teatro Colón   39

3.   Photo of María Bibiana Uribe that ran in U.S. and Mexican
     newspapers   41

4.   Carmen Aguilera, the working-class queen of the Fiesta de Flores
     the year of the festival's rebirth   55

5.   *Indias bonitas* and *chinas poblanas* with almost indistinguishable
     styling   58

6.   Matilde Urzais "personifying" an Indigenous woman from
     San Pedro Ixcatlán, Oaxaca   64

7.   Announcement of María Palma's victory   71

8.   Judges appraise pageant contestants   74

9.   Elena Sánchez Valenzuela in character for the film *En la hacienda*   83

10. Sergei Eisenstein directs the filming of *Que viva México*   85

11. Still from the 1938 film *La india bonita*   89

12. Mexican Tourist Association poster ca. 1910–1959   106

13. Advertisement for Xochimilco featuring modern transport, water,
     and an *india bonita* in equal measure   108

14. Dolores del Rio at a baptism in Xochimilco   112

15. José María Fernández Urbina's *El fuente de los cántaros* (1927)   123

16. José Clemente Orozco's *Cortés and Malinche*, in the Colegio del San Idelfonso featuring a depiction of Luz Jiménez   132

17. Luz Jiménez and her daughter Concha with a group of well-to-do compatriots   136

18. Luz Jiménez with the painter Manuel Rodríguez Lozano in the courtyard of a school where they worked together   141

19. Photograph Luz sent to Jean Charlot in 1962   142

20. Display in the 2018 Museo Nacional de Antropología exhibit *La flor en la cultura mexicana*   147

ACKNOWLEDGMENTS

AM INDEBTED FIRST AND FOREMOST to the Indigenous women whose stories fill these pages. Luz Jiménez, María Bibiana Uribe, María Palma, Petra Hernández, the unnamed actress in "La campesina," and so many others. I also thank the families of the people I write about and especially Jesús Villanueva Hernández, who opened his personal archives to me and who so generously shared his perspectives on his grandmother's life.

This book would not have been possible without support from mentors, colleagues, family, and friends. I am deeply grateful to Kelly McDonough for helping to define the path I took in my research, for introducing me to the family of Luz Jiménez, and for providing guidance and encouragement throughout the dissertation and manuscript revision process. In addition to Kelly, I am indebted to others in the Indigenous studies scholarly community, many of whom I connected with initially through my work as program coordinator for the First Peoples: New Directions in Indigenous Studies publishing program. That position and my engagement with the Native American and Indigenous Studies Association (NAISA) exposed me to ideas and conversations for which I will forever be grateful.

Several individuals from the NAISA community have been particularly influential: Philip Deloria, Shannon Speed, Emil Keme (aka Emilio del Valle Escalante), J. Kēhaulani Kauanui, Michelle Erai, Rose Stremlau, Robert Warrior, Damien Lee, Karyn Recollet, Coll Thrush, Jean O'Brien, Jennifer

Denetdale, Qwo-Li Driscoll, Scott Morgenson, Kyle Mays Wabinaw, Joseph Genetin-Pilawa, Jim Buss, Rayna Green, Cutcha Rising Baldy, Lisa Kahaleole Hall, Angela Pulley Hudson, Margo Tamez, Beth Rose Manning, Tsianina Lomawaima, Daniel Heath Justice, Chris Andersen, Danika Medak-Saltzman, Mishauna Goeman, Jodi Byrd, Amy Lonetree, Leah Sneider, Alyssa Mt. Pleasant, Malinda Maynor Lowery, and countless others.

Faculty members at the University of Arizona have generously counseled me throughout the process of writing this manuscript. William Beezley has enthusiastically fostered the development of this project from the outset. Jennifer Jenkins pushed me intellectually while also providing warm encouragement and mentorship. Kevin Gosner encouraged me to think about postrevolutionary Mexico in a broader historical and global context, while Thomas Sheridan encouraged me to seek out and include Indigenous voices whenever possible and modeled this admirably in his own work. Katherine Morrissey helped me develop a framework for interpreting photographs and provided sage counsel on numerous occasions. Melissa Fitch provided a cultural studies education that allowed me to read popular culture images more deeply. Her early enthusiasm and encouragement motivated me to pursue the PhD. Maribel Alvarez, Martha Few, and Stephanie Buechler also shaped the project through conversation and mentorship.

This book has also benefited from fellow alumni of the University of Arizona history department: Pete Soland, Rocio Gomez, Joshua Salyers, Allison Huntley, Anabel Galindo, Marco Macias, Shayna Mehas, David Wysocki Quiros, Kelley Castro, Kathryn Gallien, Amie Kiddle, Ryan Kashanipour, Adrian Mendoza, Lisa Munro, Ageeth Sluis, Diana Montano, John Klingemann, Aurea Toxqui, Elena Jackson Albarrán, Jeffrey Bannister, Ryan Alexander, Matthew Furlong, Tracy Goode, Collin Deeds, and Stephen Neufield. María Muñoz has been a mentor and friend by pointing me to critical sources, asking well-timed and incisive questions, and introducing me to *mezcalinis* and other wonders of Mexican cuisine. Cory Schott has been supportive as a sharp-witted friend and confidante, both in Tucson and in my new home in the Pacific Northwest. Michael Matthews familiarized me with Mexico City archives, including the Archivo General de la Nación and the Biblioteca Lerdo de Tejada, and made my first summer of research in Mexico City infinitely more interesting than it would have been without him there.

At the Oaxaca Summer Institute, I had the opportunity to immerse myself in fruitful conversations with an inspiring group of scholars. David Wysocki

Quiros and David Reid felt like family for a summer, and conversations with them broadened my thinking about my research and about Mexican history in general. I also cherished the intellectual exchanges I had with other participants, organizers, and scholars: Bill French, Ricardo Pérez Montfort, Anne Rubenstein, John Mraz, Mary Kay Vaughn, Monica Rankin, Ann Blum, Kevin Chrisman, Megan McDonie, Janett Barragán Miranda, Tyler Shooty, and Itandehui García López.

I am grateful to have had the counsel and support of numerous other scholars along the way, including Zeb Tortorici, Laura Gutiérrez, Nicole Guidotti-Hérnandez, Julie Prieto, Yunuen Rhi, Rick López, Luke Smith, and Kirstin Erickson. In the Pacific Northwest, José Antonio Lucero, Adam Warren, and John Lear have brought me in to their university communities and enriched my work through conversation and feedback. Vanessa Freije has been a dear friend and writing partner whose counsel and comradery have been essential to the completion of this manuscript.

My friends and colleagues at Densho, especially Tom Ikeda, have been immensely supportive of my work and allowed me the time and space necessary to pursue research opportunities and occasional writing retreats. Further, the racial equity training and facilitation work I have been supported in doing at Densho have deeply informed my frameworks for examining the historical roots of racism and settler colonialism. Barbara Yasui, Daryn Wakasa, Michael Ishii, Nancy Ukai, Nina Wallace, Erin Shigaki, Caitlin Oiye Coon, Janet Hayakawa, Danielle Higa, Jason Matsumoto, Tsuya Yee, Satsuki Ina, Stanley Shikuma, Frank Abe, Sharon Yamato, Joemy Ito-Gates, Chizu Omori, and especially Hana Maruyama are all due special recognition in the development of my intellectual growth in this area.

Research trips to Mexico City were more productive and fun thanks to historian friends with whom I've shared that time. I thank Susan Deeds for sharing her warmth, wisdom, brilliance, cooking, and hospitality. And thanks to Carmen Nava for sharing her encyclopedic knowledge of Mexican history and so kindly letting me consult her home library. Thanks also to Tracy Goode for providing research support in several archives and for hosting her famous pizza parties that helped so many of us historians connect with one another in Mexico City.

My deep thanks to my editor and friend Kristen Buckles for being an early advocate for my work and for so ably advising me as I worked to revise my dissertation into a publishable manuscript. Thanks also to everyone else at the press who has shepherded this project through to completion: Stacey Wujcik, Leigh McDonald, Kathryn Conrad, and Abby Mogollon. The five anonymous peer reviewers who commented on my book proposal and manuscript offered invaluable insight that fundamentally shaped this project. I am deeply appreciative of the time and consideration they gave to my work. And thanks to Myla Vicenti Carpio and Jeffrey Shepherd for including my work in the Critical Issues in Indigenous Studies series and for the helpful feedback and support they offered as editors of that series.

Other friends in the publishing world have also supported my academic and professional pursuits for more than a decade. Christine Szuter was so inspiring in her integrity and leadership that the examples she set have influenced my scholarship and my entire professional career. Mark Simpson Vos, Jason Weidemann, Mary Braun, Lisa Pacheco, Lela Scott MacNeil, Scott DeHerrera, and James Brooks all shared professional insights and tips that have strengthened my book project.

Many thanks to all the archivists whose meticulous work allows us historians to do what we do, but especially to Bronwen Solyem. During my trip to consult the Jean Charlot collection, her knowledge was invaluable to my research on Luz Jiménez. My thanks to the Jean Charlot Foundation for providing funding that made that trip possible. Essential funding for the completion of this project also came from the Lewis Hanke Post-Doctoral Award offered by the Conference on Latin American History, so I thank the awards committee for selecting my project.

I am fortunate to have gifted writers and thinkers in my life whose intellect, friendship, love, and wisdom have sustained me and made me a better writer. Thank you Gina Balibrera Amyx, Brenna Fitzgerald, Mari Hayman, and Shaun Scott. Angilee Shah, my first editor at Public Radio International and now a friend, also offered incisive and unflinching feedback that has taught me invaluable lessons on how to write about history in a way that is digestible for general audiences.

This book is dedicated to my family, whose love has fueled my curiosity and drive from the beginning: to my sister Alana Varner, whose intellectual interests and passions are so closely aligned with mine and never cease to inspire me; to my dad, whose work with the Navajo Nation exposed me to the complexities of Indigenous and settler histories long before I had the words to talk about them; to Sarah Wolter, who is more sister than cousin, and whose friendship and love are foundational to everything I do; to Kathy, who is more soul mother than aunt and who fostered a lifelong sense of adventure and appreciation for writing craft; to my grandmother, Victoria—I think about you every day and wish you were here to see this; to the entire Allen family for cultivating a sense of justice, kindness, and a deep appreciation for writing and the arts, all with a healthy dose of humor and joy; and to my mom and Bob, whose love and support made this all possible.

LA RAZA COSMÉTICA

INTRODUCTION

N THE OPENING SEQUENCE OF the 2010 Miss Universe competition, eighty-three bombshells wearing cartoonish renditions of their national symbols shimmied and strutted across television screens. There was a leather-clad Italian gladiator, a leggy Peruvian scissor dancer, and a sultry Costa Rican peacock. In this parade of hypersexualized nationalism, Miss Mexico appeared a world apart. Ximena Navarette, who hails from Guadalajara, walked stiffly onto the stage, straining to balance an enormous sequined headdress topped by an undulating crown of feathers. Navarette's costume, according to its designers, was fashioned to invoke Yum Kaax, a Mayan god associated with wilderness, forests, and agriculture.[1] At stage center she paused to display her costume and stiffly turn her head from side to side, lips pursed into a tight smile.

This awkward embodiment of a Mayan deity might have left uncritical viewers thinking it was simply a sign of Mexico's pride in its Indigenous heritage. Perhaps the beauty queen's embrace of Indigenous iconography tugged at the patrimonial heartstrings of Mexican viewers, but the costume also pointed to a paradox with deep historical roots. Beneath the golden aura of sequins laid a tangled web of appropriation, representation, erasure, and dispossession that has characterized the position of Indigenous peoples in Mexican national identity narratives since the nation's inception.

While Miss Mexico's 2010 costume may have feigned to celebrate Mayan religion, Mayan women themselves were all but explicitly barred from entry in the pageant. The qualifying competition for Miss Universe, Nuestra Belleza de México, limits participation to contestants who are five feet, five inches or taller and requires competitors to cover their own travel and costuming costs.[2] As a result, only a certain class and type of woman can participate. And a survey of recent winners makes clear that only lighter-skinned mestizas even have a shot at winning.

Twenty-one-year-old Ximena Navarette went on to win the Miss Universe crown in 2010. It was a happy coincidence for Mexico since the country was in the midst of a nationalist reverie celebrating the centennial of the start of the revolution and the bicentennial of Independence. The newly crowned beauty queen returned home to adoring fans and dignitaries. President Felipe Calderón hosted her in the presidential palace and praised her, saying "This will serve Mexico and our image as a country."[3] Navarette appeared as a guest of honor at the centennial and bicentennial celebrations later that fall.[4] She was the woman of the moment, but the melding of appropriated Indigenous symbolism, European beauty standards, and *Mexicanidad* that carried her to victory was nothing new.

This book turns to an era that was critical to the contemporary creation of Mexican national identity. It examines the Cultural Revolution (1920–1946) as a project of settler colonialism that continues to reverberate today.[5] Through a focus on popular beauty culture—from beauty pageants, cinema, and tourism propaganda to photography and murals—I show how Mestizaje and popular understandings of Indigeneity were fundamentally structured by legacies of colonialism as well as shifting ideas about race, place, and gender. In a complex interplay of appropriation and erasure, Indigenous peoples were, as María Josefina Saldaña-Portillo puts it, "at once summoned to appear everywhere as the foundation of Mexican character and instructed to disappear into the more perfect union of Mestizaje."[6] And although Indigenous women were rarely granted opportunities for self-representation, I center their voices whenever possible in order to show that they weren't merely passive recipients of an imposed identity. On the contrary, reading against the archival grain reveals the many meaningful ways Indigenous women strategically engaged with and resisted the currents of postrevolutionary nationalism.

FROM "INDIAN PROBLEM" TO AZTEC NATIONALISM

Over the course of a decade of revolutionary warfare that began in 1910, as many as two million men, women, and children lost their lives. As the violence waned, Mexican leaders turned to the urgent task of rebuilding their nation. In order to stabilize their country, they needed to integrate a diverse populace, quell ongoing battles, and restore their economy and international reputation. A unifying narrative of national identity could help by constructing a foundation on which postrevolutionary society could be built. Mexico had crafted an origin story before—following Independence and again during the regime of Porfirio Díaz (1876–1910). Leaders of the fledgling postrevolutionary state had material to work with, but what good is a revolution if it doesn't change everything? Leaders turned to invented traditions and formulas that had been successful in the past but polished them with a modern, populist veneer.[7]

Parallel to the concerns of restoring peace and crafting a unified identity was an issue framed in the racist rhetoric of the time as the "Indian Problem." This "problem" posited that poor and often rural-dwelling Indigenous peoples whose ancestors had survived centuries of colonization were innately backward and an impediment to national progress. Efforts to control and contain this population began with the conquest and were later absorbed into the foundations of Mexican nationhood. The 1857 constitution attempted to simply write the Indigenous population out of existence by eliminating the term *Indian* and by making organizations based on race or ethnicity illegal.[8] Later, Porfirio Díaz and his cronies took extreme measures in order to displace, dispossess, and eliminate Indigenous peoples.

The violent tactics of the Porfiriato existed in tandem with celebrations of select aspects of Indigenous cultures. In the Porfirian universe, this symbolic inclusion privileged stone relics of past peoples, an impulse that particularly favored the Aztecs.[9] This selective glorification rested upon a racist hierarchy that ranked Indigenous groups according to European models of progress—since the Aztec system of governance and rule was in some ways relatable to European empires, they were presumed to be more civilized than other Indigenous groups. While Díaz helped popularize the celebration of Aztec heroes, the thinking that informed his actions long predated his rule. During the French occupation, Emperor Maximiliano (1864–1867) deemed Aztec artifacts worthy of display in the Louvre and identified Cuauhtémoc as a hero.[10]

This campaign resonated enough that in a speech delivered shortly after Maximiliano's execution, President Benito Juarez, himself a Zapotec, identified Mexicans as the heirs to "the Indigenous nationality of the Aztecs."[11] The publication of the massive historical tome *México a través de los siglos* (1887–1889) further established the Aztec empire as a precursor to the modern nation in the Mexican imaginary.[12]

The ideology that wed Aztec identity with Mexican nationalism may have had deep roots, but Díaz expanded the trope. Over the course of his thirty-five-year regime, he recognized that adopting the discourse introduced by Maximiliano and aligning himself with the progenitors of the nation would strengthen the legitimacy of his dictatorship and potentially improve his nation's standing in the world.[13] Implementing this vision, Díaz's government funded major archaeological digs, hosted public festivities on the occasion of notable discoveries, and created monuments and museums that helped link his regime to a noble past. Mexico's pavilion at the 1889 Paris World's Fair brought the modern reinvention of the Aztecs to a global stage and left a legacy of relics and statuary that to this day stand as enduring reminders of the Porfirian reimagining of the nation's most revered heritage.[14]

Beginning in the 1920s, the postrevolutionary elite "revised but did not abandon Porfirian national memory" in their quest to unify the nation.[15] They saw that violence, property seizures, and forced removals of Indigenous peoples ultimately stoked unrest. While Mexico didn't retire these tactics, those in power began employing more subtle means of enacting submission and erasure. Aware that certain aspects of Indigenous material culture could be of value in the process of retooling Mexican national identity, those leading the efforts expanded from pre-Hispanic stone relics to include elements of contemporary cultures. A new paradigm based on appropriation and assimilation gained popularity among those most concerned with rebuilding the nation and fixing the "Indian Problem." Like Porfirian formulations, postrevolutionary nationalism often favored Aztec heritage. In many early postrevolutionary endeavors especially, Nahuatl-speaking peoples were favored over other Indigenous groups because they were seen as being the closest living heirs to the Aztec empire.

Thanks to developments in the social sciences, timeworn national identity concerns and efforts to control Indigenous populations could be incorporated into the "modern" pursuit of knowledge. By the early 1920s, the field of anthropology had expanded beyond its grave-robbing origins to encompass the study of living peoples and their languages, bodies, and material cultures. Mexico's high priest of anthropology, Manuel Gamio, interpreted the revolution as a "popular mandate for the fusion of the races" and positioned his field as being the discipline most fit to help the postrevolutionary government become "unified, healthy, and progressive."[16] Gamio's work was critical to the development of postrevolutionary nationalism and Indigenismo,[17] a complex network of policies and practices that valorized select components of Indigenous heritage while also imposing misguided reforms intended to better Indigenous lives.

Gamio advanced ideas that shaped Indigenismo for decades to come, arguing that Indigenous peoples were not inferior and that their cultures needed to be documented, salvaged, celebrated, and incorporated into broader society.[18] He and the anthropologists that followed in his footsteps helped define popular understandings of Indigenous authenticity, codified cultural ideals and hierarchies, and disseminated those ideas to the masses through widely translated publications, pageants and other public events, photography, and film. Western intellectualism was thought to be objective and modern, so the field of anthropology was cast as a potential panacea for all social ills. And much in the same way that Orientalism was a manner of restructuring and exerting power over Asia and the Asian diaspora,[19] so, too, did Indigenismo utilize Western theory and praxis to fabricate new understandings of Indigeneity. This, in turn, was used to establish the superiority of Western systems and helped extend the state's reach in governing Indigenous peoples, all with the aim of more thoroughly incorporating them into the nation.

Scholars have tended to view Indigenistas sympathetically, acknowledging their shortcomings but crediting them with at least seeing Indigenous peoples as human. For example, given that Alexander Dawson's work on institutional Indigenismo acknowledges that their assimilationist aims were ethnocidal, his willingness to credit Indigenistas for their good intentions is too generous.[20] Judging the impact of their actions rather than the intent of their words—and doing so within the framework of hemispheric settler colonialism—makes such a benevolent interpretation less viable.

Complementing the integrationist desires of Indigenismo, an ethos of Mestizaje became more finely tuned to fit the needs of the postrevolutionary state. In her book *Indian Given*, Saldaña-Portillo masterfully illustrates how the logics of Mestizaje had been at work for centuries encoded into colonial land-grant laws that favored Spanish-born *peninsulares* who married their Indigenous concubines as a means of remapping the land under Spanish rule and later as an answer to the rigid Spanish caste system.[21] Mestizaje morphed over time, but some version of it remained a constant in Mexican political philosophy. During the Porfiriato, the Científico thinker Justo Sierra posited that cultural and biological mixing were essential to the betterment of the "Mexican race." He argued that miscegenation could serve to temper the less desirable Spanish tendencies and, as Kelly McDonough writes, "in a strange sort of alchemy, remove Catholic dogma, greed, and the perpetuation of social stratification and discrimination, while leaving intact other desirable attributes."[22]

After the revolution, José Vasconcelos further refined and popularized ideas about Mestizaje. In 1925, between stints as the secretary of education and a run for president, Vasconcelos published his manifesto *La raza cósmica*. The book spun a utopian racial fantasy that imagined a new "cosmic race" that blended all of the world's existing races into a "happy synthesis" superior to all others. While this might initially seem progressive in comparison to the antimiscegenation laws in place in the United States at the time, Vasconcelos's plan for social progress ultimately just reproduced white supremacist racial hierarchies. Vasconcelos's imagined *raza cósmica* would be a white race made even greater by appropriating select Indigenous, Black, and Asian traits while simultaneously eradicating the qualities thought to be aberrant in each of those populations.[23] And, as Rick López notes, Vasconcelos was primarily interested in appropriating the "spiritual" qualities of Indigenous peoples.[24] "The Indian," Vasconcelos wrote, "will have no other choice but to diffuse and perfect himself in each of the superior varieties of the species."[25] This new brand of Mestizaje was the ultimate answer to the age-old "Indian problem" in that it promised to erase—or at least dilute—Indigenous populations under the guise of integration and progress.

In addition to Gamio and Vasconcelos, other—mostly male—members of the social elite also had the power to shape and implement the ideals of Indigenismo and Mestizaje. José Puig Causaranc, for example, served the identity project in various capacities: as the author of editorials, as a beauty pageant judge, as the founder of the Casa del Estudiante Indígena experimental school, and as the first mayor of Mexico City once it was incorporated in 1929. By the 1930s, these paradigms had become increasingly institutionalized. President Lázaro Cárdenas (1934–1940) departed from Indigenista thinking in some ways but nevertheless embraced assimilationist arguments that Indigenous peoples were simply "backward proletarians" in need of better government intervention in order to make them fully modern members of the citizenry.[26]

As these identity ideals took shape, leaders and intellectuals grappled with how best to implement them. As a result of competing interests and shifting scientific and social paradigms, there was initially little consensus about how best to move forward with creating a suitably mixed national polity. In fact, there was little agreement about what *Indigenous* even meant. Even though Indigenistas often claimed it was an identity pinned not to race but rather to culture, class, location, and language, they often turned to biological factors and racializing logic in the implementation of their ideas.[27] Well into the 1940s, individuals with divergent visions for social progress grappled with these ideas, and it was not uncommon for them to contradict even their own thinking as slippery definitions of race and ethnicity shifted and evolved. But while the ideas and methods of implementation behind Mestizaje and Indigenismo were in constant flux, they were always after the same thing: the disappearance of Indigenous peoples into a perfectly blended, "modern" society.

Mestizo men were the primary evangelists of Indigenismo and Mestizaje, but the burden for achieving biological and cultural mixing was largely placed on Indigenous women.[28] In the project of "improving the race," Indigenous women's bodies were seen as the necessary channels through which the country would be whitened, modernized, and integrated. In his 1916 book, *Forjando patria*, Gamio described several types of women and selected one—the "feminine type"—as being the ideal progenitor of the new nation. This influential work deemed certain types of Indigenous femininity as being "worthy not just of emulation but of incorporation."[29] Since the dawn of colonial conquest, women had long been imagined as the ones responsible for, quite literally, birthing a new nation. Gamio's assertions gave voice and the authority of scientific objectivity to their role in Mexican nation building. In keeping, healthy motherhood was also of utmost importance in the Indigenista agenda.[30]

The formula for this model of racial progression was encoded in centuries-old colonial logic, at least as old as the story of Hernán Cortés and Malintzín, whose union purportedly resulted in the birth of the first mestizo in 1523. Social taboos prevented Indigenous men from pursuing white or mestiza women, but for European men the act of transgressing racial boundaries to exploit Indigenous women sexually was taken as a right of their colonial inheritance.[31] By the late 1800s, the idea that mestizos were born of unions between white men and Indigenous women had even made its way into American travel writing.[32] Applied to postrevolutionary identity projects, these tendencies grounded abstract discussions of race and ethnicity in individual bodies as the nation searched for solutions to its "Indian Problem."

Under sway of the early twentieth century vogue for all things Aztec, Nahua women were often seen as being most fit for producing the new nation.[33] Social scientists, artists, and intellectuals confirmed this indigenist hierarchy, placing a premium on the racial purity and ethnic authenticity of these "descendants of Moctezuma" as the ideal subjects for incorporating into the national polity.[34] Women from the Isthmus of Tehauntepec, with their famed beauty and iconic starched white headdresses, were also popular symbols of Indigeneity, but they were more often seen as "exotic" than as viable elements of modern society.[35] Where Tehuanas were marked as "fearless" members of a supposedly matriarchal society, Nahua women were consistently presented as being meek and docile. By the 1930s, as the challenges of assimilation became more apparent, bureaucrats and intellectuals turned to more concerted studies of Indigenous diversity in order to better manage the "Indian problem." But even as regional ethnographic studies began to influence policy and official rhetoric, all things Aztec reigned supreme in popular culture emanating out from the nation's capital.

As much as the projects of Indigenismo and Mestizaje purported to be about social improvement, the focal points of these discussions careened around biology, ethnicity, class, superficial mannerisms, and ethnic traits. A specific set of codes and characteristics marked what came to be considered the "authentic" Indigenous woman. This invariably included elements of *traje* (Indigenous dress) such as embroidered huipils (woven blouses), sarapes (shawls), woven belts, long skirts, and sandals as well as braided hair and demure mannerisms. The reliance on these highly gendered ethnic markers underscores the fact that Mestizaje and Indigenismo were not just about race or ethnicity. Instead, ethnic identity, locality, class, and gender mutually constituted these idealized identities. For postrevolutionary nation builders, the solution to the "Indian problem" and an alluring formula for national identity seemed to lie somewhere at the intersection of those overlapping spheres.[36]

CULTURAL REVOLUTION AT THE DAWN OF MASS MEDIA

As postrevolutionary nationalism evolved, the image world of the average Mexican was also being revolutionized. In the early 1920s, a boom in technology introduced a sudden proliferation of images on the streets and in homes:

there were more photographs in newspapers, cinemas cropped up across the country, and printing houses mass-produced calendar art and postcards. Even the murals commissioned by José Vasconcelos for the interior walls of the secretary of public education building were photographed and circulated widely beyond the government offices that housed them.[37] Cameras were lighter, flashes were better, prints cost less to reproduce. The rotogravure replaced the printing press, allowing for images in much finer detail and with more dramatic emphasis of light and shadow.[38] By the 1930s, 35 mm cameras from Europe were in wide use. Filmmaking materials became more affordable, and the government funded a national film industry to produce more domestic films. Sound technology entered the Mexican film scene in 1931, making movies intelligible even to the many illiterate viewers unable to read title cards. By the dawn of the 1940s, novice cameramen and tourists with home movie cameras abounded, and the film industry had entered its golden age.

The postrevolutionary elite saw this tectonic shift in the world of image making as an opportunity. They used the emerging technologies as the scaffolding upon which to construct a complex visual economy of national identity, gender, and racial ideologies.[39] Because illiteracy was so rampant, this popular visual culture was necessary to reach the masses. Following the work of Rick López, this book treats the realm of visual culture as a critical site for exploring the postrevolutionary production of nationalism and identity.[40] The cultural elite used everything from calendar art and postcards to film, photography, and fine art to flood the nation with images and ideals that epitomized their new brand of national identity. Pageants, performances, and festivals, which could now be promoted widely through newspaper photographs and articles, also became critical sites for educating and engaging the populace.

It was not just the proliferation of images that mattered; it was also the means by which those images were generated. The plethora of new gadgets that facilitated mass reproduction appealed to those interested in modernizing the nation. To many, technological advancement signaled objectivity and authenticity. Photography and moving images, in particular, were seen as neutral media that could truthfully represent their subjects. In reality, the producers of these images developed techniques that allowed them to manipulate the affect of their work. Photographer Hugo Brehme, for example, smeared glycerin on his camera lens to blur the image when he wanted to create a dreamy, romantic feel in a photograph.[41] Similarly, filmmakers used camera angles, lighting, and shot construction to manipulate meaning and message. Film and photography were anything but neutral. Even so, these emerging forms of media maintained their reputations for accurately and objectively reproducing reality.[42]

As the nascent postrevolutionary government was occupied with broader pacification endeavors, businessmen who mastered new media technologies were among the crop of leaders who rose to answer the call of unifying the nation in the public sphere. They, too, recognized that integrating the Indigenous populations was key to national stability as well as to the success of their own investments.[43] *El Universal* newspaper publisher Félix Palavicini was one such leader. Palavicini, a self-appointed ambassador of revolutionary doctrine, had cut his teeth as minister of education under the brief administration of Venustiano Carranza, was a signatory of the 1917 constitution, and later ran an unsuccessful campaign for political office.

Palavicini founded *El Universal* in 1916 to be the voice of revolutionary thought and used the paper to host a number of civic contests, congresses, and gatherings throughout the early years of reconstruction.[44] These efforts were aimed at addressing what he saw as some of the nation's most onerous problems, including the incorporation of Indigenous peoples into the national polity. By amplifying his publication's role in nation building, Palavicini enjoyed the added benefit of increasing his newspaper's standing and sales. As such, Palavicini was one of the first civic leaders to successfully marry revolutionary values with capitalist pursuits.[45] And with the constant changes in national leadership throughout the revolution and its early aftermath, Palavicini and his newspaper served as more consistent voices of authority than any state actors. *El Universal*'s national reach meant the paper had the potential to create a sense of unity and cohesion among a disparate populace. The ideologies promoted in the pages of the paper, then, must be weighed in accordance with the pseudostate function it performed.[46]

INVENTING THE *INDIA BONITA*

In keeping with the broader identity projects of the era, women took center stage in visual culture. Flappers, vixens, and *chicas modernas* became increasingly popular icons despite the tremors of moral panic and violence triggered by their bare legs and "unladylike" short locks.[47] *Chinas poblanas* and *Tehuanas* graced screens, stages, and society events. The *india bonita* emerged as another major archetype of the postrevolutionary era. These "pretty Indians" were not real women but rather figments of a nationalist longing for docile Indigenous women who could be neatly folded into the Mexican social order. *Indias bonitas* had existed in the colonial imaginary for centuries, but details of the trope ossified in the aftermath of the revolution. As Adriana Zavala and others have shown, *indias bonitas* were often presented as being passive, meek, and docile; sometimes hypersexualized, sometimes childlike, and often helpless.[48] And because the cultural markers signaling idealized Indigenous femininity had been so clearly defined, anyone could copy and perform them.

India bonita images that proliferated in Mexican calendar art, films, murals, postcards, and advertisements wed select symbols of Indigenous culture with the biological ideals of Mestizaje. When projected onto mestiza bodies, the dress and mannerisms that marginalized and "othered" Indigenous women were rewritten as quaint and desirable. The *india bonita* trope was at times strategically performed by Indigenous women, but increasing numbers of white-coded mestiza women donned these costumes to "play Indian," borrowing Philip Deloria's turn of phrase. *Indias bonitas* signaled the desired racial progression from Indigenous to mestiza with the dual function of romanticizing the Indigenous past that Mexicans hoped to overcome and projecting the mestizo future they could look forward to.

Although the *india bonita* trope was meant to invoke Indigenous women, it was more a project of erasure than one of fair representation. Indigenous cultures were distilled, appropriated, narrowed, and incorporated into postrevolutionary identity on the assumption that Indigenous peoples needed to be integrated to the point of disappearance. This logic allowed for actual Indigenous peoples to be effectively written out of the narrative of national progress. And supplanting Indigenous women with mestiza women in popular culture was yet another means by which Indigeneity was visually erased from the construction of *lo Mexicano*.

Scrutiny of postrevolutionary beauty and identity ideals exposes the reductive and racist logics that undergirded them. By imposing a framework of authenticity to determine who and what counted as legitimately Indigenous, the postrevolutionary elite established a set of constrictive boundaries and binaries that governed what Indigenous female comportment and cultural practices were to look like. The standards of biological and cultural purity against which living Indigenous women were measured inherently bound them to the past. This ideal privileged a conquered empire and dead Indians over the multifaceted realities of living Indigenous peoples, and it dictated that

Indigenous peoples were no longer truly Indigenous once they donned Western dress, engaged in "modern" activities, or moved away from rural spaces.

As Jean O'Brien and Shannon Speed argue, these narrowing parameters of "authentic" Indigeneity operated as a sort of inverse of the "one-drop rule" in the United States.[49] In the U.S. context, the rule dictated that anyone with even a single traceable drop of Black blood would always be Black. This effectively grew the class of people who could be denied property and civil rights in America's legally encoded systems of racial violence.[50] In Mexico, the slightest entanglement with the "modern," be it urbanity or Mestizaje, could—discursively, at least—negate one's Indigenous identity.

While much of this identity project circulated in the boundless realm of intellectual exchanges, easily reproducible images, imitable performances, and social codes, it was also firmly rooted in place. Analyzing projects of Indigenismo and Mestizaje as they existed in Mexico City reveals the material impact these ideologies had on everyday people. This book takes a regional view of Mexico City, seeing it less as a monolithic urban space and more as a compilation of distinct regions, some of which were deliberately cultivated for their association with "Mexico Viejo." I show how the cultural elite manufactured an identity that was both shaped by and, in turn, shaped the city itself. Local Indigenous traditions were appropriated, reimagined, and revalued in a way that wed urban growth and enterprise with nationalist objectives. Regions and cultural practices affiliated with Tenochtitlan and the Aztec empire became founts of popular culture and invented tradition. In turn, certain parts of the city were classed and preserved as what Ageeth Sluis calls *camposcapes* while others were destined for urbanization.[51] "Modern" folk could transgress these boundaries, but Indigenous peoples were only considered authentically "Indian" when they occupied rural spaces and markets, wore *traje*, and engaged in specific behaviors. Examining this ethnic double standard as it played out in Mexico City provides even greater evidence that postrevolutionary unification was ultimately a project of Indigenous erasure.

Indigenous peoples were not passive recipients of these projects. As Ardis Cameron writes, "looking is always a constructive practice" that allows an active viewer to impose narrative, meaning, and desire on whomever they are viewing.[52] But that does not mean that those being viewed are entirely powerless. Rather than silently accepting imposed narratives, Indigenous peoples strategically engaged with, resisted, shaped, reinforced, and detracted from the currents of Mestizaje and Indigenismo. Despite persistent attempts to disappear and disenfranchise Indigenous peoples, they persistently adapted to and covertly shaped postrevolutionary identity discourses. In several cases included in the chapters that follow, they reappropriated the *india bonita* construct for their own benefit. Even so, Indigenous agency within broader systems of settler colonialism must not be confused with liberation. Rather, this book includes a range of Indigenous interventions into broader national identity projects in order to disrupt top-down understandings of identity construction and to "people" this history with voices that have all too often been entirely ignored.

SETTLER COLONIAL NATIONALISM

I trace postrevolutionary constructions of beauty, race, and identity as extensions of settler colonialism because that framework is necessary in order to fully grapple with the complexity and longevity of the questions engaged here. Systematic attempts to reproduce Mestizaje, to assimilate Indigenous peoples into the national polity, and to normalize Native appropriation and erasure were all manifestations of settler attempts to orchestrate Indigenous disappearance while also affirming their own belonging. As historian Patrick Wolfe puts it, "settler colonialism is a structure not an event."[53] In the Mexican context, vestiges of colonialism continue to shape social systems even though the days of Spanish conquest and the shifting regimes of violence, domination, extraction, and exploitation employed throughout the colonial era have come to an end. The aims of conquest—taking lands, resources, and autonomy from Indigenous peoples while normalizing settler ownership—were engrained first in New Spain's and later in Mexico's social order, economy, and politics. In other words, acts of colonialism did not just happen during conquest—they were embedded into the very foundations of New Spain and Mexico.

This book shows how ostensible celebrations of Indigenous heritage in postrevolutionary nation-building projects often worked to narrow the boundaries of what counted as "true" Indianness. These "logics of elimination" at once advanced Indigenous erasure and affirmed the settler right to inherit all that which was once Indigenous.[54] In adopting an origin story that centered noble Aztecs and their descendants, nation builders aligned themselves with a national mythology that normalized their own belonging to place while also obscuring the enduring violences of occupation. They attempted to define and delineate Indigenous authenticity in order to discursively shrink the existing

Native population while pop culture simulacra featuring white-coded women as sultry *indias bonitas* further normalized the idea that mestizos were the new Natives.

This book also looks to a growing body of Indigenous and Latinx scholarship that critically examines both Indigeneity and settler colonialism in the context of Latin America and its diaspora.[55] Wolfe's framing largely obscures the theory's applicability to Latin America by arguing that settler colonialism rests on the act of first dispossessing Native populations of their land and then importing foreign slaves to work that land.[56] In much of Latin America, however, Native peoples were first dispossessed of their land and then made to work it alongside foreign slaves and itinerant immigrant labor forces. But as Shannon Speed argues, that doesn't mean that what happened in Latin America wasn't a function of settler colonialism. It simply means that settler colonialism is more varied and expansive than Wolfe would have us believe.[57]

As Speed claims, the ways in which systems of elimination have played out north and south of what we now recognize as the U.S.-Mexico border have more in common than not.[58] Though policies north of the border leaned in the direction of isolation and those south of the border tended toward integration, Speed argues that "the way Indigenous people were racialized across the Americas bears a striking resemblance: savage, unfit for modern life, and destined to fade into extinction."[59] To delimit critiques according to the arbitrary, shifting boundaries of nations undermines our ability to grapple with the full hemispheric scope of the violences that systems of racism and colonization have enacted.

Although the settler-colonized binary in Mexico is not always clear because of centuries of cultural and racial mixing,[60] Mestizos in postrevolutionary society—especially those privileged by wealth and whiteness—were more likely to be complicit in systems that disenfranchised, erased, and exploited Indigenous peoples.[61] I follow the work of Shona Jackson, María Josefina Saldaña-Portillo, M. Bianet Castellanos, Richard Gott, Shannon Speed, and Gabriela Spears-Rico, who examine how both Creoles and mestizos became complicit in settler colonial systems.[62] Hierarchies of class, color, gender, race, and ethnicity were all by-products of settler colonialism that ultimately worked to reinforce and reproduce settler power at the expense of Indigenous lives, rights, and sovereignty. Viewing the deliberate production of these social categories as extensions of settler colonialism's long reach helps make sense of some of the perplexing contradictions of the era. It also sheds light on the subtle and not subtle ways in which power and belonging to place were produced for some Mexicans while being systematically denied to others.[63]

J. Kēhaulani Kauanui argues that Wolfe's "structure not an event" formulation can't be fully understood unless it is put in conversation with the social construct of Indigeneity.[64] In doing so, my work is situated within a body of scholarship that examines how settler colonialism lingers and reproduces itself throughout the Americas while at the same time recognizing the inherent fluidity and complexity of Indigenous identities. As Maylei Blackwell, Floridalma Boj Lopez, and Luis Urrieta Jr. put it in their introduction to *Critical Latinx Indigeneities*, "indigeneity is defined and constructed across multiple countries and, at times, across overlapping colonialities."[65] In her contribution to the volume, Saldaña-Portillo advocates for a hemispheric view of settler colonialism that reads immigration, mass incarceration, and other systems that disprivilege some while elevating the power and privilege of others as manifestations of the same colonizing structure. The present volume traces the logics still at play in these systems back to a critical point in their contemporary development in order to better understand the ways they continue to shape the lives of Indigenous peoples throughout the Americas today.

This framework allows postrevolutionary identity projects to be seen as part of a longer trajectory of Mexican history. Spanish conquest and the relentless waves of death and disease it enacted; epidemics of violence against women; attempts to define racial identities through *casta* (caste) paintings; Indigenous dispossession and forced labor through encomienda, repartimiento, and hacienda (Spanish systems of regulating labor and land); the appropriation and erasure visible in the 2010 Miss Universe pageant; and contemporary anti-Indigenous attitudes—all of these are part of a system meant to displace and disappear Indigenous peoples in order to make way for settlers and their heirs. Viewing these disparate things as manifestations of a single system underscores the enduring, embedded nature of colonial violence. And, as Speed argues, recognizing the ongoing nature of settler colonialism is a necessary first step toward decolonization.[66]

Beyond the scholars already cited, this book's theoretical framework draws from the field of Indigenous studies. Philip Deloria's *Playing Indian* and *Indians in Unexpected Places*, as well as Jean M. O'Brien's *Firsting and Lasting: Writing Indians out of Existence in New England* have been particularly influential.[67] These works deal primarily with U.S. history, but the frameworks they deploy are applicable in the Mexican context because the postrevolutionary elite often turned to the United States in looking for solutions to the "Indian Problem." Additionally, many intellectuals and artists of the era received education and training in the United States. And ideas about Mexico's Indigenous peoples were shaped, in part, by the imperialist, enterprising gaze of Americans writing about and promoting tourism to Mexico since the Porfiriato.[68] This book is conceived as a transnational study, then, because the flow of ideas—if not always people—paid little heed to national borders. And although this is primarily a cultural history grounded in Indigenous studies, I employ film theory and cultural studies critique as tools for deeper readings of historical images and popular ephemera.

Following Deloria's lead, I treat the *india bonita* trope as an ideology rather than a stereotype. As he explains, ideologies reflect power, domination, and acquiescence; and they socially construct expectations about how certain groups are going to act. This, he argues, is an important rhetorical distinction from stereotypes, which speak to replication but not to the complexity of construction that shapes their impact on the material world.[69] This interpretation complements another framework I employ: Deborah Poole's conceptualization of "visual economies" in which images are interpreted within a network of "social relationships, inequality, and power."[70] In visual economies, images circulate across national, cultural, and class boundaries with implications for the material and social realities of both the viewers and the subjects of their view. Though I use the word *representation* at times, it should be taken as shorthand for the more apt but cumbersome "visual economy."

In my critique of postrevolutionary images and discourse, I hope to illuminate false binaries while at the same time avoiding the reification of the problematic boundaries they worked to reinforce. Commonly used derogatory terms like the "Indian problem," *raza de bronce* (bronze race), and "backward Indians" reflected racist and paternalistic attitudes toward Indigenous peoples. They are referenced with caution throughout this work and only when necessary in order to illustrate how settler colonial ideology was manifested throughout postrevolutionary thinking.

Similarly, I identify how and by whom popular understandings of "tradition" and "authenticity" were determined and the way those labels were employed in the quest to produce postrevolutionary identity. I reference the term *traditional* to demonstrate how the cultural elite conceived of it: as a signifier of the past that either needed to be eradicated or incorporated into the cultural celebrations. "Authenticity" was not so much a static or objective concept but rather used as a measure of individual and community engagement with a specific set of Indigenous cultural practices. As a construct of postrevolutionary identity discourse, authenticity became a tool of erasure dictating that "real" Indigenous peoples lived, behaved, talked, and appeared differently than the mestizo population.

Modernity, too, was a postrevolutionary construct still under the influence of the Porfirian penchant for efficiency and progress. Being "modern" meant adopting Western knowledge systems, development, and technological innovation. It allowed upwardly mobile mestizos to distance themselves further from Indigenous peoples because modernity was constructed as being antithetical to Indigeneity. At the same time, the concept left enough room for Indigenous people to "become" modern and mestizo if, according to Indigenista logic, they were healthy, urban, and adequately integrated into the nation.

Historical analysis of racial construction through visual culture presents the temptation to assess race based on physical features, but to do so would replicate the logic of racial determination that this book critiques. That said, certain characteristics were routinely assigned symbolic value as being European or mestizo and others that were routinely used to symbolize Indigeneity. Light skin, high cheekbones, and narrow noses, for example, were adopted from Old World statuary and global visual discourse to signal classic European beauty. Meanwhile, rounder faces, dark hair and skin, braids, and shorter statures were typically associated with Indigeneity. In reality, of course, race and ethnicity are extremely fluid, and these characteristics are not so neatly assigned. I do not subscribe to the narrowing ways in which racial identity was fixed but instead identify the physiological characteristics and symbols that came to be associated with groups along ethnic and racial lines in order to better critique the confines and limitations of that logic.

Place is paramount to this study, and my focus on Mexico City is not meant to elide the importance of cultural production in other parts of the country nor to reject a growing body of scholarship that shows how "microcosms of power" on the periphery of the capital shaped Mexico too.[71] Jennifer Jolly's and Gabriela Spears Rico's recent works on Pátzcuaro and Deborah Poole's work on Oaxaca, for example, show how *patrias chicas* contributed to and resisted the nation-building process.[72] Like Spears Rico, I hope to make an intervention that illustrates the necessity of engaging settler colonial theory and Indigenous contributions to understanding postrevolutionary identity projects. As Mexico City remained an epicenter for mass production of visual culture, it is a logical place to start, but I hope that this work contributes to the growing foundation of scholarship examining how similar projects played out across the nation and throughout Latin America.

Finally, I acknowledge that as an Irish American settler scholar from the southwestern United States, there are limitations to the critical intervention I am able to make to this field of study. I strive to treat the topics I address here with sensitivity and to be accountable to the people, both past and present, who were and still are directly affected by these identity constructs. And I hope that by turning my attention to untangling the (il)logics of the broader settler colonial systems my own ancestors were complicit in building, I have written a book that might contribute to ongoing Indigenous and Latinx-led conversations about decolonization.

ORGANIZATION

This book traces how settler colonial ideology moved through postrevolutionary society, and the organization of the book is intended to reflect that trajectory. The early chapters focus on the emergence and evolution of an ideology, while later chapters follow how it was widely deployed and replicated. In the final chapters, I examine how settler colonial tropes were manifested and resisted in deeply embodied and place-based ways.

Chapter 1 follows the India Bonita contest, a serialized pageant that appeared in the pages of the *El Universal* newspaper over much of 1921. I examine how Manuel Gamio and his fellow judges used race science and anthropology to inform their selection of a pageant winner and, in doing so, used their positions of authority to brand a narrow view of "authentic" Indigeneity. While romanticized ideals of Indigenous women had been circulating for centuries, I argue that the 1921 pageant created the prototype for the *india bonita* trope as it would be reproduced throughout the era of postrevolutionary reconstruction. While the trope was necessarily mutable, the conversation and the people authorized to have that conversation were firmly fixed by the pageant. This chapter also mines the archive of contestants in order to present counternarratives to the pageant by attesting to the complexity and diversity of Indigenous women's lives at a moment of major social change.[73]

Chapter 2 traces the creation of the Flor más Bella del Ejido pageant, an annual India Bonita–like contest in which young Indigenous women donned specific *traje* and competed in front of a panel of judges. The event, which is still produced today, is rooted in pre-Hispanic tradition but was co-opted by postrevolutionary elites in the early 1920s and molded to become a major component of Mexico City's indigenist celebrations. This reinvention, which evolved over the subsequent decades, sheds light on the in situ production of *Mexicanidad*. As the city swelled in size and became more urban, bureaucrats and Indigenous peoples alike strove to carve out select spaces to mark Aztec origins and to maintain contemporary Indigenous cultural practices. Testimonies from pageant winners illustrate some of the ways in which Indigenous women strategically—and, at times, cynically—engaged with these projects. However, media coverage of the pageant reified beliefs that Indigenous authenticity could be determined by a narrow set of gender, racial, and geographic factors.

In the decades following the revolution, cinema became an increasingly attractive means with which to disseminate nationalist ideals to the masses. Chapter 3 follows the development of *cine folclórico* films and the *india bonita* trope that helped characterize the genre. I decode on-screen representations and performances along with casting decisions, film techniques, and media coverage within four different types of *cine folclórico* films in order to highlight the complex ways in which the medium helped to normalize emerging discourses on Mestizaje and Indigenismo. Like beauty pageants, film trained viewers to focus on specific, superficial sources of visual pleasure while a complex set of race, gender, and identity ideals were being asserted just beneath the surface. The chapter includes analysis of rare and little-known films, including a series of documentaries by Manuel Gamio; a *comedia ranchera* rendition of the India Bonita pageant; and a Mexican-produced pornographic film from the silent era. I also mine the vast media coverage of the 1930–1931 production of Sergei Eisenstein's *Que viva México!* to show how the film influenced Mexican movie making decades before its eventual release in 1979.

Over the course of revolutionary reconstruction, Xochimilco was cultivated as a tourist destination and also served as a critical source of potable water for a rapidly growing Mexico City. Chapter 4 shows how postrevolutionary identity projects in Xochimilco paralleled and reinforced regional development interests. Mutually constitutive representations of the place, water, and women of Xochimilco all tended to center on the concept of purity. I evaluate these overlapping discourses in films ranging from home movie footage to the classic *María Candelaria* as well as tourism campaigns and urban environmental history. I argue that in Xochimilco, the *india bonita* trope was central to efforts to bridge the "modern" (potable water, sanitation, transportation, filmmaking) and the "traditional" (Indigenous authenticity, living memory of the Aztec empire). At the same time, I show how the trope and the stereotypes it generated were strategically employed by residents of Xochimilco to gain a modicum of autonomy and empowerment within systems that otherwise worked to disenfranchise and disappear them.

Chapter 5 turns to the legacy of Doña Luz Jiménez, a Nahua woman who modeled for Diego Rivera, Fernando Leal, Jean Charlot, Jose Clemente Orozco, and many other members of the postrevolutionary artistic vanguard. To them, Jiménez was the epitome of Indigenous female beauty, and depictions of her face and body still grace countless murals and works of art across Mexico City. She was also a gifted teacher, weaver, intellectual, and storyteller. Her words linger in children's books, anthropology texts, and in the scores of letters she sent to Jean Charlot. But despite this hypervisibility, her name is largely absent from the bodies of work she helped to define. In this chapter I take a critical view of how Jiménez was represented by artists, and I mine her personal letters, family archives, and artist recollections to depict a more intimate side of settler colonialism. While interrogating Jiménez's erasure from the historical record, this chapter also engages her own words and images to show the extent to which she deliberately engaged with postrevolutionary identity projects and to examine how she represented herself.

This book illuminates a world in which elite and upwardly mobile members of society created and viewed images that allowed them to unify the nation while measuring mestizo modernity against the Indigenous other. These images and the ideologies that undergirded them attempted to fix identities that had been in flux for centuries, all in the service of normalizing settler colonial belonging and writing Indigenous peoples out of existence. Between these convoluted layers of appropriation and erasure, Indigenous people enacted myriad counternarratives and strategically engaged with these projects.

The traditions and tropes written into existence in the decades of revolutionary reconstruction still loom large in Mexico's cultural imaginary. Even today, a nostalgic romanticism dictates that "real" Indigenous peoples engage in specific activities, live in certain spaces, speak Indigenous languages, and wear *traje*. Calendar art and more contemporary media ranging from *telenovelas* to YouTube videos continue to center sexualized white-coded mestiza women in Indigenous dress. Beneath what might at first appear to be small celebrations of Indigenous heritage or benign impersonations are centuries-old legacies of violence, erasure, and dispossession. In peering into this past, I hope to contribute to conversations that ultimately undo these ongoing systems of settler colonialism.

LA REINA DE LA RAZA

The Making of the *India Bonita*

A S THE FATES OF NATIONS go, 1920 was a horrible year for Mexico. Following a decade of violence and bloodshed in revolutionary battles, waves of disaster and disease took additional tolls on its citizenry. In January a deadly earthquake took nearly three thousand lives; there was a major flu epidemic as well as outbreaks of yellow fever and bubonic plague; workers went on strike and left for the United States en masse. Even the iconic volcano Popocatépetl erupted.[1] At the end of this vertiginous year, Álvaro Obregón, a one-armed revolutionary from the northern frontier, took office as the divided nation's new president.

For those invested in postrevolutionary nation building, 1921 presented an opportunity to start anew. It marked the centennial of independence from Spain and a decade since the start of the revolutionary war. It was a moment for celebrating the nation's accomplishments and for forging new national mythologies. In the first weeks of the new year, Mexico City's daily newspaper, *El Universal*, announced the India Bonita contest.[2] Appearing under the no-nonsense headline "Who Is the Most Beautiful Indian?," the paper urged its readers to turn their attention to the "strong and pretty faces of the countless Indian women who occupy the lowest ranks of society." After recounting recent *El Universal* serialized contests that had sought to find the most beautiful woman or the kindest worker, they admitted that never before had they thought to adorn their pages with the "strong and pretty" faces of Indigenous women.[3] Thus, the paper was inaugurating the India Bonita contest and, through it, they hoped to discover the most beautiful Indian. In the same patronizing tone that characterized much of the newspaper's writing about Indigenous peoples, they assured readers that even these women had aspirations in their "little hearts" and that this "racial contest" would surely elevate their spirits.

Though framed as a charitable effort, the pageant would ultimately become part of larger identity projects that sought to define and appropriate select aspects of Indigenous identity. This chapter shows how, in its focus on select visual markers of Indigeneity, the India Bonita contest ultimately helped to narrow popular understandings of authentic Indigeneity. The pageant also played into broader efforts to solve the so-called Indian Problem by situating ideal Indigeneity in the rural past, favoring Aztec heritage, and positioning mestizos as the race of the future. In contradiction to the conclusions drawn by the orchestrators of the India Bonita contest, the pageant archive provides glimpses into Indigenous women's lives and shows the multifaceted contributions they made to the national conversation about what it meant to be Indigenous.

When it came to discussions of Indigenous peoples, articles published by *El Universal* in the weeks leading up to the announcement of the pageant were rife with racist and assimilationist ideologies. A January 1921 editorial penned by politician and *El Universal* cofounder Emilio Rabasa lamented what he called "the problem of the Mexican Indian." He contended that "three million Indians, morally and intellectually inferior to Moctezuma," represented a substantial burden to the "civilized half of society." Since their blood had been so diluted by centuries of miscegenation, he argued, it was impossible to isolate them to reservations as the United States had done.[4] Rabasa concluded that the only viable solution would be a more thorough integration.

Another article published the same week by J. M. Puig Casauranc, an Indigenista and prominent public figure who would go on to become the secretary of public education, also compared U.S. and Mexican Indigenous populations.[5] Casauranc stated that American Indians were "robust men and women with faces full of intelligence and health" as opposed to Mexican Indians who, he said, occupied themselves with "the passive contemplation of nature." He argued that while American Indians had access to what he considered a brilliant boarding school system and had many opportunities for cultural, intellectual, and moral growth, isolating them on reservations tragically impaired their ability to fully integrate into broader society. Casauranc concluded that despite being a "backward people," Mexican Indians were actually better off than American Indians because they had genuine opportunities to become integrated into modern society.

These essays reflected a widespread belief that in order to quell the violence of the revolution, nation builders had to solve the so-called Indian Problem once and for all. Since it would be nearly impossible to isolate Mexico's diverse Indigenous population, more thorough cultural and biological integration emerged as a desired alternative. In order to do this effectively, civic leaders and intellectuals were compelled to identify aspects of Indigenous culture they felt were worthy of incorporation while simultaneously weeding out traits thought to be regressive. The India Bonita pageant was an opportunity for the paper to advance this project and educate readers about "ideal" aspects of Indigeneity. While the pageant was introduced as a celebration of Indigenous women, it was actually part of a larger attempt to racially and socially engineer a modern mestizo nation.

SEARCHING FOR THE "QUEEN OF THE BRONZE RACE"

Shortly after the pageant announcement, *El Universal* sent a team of reporters and photographers into the populous San Antonio Abad neighborhood in search of contestants. Armed with pens, cameras, and a fierce sense of nationalism, the intrepid reporters set off into the city in search of viable contestants. After searching without success for an hour, they finally encountered what they were looking for: "an Indian with large and dark eyes" by the name of Emma Garduño.[6] Promising the potential of a three-thousand-peso award, they asked Garduño if she'd pose for a picture. They describe her as being dumbfounded and slow to respond but ultimately acquiescing to their pleas. A few days later, on January 25, 1921, Garduño's portrait appeared on the front page of the paper's interior section. Wearing simple clothes and hair styling, the young woman in this first pageant entry did not bear any of the material markers popularly associated with Indigenous womanhood.

The *El Universal* team continued its search. In another foray into the San Antonio Abad neighborhood, they describe chasing down Natalia Estrella on her way to work at a cardboard box factory. Though she slipped inside the factory before they could catch her, they enlisted her employer to fish her out, then convinced the woman they called a "spirited" member of the "humble race" to pose for a picture.[7] The group encountered their next contestant, Guadalupe Viveros, at the crowded Mercado de San Juan. Admiring her "childlike manner" and "Indigenous nature," the newspapermen staged a portrait in a garden adjacent to the market.[8] While these early contestants seemed willing enough to participate in the pageant, they were never quoted directly by *El Universal*, so it is impossible to know whether they participated out of pressure or genuine interest.

Spurred by this string of successes but desiring more "traditional" contestants, the reporters ventured farther out to Xochimilco, the picturesque region thought to retain some of México Viejo in its intricate network of canals and chinampas (floating gardens). With dramatic flourish, an unnamed *El Universal* journalist relayed how his team traveled to the region they were certain would be "full of legitimate Indians." The anticipated romance of the scene was quickly dispelled when the team was met with a hostile reception from the Indigenous people they attempted to photograph. In lurid detail, the author described how they approached one possible contender, explaining to her that they were looking for the most beautiful Indian in Xochimilco. The woman refused to be photographed and told the reporters, "It is not my will." The team persisted until finally a man in a boat came to the woman's aid, waving a stick at the reporters and attempting to throw their camera in the water.[9]

Finally moving on, the team worked their way back to the region's main market. There they found Matiana Morreno, who was willing to have her photograph taken and whom the reporter described as being perfect for the pageant: "[we found in] one of those woolen rebozos, a precious Indian with a perfectly oval face, full of color, with impeccable teeth, jet black braids, and a peaceful and serene gaze."[10] Morreno's perceived passivity, combined with just the right facial characteristics and dress according to a calculated assessment, made her an ideal candidate in the eyes of the reporters. These early entries show that while the newspapermen may have wanted to celebrate Indigenous women, they certainly did not respect them.

The drama and intrigue of the early pageant reporting helped build a public enthusiasm that would be sustained over the months to come. The paper encouraged engagement from their readers, urging those who employed young Indigenous women to continue notifying the publication about potential candidates. In order to incentivize individuals to submit nominations, they launched a parallel contest that would recognize the best photograph of an India Bonita.[11] Entries started pouring in from readers who felt they, too, might be able to discover the nation's prettiest Indian as well as from young women nominating themselves for the prize. For the next seven months, the newspaper featured these photographs of contestants on an almost daily basis. By mid-March reporters noted that they were so overwhelmed with entries that they were having trouble keeping up with printing them all.[12]

The daily profiles of India Bonita candidates followed a simple formula: a portrait of the young woman would appear alongside a brief description of the woman or a short story about how she came to be nominated. At times, the paper would share select details about the candidates—their aspirations for the future, or where they were from. Other entries focused more on narratives about the employers or photographers who nominated them. While the contestants and the entries themselves varied, some clear patterns emerged. The majority were very young working women in Mexico City. A good number of them were teens, some as young as fourteen years old, while none of the contestants were older than twenty-five years of age. More than half were migrants who worked as nannies or housemaids in the homes of more established city dwellers.[13]

The contestants reflected the wide range of styles, lifestyles, and physical characteristics that existed among Mexico's diverse Indigenous population. Throughout the course of the pageant, many women wore clothing that was recognizably "traditional," such as embroidered blouses and Tehuana head-dresses, but others sported of-the-moment fashions including flapper-style bobbed hair, headbands, and long pearl necklaces. Meanwhile, working women were often pictured in nondescript work clothes or uniforms with lacey frills that had an almost Victorian air to them. What emerged was a collective snapshot of a group of women as diverse as any other, but pageant organizers nevertheless drew the conclusion that one type of Indigenous woman was more Indigenous than others.

Although non-Indigenous men orchestrated the pageant, it nevertheless provided opportunities for some of the women and girls who participated in it. For instance, several candidates expressed the desire to compete so that they would have a way to show people back home that they were successfully making their way in the city. With cameras still a rare commodity and studio portraits unattainable for most members of the working class, the pageant presented an opportunity for migrant workers to obtain a portrait—and

FIGURE 1. Gudelia Castillo. She said she planned to buy multiple copies of the newspaper and send it to friends and family at home. *El Universal*, April 22, 1921. Biblioteca Lerdo de Tejada.

multiple copies of it—that could be shared with friends and family back home. Gudelia Castillo, a domestic worker originally from the village of Zumpango in Mexico State, spoke of her plan to buy several copies of that day's edition of the newspaper to send to her homeland (*mi tierra*) so that her family could see that she was "a good girl who had proudly appeared in our racial contest" (fig. 1).[14] But whatever agency Indigenous women had in the pageant, it was still framed by and filtered through racialized ideologies of the era.

Despite the fact that the pageant was supposed to be about Indigenous women, the voices of the cultural elites who supported the endeavor dominated the discourse around the pageant. Many entries focused on those who nominated contestants, on the photographers of the portraits, or on the newspaper's role in the pageant. In some cases, search teams made up of members of the upper class would nominate contestants. These entries often detailed their process of seeking out *indias bonitas* as though it were an entertaining diversion. Employers nominating their workers sometimes highlighted how well they cared for their servants, perhaps hoping to evidence what decent and kind people they themselves were. They also found ways to promote their own interests under the guise of participating in this seemingly benevolent project. A May 1921 entry featured Concepción García, a twenty-year-old from Mexico City who worked as a shop girl in a perfume boutique.[15] Her employers nominated her and, probably seeing a good opportunity to promote their own business, they offered to donate a case of Heno de Persia soaps and perfumes to the winner. This product-name donation points to an undercurrent of commercial interest that was consistent throughout the pageant.

The India Bonita pageant entries were full of complexities and contradictions, but one thing they were noticeably lacking was any concrete discussion of the contestants' beauty. Similarly, Indigenous beauty was left out of mainstream dialogues and visual representations of beauty culture at the time. The pages of a women's section that appeared weekly in *El Universal* during the course of the pageant were illustrated with images of lean, fair-skinned women with what Ageeth Sluis calls "deco bodies."[16] Beauty contraptions to help narrow the nose or lighten the skin promised to help women attract a beau. Indigenous beauty was presented as a quaint way to celebrate isolated, desirable aspects of Indigeneity rather than a standard other women should strive to attain.

This absence of conventional beauty culture distinguished the India Bonita contest from other beauty pageants featured in the pages of *El Universal*. Concurrent national and international beauty pageants celebrated women with European features and employed different terms and measures than those reserved for the India Bonita contestants. For example, the winner of a contest to represent Mexico in an international beauty pageant was the epitome of the *chica moderna*, with a pageboy haircut and carefully made-up face.[17] The journalist covering the story praised the grace and serenity of the women's countenance that, he claimed, harkened back to the classic Greek and Roman beauties that had been immortalized in marble and bronze.

Similarly, the Mexicana más Bella contest—a 1920 *El Universal*–sponsored predecessor to the India Bonita pageant—focused almost entirely on European beauty standards. In one article, a journalist discussed the amazing range of beauty seen in Mexico but focused solely on the disparity between women from Northern Europe ("tall, white, intensely blue eyes, and blond hair") and those from Spain ("more short than tall, sensual lips, dark hair, and undulating, lively movements").[18] Photographs of the Mexicana más Bella contestants showed them striking dancerly poses under dramatic lighting that accentuated the long lines of their necks and arms. They were commonly pictured draped in cloth, reminiscent of Greek statuary, and with emphasis on their faces and bodies rather than their clothing.

Meanwhile, the India Bonita contestants were almost always pictured facing the camera directly with their heads sometimes turned slightly to the left or right. In some cases, full-body portraits showed off ornate clothing, studio props like pottery or painted gourd baskets, and bare feet. These images were more akin to racial "type" photographs and postcards than the conventional portraits of beauty queens and movie stars.[19] Descriptions of the women that accompanied the photographs focused on contestant mannerisms like subservience, piety, melancholic dispositions, and humble or shy behavior. In the rare moments in which beauty was discussed specifically, it was often done in a condescending manner: "We can comfortably say that the beauty of our race is not depleted, it's just necessary to have the patience necessary to find *indias bonitas* worthy of our national contest," commented one *El Universal* writer.[20]

Where discussion of beauty was lacking, an interest in racial purity took center stage. Contestants were often linked to Aztec identity through words and phrases like "la raza de Moctezuma Ilhuacamin" and "la Reina Xochitl."[21] Other Indigenous groups were referenced occasionally but with little specificity. For example, Virginia Quielva was identified as being a "Oaxacan of pure race," but her entry offers no detail about which of the dozens of Indigenous groups in Oaxaca she was affiliated with.[22] So while Indigenous women were ostensibly being celebrated for their beauty, the contest actually served to reinforce racial and ethnic stereotypes. It also further normalized Aztec affiliation while casting most other Indigenous identities as generically exotic "others."

The entries reinforced ideas about Indigenous racial purity by drawing attention to clothing or facial features that were thought to look Indian. In nominating her domestic worker, fifteen-year-old Domitila Hérnandez of Chalco, for the pageant, a woman who identified as Señora Carmen F. viuda de Bandala wrote, "as you can see in the photograph, she has well defined features of our primitive race . . . and she is the daughter of Indians pure in race."[23] The accompanying portrait shows a young woman robed in an embroidered blouse and belt with bows in her hair and elaborate jewelry, material markers of Indigeneity that would have reinforced the Señora's claims of authenticity. Another contestant was said to have "the nostalgia of the raza printed in her large, dark eyes."[24]

Contestants who donned Western dress or otherwise strayed from easily recognizable markers of Indigeneity often appeared in *El Universal* alongside written entries that verbally asserted their legitimacy. Aurora Azarte, for example, had a lighter complexion than other candidates. The author of her entry anticipated readers exclaiming "This isn't an Indian!" upon seeing her image but assured them that "fortunately Indians still existed who exhibit the proud features of Moctezuma" and that she was one of them.[25] "Very few people who see this delicious photograph would believe that she is an Indian," said the nomination letter, "but indeed she is. She has green eyes but is pure in race because she is the descendent of legitimate Indians." The author's claims to racial purity indicate the extent to which criteria used to determine "real Indians" were nebulous and inconsistently applied, at least at this stage of the pageant. In the case of Aurora Azarte, readers of *El Universal* were to see her as Indigenous simply because the reporter said so. As was typical of the contest, Aurora herself was not afforded the opportunity to self-identify her own ethnicity or cultural affiliations.

While the pageant included a diverse group of contestants, the greatest praise was reserved for those who most closely conformed to the popular ideals of Indigenous femininity. Signifiers of this identity included braids, embroidered blouses, long skirts, sandals, and the occasional prop such as a hand-decorated Olinalá bowl or a replica of a pre-Hispanic artifact. The newspaper simultaneously discouraged contestants from wearing contemporary fashions by turning away some submissions that editors deemed too modern. As these criteria became more clear, contestants took measures to "look Indian" by wearing Indigenous dress or by including other recognizable markers of Indigeneity. While *traje* may have been the daily wear of some contestants, others clearly donned costumes and props that they (or the studio photographers) thought would make them appear more authentically Indian.

The photo of fifteen-year-old Eleuteria Palato provides a good example of how Indianness was staged in some portraits. The props, background, and lighting indicate that it was a studio portrait. The position of the ceramic pot she holds suggests that someone placed it in her hand for the photo, because it would have been nearly impossible for her to maneuver her hand and the pot into that position on her own. Even in this portrait that speaks to many of the conventions associated with Indigenous identity at the time, the written entry defied the ideology of the humble Indian maiden. It stated that, in addition to being pretty, Eleutaria was well educated and read *El Universal* on a regular basis.[26] When asked about her desire to win the contest, she responded thoughtfully by saying that if she did not win, she hoped that someone from her region would because she thought it would honor her community.

One contestant went beyond all the others in demonstrating her knowledge of Indigenous dress and language. María Bibiana Uribe first submitted an entry to the pageant that showed her in Western dress. It was rejected, but she was encouraged to submit another photo in which she was wearing more "authentic" clothing.[27] She complied, submitting a photograph that featured her wearing recognizably Nahua clothing. The letter that accompanied this new photo was written by Bibiana's godmother and went into more detail about Indigenous identity than any other entry. The godmother stated that María Bibiana had "wheat-colored skin" and was a descendent of the "fierce Aztec race."[28] She described what Bibiana wore, emphasizing the fact that the contestant had made much of the clothing by hand. She also identified every article of clothing by its Nahuatl name, and the paper printed the words in bolded typeface.

As the contest neared its close, *El Universal* assembled an all-male jury of artists, intellectuals, and public figures to select the winner of the pageant: Jorge Enciso, an acclaimed artist famous for his drawings of Indigenous peoples and nationalist themes; Manuel Gamio, a Columbia University–trained anthropologist known for his seminal publication *Forjando Patria*, anthropological studies, and as a proponent of Indigenismo;[29] Aurelio González Carrasco, a playwright whose bawdy skits drew large audiences to cabarets and other popular theaters; and Carlos M. Ortega, another playwright popular among the working class. The jury also included journalist Rafael Pérez Taylor (who wrote under the pseudonym Hipolito Seijas), the orchestrator of the India Bonita pageant and the author of most of *El Universal*'s coverage of it. They gathered in August 1921 to evaluate the 171 photographs of hopeful contestants that had graced the pages of the newspaper over the past several months.

The competition that had begun as an attempt to find the *prettiest* Indian woman had morphed into a search for the most *legitimate* Indian. Dalevuelta went so far as to write that "the selection was based solely on Indigenous features and was in no way motivated by the beauty of the contestants."[30] Pageant judge Manuel Gamio served as the arbiter of Indigenous authenticity. Having trained under U.S. anthropologist Franz Boas, Gamio is known as being the father of Mexican anthropology. He argued that the nation needed to civilize and economically improve its Indigenous population in order to quell revolutionary violence and to prevent it from falling prey to the socialist influences of the Soviet Union.[31] Gamio's language in interviews and in the numerous editorials he penned throughout the course of the pageant indicated a belief that science could be employed to determine the cultural and physiological features of true Indians.

Although Gamio claimed to be sympathetic to Indigenous causes, his perspective often rested on racist hierarchies. In an article he published in *El Universal* just a week before the winner of the India Bonita contest was selected, he opined that the true failure of European conquest was that the colonizers had not more thoroughly integrated Indigenous and European races: "The remedy is to melt these races together, modernizing the backward [*retrasada*] Indigenous civilization and incorporating them with the European type, which is more advanced and efficient."[32] Gamio then went on to make the case that this more thorough mixing of Indigenous and European races should happen now, but he advocated for a cultural, not racial, fusion. Like his contemporary Indigenistas who subscribed to the ethos of Aztec nationalism, Gamio favored Aztec ancestry over other Indigenous identifications. To him, the most worthy Indians were the descendants of Moctezuma.

Against this backdrop of identity projects, scientific racism, and the Aztec vogue, ten pageant finalists were selected from the diverse group of contenders. On August 1, 1921, the finalists convened in the offices of *El Universal*, where the jury could "study them carefully."[33] A photograph shows these young women assembled in front of the unmistakable outlines of pyramids, providing a clear visual referent to the Aztec past and no doubt bolstering the perceived authenticity of the contestants and the pageant in which they were participating. Despite the vast diversity of contestants seen over the course of the pageant, the photograph shows a notably homogeneous-looking group of young women.[34] The finalists all wore rebozos, braids, bare feet, and embroidered huipils and belts. Upon arriving for the photo, their faces had been wiped with a moist cloth in order to ensure that they were in their "natural state" and not wearing any makeup.[35] Considering the jubilant verbiage seen throughout the pageant, the portrait of the finalists is remarkably somber.

At the center of the photo stands a young woman described as an "obsidian-eyed princess" ensconced in a lacy white scarf and holding a painted Olinalá-style gourd bowl in her hands. This was sixteen-year-old María Bibiana Uribe, newly anointed the "queen of the bronze race" and the winner of the India Bonita title. She had traveled to Mexico City from her hometown of San Andrés Tenango, Puebla, along with her grandmother and godparents. Dalevuelta wrote that from the moment he saw her, he could not imagine that any other contestant would so elegantly display the "beauty, pure Indigenous blood, youth, and discretion" that she exhibited.[36] In announcing her victory, *El Universal* claimed that this "fine and sweet little figure" exhibited all the characteristics of the race: "dark skin, black eyes, short stature, delicate hands and feet, long black hair, and so forth."[37] As yet another reminder that this beauty pageant had little at all to do with beauty, these physical descriptors paid little heed to María Bibiana Uribe's physical attractiveness and focused instead on portraying her as a pure cultural specimen.

Though Bibiana's "Aztecness" was mentioned throughout the pageant, it was highlighted anew after her victory. Manuel Gamio confirmed that she was a descendent of "Moctezuma's race," evidenced as much by her physical characteristics as by her ability to speak Nahuatl. *El Universal* also made a point of noting that as a speaker of Mexicano (a colloquialism for Nahuatl language), she was a member of the "Aztec family." And Bibiana herself affirmed this identity. After winning the title, she held court in the offices of *El Universal* and schooled the journalists on the names of the various articles of clothing she was wearing: *kiskume* for covering the head, *titixtle* around the waist, and a silk blouse. She paused to point out the animals that adorned her *kiskume* to a rapt audience of typically skeptical male journalists.[38]

LIKE A VIRGIN

The attention to physical traits and Aztec descent fit neatly within the trajectory of postrevolutionary identity discourse. But another discursive turn broke from this predictable pattern. Questions about and assertions of Bibiana's virginity, romantic availability, and sexual appeal began to pepper *El Universal* articles that were otherwise focused on her cultural and racial identity. The contestants' virginity had not been stipulated as a criteria for winning the pageant, nor had it been publicly discussed at any previous point throughout the pageant. Even so, the jurors and reporters immediately began referring to María Bibiana Uribe as the *virgen indígena* or the *virgen morena*. Post-pageant portraiture underscored this correlation with the sixteen-year-old often appearing with a lacy veil and eyes cast to the heavens. Bibiana, who was a devotee of the Virgin of Guadalupe, would have likely eschewed this correlation out of the pious respect and deference with which she spoke of the Virgin Mother in interviews after the pageant. At one point she deflected a reporter's praise by saying "I am not pretty, sir. She [the Virgin of Guadalupe] is."[39]

In a newspaper interview conducted the day she was awarded the title, reporter Fernando Ramírez de Aguilar—using the pen name Jacobo Dalevuelta—described María Bibiana Uribe as a delicate *flor de campo* who had the "candor of a virgin, the beauty of a flower of Yolochilt, and the good looks of a Sultan's favorite harem consort."[40] Beauty was finally a part of the discussion, but it was mired in sexual innuendo. Dalevuelta interrogated her about her relationship status, repeatedly asking her if she had a boyfriend. He described Bibiana as refusing to answer, blushing, lowering her eyes, and seeming nervous. When asked again about whether or not she had a boyfriend, she replied that she did not know. Unrelenting, he assured Bibiana that she would see her boyfriend again. He noted in the paper that she didn't provide information about this supposed love interest, but that she didn't correct the assertion either. In explaining why he picked Bibiana as the India Bonita, playwright and pageant judge Aurelio González Carrasco's comments were particularly licentious. He even went so far as to suggest that one of the judges or newspapermen should take advantage of the opportunity and marry the teenage queen.[41]

The fact that interest had moved from cultural and physical assets toward Bibiana's romantic life and sexual history underscores the integrationist undercurrents of postrevolutionary identity projects. What started off as an effort to identify and celebrate Indigenous beauty became a civic education project aimed at defining Indianness and, in its final moments, an opportunity to depict the ideal Indigenous woman as being pure, sexually available, and worthy of the attention of non-Indigenous men. The discussion of Bibiana's sexuality and romantic availability, then, fit within broader efforts to cast Indigenous women as worthy objects of mestizo male sexual appetites in an effort to "modernize" the Mexican people through more thorough integration.[42] While public intellectuals like Gamio were adamant that integration should take place only at the level of material culture, the subtext of the pageant made it clear that biological integration would be welcome too.

QUEEN FOR A DAY

The Indigenous woman as object of desire was one narrative that emerged from the India Bonita contest, but there were others as well. Another line of postpageant discourse pictured Indigenous peoples as helpless children in need of moral guidance and racial betterment. In this narrative, the newspaper cast María Bibiana Uribe as a child in need of well-appointed Spanish *padrinos* (godparents) who could take her in and ensure a good education. *El Universal* selected Don Andres Fernández and his wife, Doña Esperanza M. de Fernández, for the job.[43] Bibiana visited the family home, along with her mother and journalist Rafael Pérez Taylor, shortly after winning the pageant. According to *El Universal*, the group received a warm welcome accompanied by a grand *comida* (meal). The description of the encounter emphasized the genteel nature of the hosts while portraying the two Nahua women as being out of their element. Between language barriers, class differences, and the documentation of their every move, they likely did feel uncomfortable—as anyone would—but *El Universal*'s portrayal of the event fed into tropes about Indigenous people being incapable of navigating modern society.

While the family matriarch questioned Bibiana about her hopes and aspirations, the newly crowned India Bonita was described as being shy and blushing, barely mumbling brief responses to these inquiries. Meanwhile, the journalist repeatedly mentioned Don Fernández's white skin and his wife's graciousness, casting them both as ideal representatives of the Spanish race.[44] The paper also praised the patriarch's generosity in offering to pay for Bibiana to attend school in Puebla. But in making this offer, Don Fernández reflected the racist logic that Indigenous people would become worthy individuals only through proper acculturation: "perhaps [she] possesses some great talent and with education she might become a valuable member of her family and of her society."[45] He also offered to manage her cash prizes until, he said, Bibiana had gained sufficient skills to manage her own affairs. The teen was a backward Indian, the article implied, but could be made modern enough through education and exposure to the more "civilized."

Major cinemas and theaters throughout the city joined in the feting of the new queen. Homages and tribute performances in Bibiana's honor premiered at Cine Casino, Teatro Lírico, Teatro Principal, Teatro Cine Santa María de la Ribera, and Teatro Colón, with half of all proceeds going to the pageant winner. Night after night, musicians and performers honored Bibiana, while teaming crowds turned out to catch a glimpse of the newly crowned queen. *El Universal* reported on each of these theater functions and meticulously tracked the growing sum of her winnings from ticket sales and other gift donations.[46]

The grandest of these theater events was held in the Teatro Colón, where a variety show homage to the India Bonita premiered on August 24. The show was so well received that an encore performance was scheduled for the following night, and President Obregón was personally invited to attend. Bibiana attended with a court of honor composed of three other India Bonita finalists: Petra Jiménez, Ignacia Guerrero, and Amada Guzmán. When she appeared at center stage on a throne adorned with serpents and symbols of the "ancestral race," the crowds went wild. But Bibiana was not the only star of the show.

María Conesa, a popular Spanish-born diva on the Mexican *género chico* circuit, shared the spotlight with Bibiana. Conesa's performance was an adaptation of her off-color live show "La India Bonita," which had premiered about a month into the contest.[47] Dressed in full Tehuana garb, Conesa delivered her rendition of the popular "Zandunga Oaxaqueña." She also sang couplets dedicated to Bibiana, professing her sisterly love for the *indita Mexicana* (little Mexican Indian) and insinuating that Palavicini and Pérez Taylor were mad with desire for the teenage queen.[48] Later, she appeared visibly emotional as she recited a monologue dedicated to the Reina de la Belleza Indígena.[49]

While the event was ostensibly a celebration of the India Bonita, it was also presented as a harmonious reconciliation of Indigenous and European peoples with Bibiana Uribe and Conesa standing as the figureheads of their respective races. Eduardo Gómez Haro dedicated a poem to the two Marías, casting the women as living testaments to the strength and beauty that lay at the heart of the mestizo race.[50] *El Universal* reported on a hug shared between Conesa and Bibiana Uribe as though it were atonement for centuries of violence and oppression: "In a sincere hug, the representatives of two races that were enemies for four hundred years, and that form the basis of our nationality, were united."[51] The fact that these conciliatory acts were performed in El Teatro Colón, a theater named after the father of New World colonialism, is an irony too rich to ignore.

A photo accompanying *El Universal's* coverage of this grand event shows the two women together on stage. Bibiana appears visibly uncomfortable while Conesa, costumed from head to toe as Bibiana, beams by her side (fig. 2). Playing Indian wasn't new to Mexican stages, but the Teatro Colón homage was novel for the intimacy of the impersonation. Because Indigenous identity had been reduced to a few symbols and characteristics throughout the pageant, it was easier for people like Conesa to appropriate and perform it. For non-Indians, Indigeneity was further normalized as a costume that could be taken up at will and then shed when being "modern" was more advantageous. The move from the *género chico* stage to a much larger venue with diplomats

FIGURE 2. María Bibiana Uribe and María Conesa appear on stage together at El Teatro Colón. "Esta noche se repite en el Colón el homenaje de la india bonita," *El Universal*, August 26, 1921. Biblioteca Lerdo de Tejada.

and polite society in attendance was an early instance of the *india bonita* trope moving from the margins into the mainstream.[52]

The fact that a Spaniard dressed in *traje* was celebrated alongside Bibiana suggests that performance and impersonation of Indigenous identity were central components of the postrevolutionary vision for solving the "Indian Problem." The Teatro Colón event also indicates that the pageant had morphed into a reconciliation fantasy that superficially absolved the nation of its sins of Indigenous colonization and oppression. The theaters, dignitaries, journalists, and others that celebrated Bibiana were performing acts of apology and redress without having to maneuver through the thorny complications of actual restitution for Indigenous peoples. But like much of the revolutionary reform that promised justice, the acts of charity bestowed on Bibiana were little more than symbolic gestures. Still, the hoopla allowed citizens to imagine they had healed from colonial violence without doing any of the work that that healing would require.

Businesses and individuals from across the country were eager to show that they, too, supported this project. Gift donations poured in and were carefully documented in the pages of *El Universal*. They included engraved gold medal, two coral necklaces (given to Bibiana by Conesa and her adoptive Spanish family), cases of perfumed soaps, a dozen copies of her portrait taken by José P. Arriaga, a silk cushion, a pair of black satin shoes, a banquet for one hundred guests in the Xochimilco Inn, several oil paintings, a dozen pairs of sandals, two rebozos, a mattress, five boxes of Mint Marbles gum, an "Aztec" vase, a "magnificent" silk shawl from the actress Lupita Rivas Cacho, six bottles each of wine and tequila, a dozen tubes of Anty Py-O toothpaste with three toothbrushes, and a pencil-drawn portrait of Bibiana made by thirteen-year-old Leopoldo P. Muro, among numerous other items of clothing, hygienic products, and works of art.[53] The prize listings often read like advertisements, including the name and street address of the donors. For example, the announcement of a gift of soda pop carried this zippy tagline and company plug: "A case of one hundred *Zas, que sabroso estás* sodas, made in the Aguas Gaseosas factory." For a small donation of goods, businesses across the republic were able to demonstrate concern for the pressing social issues of the day while also advertising their wares. Colonial reconciliation, it seems, could also be commodified.

Indeed, a current of commercial interest ran throughout the pageant. *El Universal*'s decision to run a popular, serialized "beauty" contest was probably as much about selling newspapers as it was about advancing its publisher's social aims. Similarly, the portrait contest gave photography studios a chance to demonstrate the quality of their work well beyond the storefront displays that had traditionally been used to attract customers. In the oversized portrait that accompanied the paper's final accounting of the pageant, María Bibiana Uribe looked particularly pious, engulfed in a broad white veil and with her arms crossed gingerly over her chest.[54] But the photo has a decidedly commercial feel to it thanks to the fact that the portraitist's name and street address are scrawled across her left arm. En route to forging new identity archetypes, *El Universal* and other business enterprises found numerous avenues for profit.

FIGURE 3. Photo of María Bibiana Uribe that ran in U.S. and Mexican newspapers. The photo was overexposed and solemn, reminiscent of portraiture of the Virgen. *Revista de Revistas*, January 8, 1922. Biblioteca Lerdo de Tejada.

While *El Universal* drove the pageant and the flurry of activity that followed, the event did not go unnoticed by other newspapers. Even the *New York Times* ran a photo spread featuring Bibiana's victory in their special rotogravure section. The photo shows the *india bonita* dressed in all white with a lacy veil covering her head (fig. 3). The print is overexposed so that the white takes on an almost ethereal quality and washes out part of her face. Her large, dark eyes anchor the photo. It is a beautiful image, but the overexposure leaves a haunting effect that conveyed a sense of ghostly otherworldliness to its international audience. Perhaps it registered among U.S. viewers familiar with the work of Edward S. Curtis as being a romantic ode to a vanishing race, and it had a similar but more moralistic currency in Mexico as well.

The popular *Revista de Revistas* reprinted the photo on January 8, 1922, along with a contribution from a special correspondent in Washington, D.C. In the article, the correspondent positioned María Bibiana Uribe as an ideal emblem of tradition and piety juxtaposed against the capricious "American girl" who imprudently "bares her chest and her legs" to the world.[55] Even beyond the discussion about Mexican identity and Indigeneity, María Bibiana Uribe's "serene" visage was used as a counterweight to the moral panic caused by the emerging flapper fad. Her image was appropriated as an antidote to modernity because this "priestess of the Virgin of Guadalupe" purportedly represented all that was good and moral about the past. Even as the cultural elite worked to solve the "Indian Problem," they romanticized a moral purity in Indigenous women that countered the ills of modernity.

While the *New York Times* praised the India Bonita contest, other Mexican newspapers viewed it with scorn and attempted to discredit both the pageant and María Bibiana Uribe herself. Veracruz's daily newspaper, *El Informador*, published an article expressing their pity for Bibiana. The paper argued that "this poor *india bonita*" had been plucked from her village and showered with prizes that would now make her the scorn of her fellow Indians.[56] The article concluded by saying she would have been better off if the newspaper had left her "humble and barefoot, with her two braids and simple dress, waiting for a beau to come ask for her hand in marriage."[57] This article echoes a popular assumption that Indians were not fit for modernity and that wealth and material possessions would only serve to complicate their lives. Despite peddling these racist and sexist tropes, the article serves as a reminder that the competition was not universally well received.

Beyond these public detractors, evidence suggests that some Indigenous peoples warmly received the woman who had been named their queen. Ixtacalco and Santa Anita—historically Indigenous agrarian communities on the outskirts of Mexico City—held a series of festivities in Bibiana's honor.[58] Members of the community decorated canoes on the Canal de la Viga, the same waterway that hosted its own contest for Indigenous "flower maidens" every spring.[59] During her reception, Bibiana was enthroned on one of these canoes and flanked with six *"inditas"* between the ages of five and six.[60] Local officials delivered official greetings, and notable members of the community hosted her in their homes. She was honored with a *comida nacional* in Santa Anita's Parque de los Sabinos and serenaded with music performed by the Compañía de Tranvías Eléctricos before being whisked back to the city.

Bibiana also became something of a popular icon as well. Months after the pageant, *El Universal* made note of "The Cult of the India Bonita." María Bibiana Uribe's portrait, they reported, was enshrined alongside the Virgin of Guadalupe in humble abodes in even the farthest stretches of the country.[61] While this could be a grandiose exaggeration from a paper eager to prove its own significance, it suggests that perhaps Bibiana's victory was meaningful to a largely disenfranchised population. Like the Virgin, Bibiana seems to have been adopted as a sort of folk hero among Indigenous people of the time. These responses to the pageant show that Indigenous peoples proudly saw Bibiana as one of their own despite the many layers of settler colonial, gendered, and racialized rhetoric the pageant organizers used to frame her victory.

Little is known about how Bibiana herself felt about the victory, but photographs and moving images that documented the pageant and its aftermath hint at her attitude. Silvio Toscano captured her as she rolled through the streets of the capital atop the *El Universal* float in the 1921 centennial parade, footage that later appeared in the classic *Memorias de un Mexicano* (1950). In two brief clips, she appears with her court of honor enthroned alongside a replica of an Aztec pyramid and a sun calendar, a wall of cacti, and a masthead featuring a robed Cuauhtémoc statue. Toscano shot the second of two short clips from a low angle, accentuating the towering effect of Bibiana's already tall throne.[62] Bibiana and her court all appear in white lace veils, and she smiles faintly while adjusting her veil. Her countenance exudes a sense of pleasure and self-satisfaction and she seems to be thoroughly enjoying herself. In an interview historian Rick López conducted with Bibiana's daughter, she reported that her mother referred to herself as *La Chingona* (The Bad Ass)[63]—the Toscano footage bears evidence to this angle of her experience.

The final feting of the India Bonita took place in the stately Esparanza Iris Theater with its stage refashioned to look like the interior of an Aztec temple. Guests included dignitaries and members of high society, all of whom were encouraged to come dressed in Indigenous clothing.[64] Bibiana was positioned at stage center on a throne from which she observed a series of speeches and performances exalting the pageant and the Indigenous race. The evening's festivities included a performance by the Orquestra Típica del Centenario under the direction of the famed composer Miguel Lerdo de Tejada.[65] A photograph that ran alongside the *El Universal's* coverage of this homage shows Bibiana Uribe on her throne flanked by members of the orchestra, including several women dressed as *chinas poblanas*. The paper's coverage of Bibiana Uribe came to an abrupt halt after this event, leaving readers to wonder what happened when she returned home, what became of all those prizes, and whether or not she decided to take up the offer to attend school in Puebla.

ORCHESTRATING AUTHENTICITY

Several months after María Bibiana Uribe's victory, a debate about the legitimacy of her Indigenous heritage broke out in the pages of *El Universal* and its competitor, *Excelsior*. The discourse employed in that debate highlighted the contradictions of the racializing logics at play in the pageant. In a lengthy article published in April 1922, *Excélsior* tried to provoke a scandal by charging that María Bibiana Uribe was not a truly authentic Indigenous woman.[66] They also discredited her title as *la virgen indígena* by revealing that just three months after her India Bonita crowning, she gave birth to a child. In a menacing tone, *Excélsior* contended that Bibiana had tricked *El Universal* and the pageant judges into thinking that she was Indigenous. Reporters bolstered their case by attempting to show just how modern she was. They argued that her hometown was no longer a traditional Indigenous community because a dam constructed outside of Necaxa by the Motriz Light and Power Company had displaced them. *Excélsior* went on to allege that Bibiana had never worn traditional Indigenous dress (*traje*) before her participation in the pageant, that she only feigned ignorance of the Spanish language, and that she carried the painted *jícara* (gourd) bowl visible in many of her postpageant portraits just for show.[67]

The newspaper's investigation claimed that the only "Indian blood" to be found in Bibiana's family came from her maternal grandmother, but that her paternal grandparents and parents were already "perfectly mestizo." As proof of this point, the reporter presented a list of what he clearly found to be damning evidence: María Bibiana Uribe had long been exposed to "civilized people," he argued, and her father was a town leader, did not speak Mexicano, and had always dressed in so-called European clothing. *Excélsior* also claimed that the *india bonita*'s typical dress—which they said consisted of silk blouses, patent leather shoes, and finely woven stockings—stood in contrast to the "fanciful, arbitrary" costume she donned during the India Bonita pageant.

To *Excélsior*, entanglement with modernity amounted to proof that Bibiana was mestiza, not Indigenous.[68] The charges belied the common misperceptions that only people living in rural, traditional homelands, speaking Native languages, and eating ancestral foods, all while remaining completely untouched by modernity, could truly claim to be Indigenous.[69] The implication that the communities who were displaced by the Necaxa dam—a major modernization project of the time—were less Indigenous because they had lost their ancestral homelands shows the insidious and self-replicating nature of settler colonial logic.

El Universal promptly answered these charges in a series of articles aimed at discrediting *Excelsior* by recounting the details of the pageant and explicitly spelling out the slippery racial calculations that informed it. *El Universal* reminded its readers that they had organized the pageant to celebrate Indigenous peoples on the anniversary of the nation's independence, that it had been judged by authorities of Indigenous race and culture, and that the finalists had been brought to the offices of *El Universal* so that the judges could personally see the candidates to avoid any fraudulent contestants.[70] Then, in bolded, capitalized typeface, the paper listed the things about María Bibiana Uribe that, to them, so clearly proved her to be a member of the Indigenous race:

BROWN SKIN, BLACK EYES, SHORT STATURE, DELICATE HANDS AND FEET, SMOOTH, BLACK HAIR, ETC. FROM A RACIAL PERSPECTIVE SHE BELONGS TO THE AZTEC FAMILY, WHICH IS DISPERSED ACROSS VARIOUS PARTS OF THE COUNTRY; HER LANGUAGE IS MEXICANO.[71]

The tone and block lettering conveyed a sense of impatience at yet again having to explain what made someone Indigenous when surely, to their minds, these points had been generously made over the course of the pageant itself. The article contended that both of María Bibiana Uribe's parents were indeed Indigenous and that her accent as well as her manner of speaking proved her identity. Finally, the author responded to *Excélsior*'s claims that the pregnancy voided her rights to the India Bonita title and instead celebrated the fact that this perfect emblem of the Indigenous race had brought another of her type into the world. This confounding reversal of the previous emphasis on Bibiana's virginity was probably a face-saving gesture, but it also serves as further evidence of the arbitrary nature of race and gender constructs in Mexican identity projects.

The following day, another *El Universal* article penned by Manuel Gamio delved more deeply into explicit race science than any previously published discourse about the pageant.[72] Gamio again spelled out the physical characteristics that made Bibiana identifiably Indigenous: her hair color and type, the color of her eyes, the specific configuration of her cheekbones and ears, and other details that, he said, would be too "tiresome" to explain. He went on to say that he could scientifically prove Bibiana's Indigenous heritage, perhaps alluding to anthropometric measurements like those he had used in his studies of the people of Teotihuacán.[73] He then ridiculed some of the racial logic that *Excélsior* had employed and especially the idea that Indigenous people in modern or European dress were somehow less Indigenous than their *traje*-wearing relatives. He conveniently declined to point out that by favoring Indigenous women who wore traditional dress, the pageant had itself relied on similar materialist calculations. Gamio concluded by stating that distinguishing the genetic differences between one race and the other was one of the greatest challenges facing anthropology but that, overall, Mestizaje and Indigeneity were not simple matters that could be defined by blood.

Gamio's views differed sharply from those he advanced during the course of the pageant. His ideology had probably been informed by the second annual International Eugenics Congress, which he attended in Washington, D.C., in September of 1921, just as María Bibiana Uribe was being crowned the India Bonita.[74] Gamio's understanding that racial and cultural identity ran deeper than material markers or blood quantum was relatively enlightened for his time. But they contradicted the pageant's previous, more enduring message that clothing, language, and the antimodern defined Indigeneity. Despite his vociferous refutation of *Excélsior*'s charges, the logic behind the victory of María Bibiana Uribe—the one candidate who most clearly demonstrated mastery of her Nahua language and dress—reinforced the conceptions of Indigeneity described in *Excélsior*.

CONCLUSION

Ultimately, the India Bonita pageant was part of a highly racialized and gendered effort driven primarily by cultural elites to place Indigenous peoples within the nascent formulations of postrevolutionary national identity. Because of prevailing beliefs that something had to be done to make Indigenous peoples a better integrated part of the nation, simply writing them out of the narrative or adopting genocidal approaches were not viable options. But there was neither clear policy nor an identifiable solution for moving forward in constructing a new identity for the nation and dealing with the so-called Indian Problem. Rather, a cacophony of voices attempted to articulate what modern Indigeneity ought to look like and what elements of it to incorporate into a modern national identity. Centering the discourse on women through the guise of a beauty contest, as the India Bonita pageant did, allowed for the incorporation of less threatening aspects of Indigeneity into national identity formation without increasing anxieties about the perceived sociocultural and physical threats posed by Indigenous men.[75]

The pageant discursively and visually narrowed the parameters of authentic Indigeneity to a particular look, linguistic category, and rural, undeveloped point of origin. Casting Indigenous peoples as rural and identifiable by distinct markers like dress and hairstyle was part of an early attempt to delineate boundaries between mestizo and Indigenous, "impure" Indians from "authentic" ones. With the judges' selection of one of the few rural-dwelling contestants as the winner, the pageant also replicated the idea that Indigeneity in its purest form existed outside of the city and that urban, mixed-race, Spanish-speaking individuals were somehow less Indigenous than their relatives in the country.

The pageant also promoted the idea that the purest and noblest form of Indigeneity existed in the past by focusing on the candidate with the clearest connections to Aztec culture and by playing up this connection with references like "Moctezuma's race." By perpetuating the idea that Aztec affiliation constituted the purest form of Indigeneity, the pageant devalued other Indigenous groups and made it easier to write those peoples out of national identity narratives. It also manufactured superficial forms of atonement and reconciliation for the legacies of colonial violence while paving the way for individuals and businesses to profit from performative apologies. Finally, the emphasis on sexuality, assimilation, and appropriation helped normalize the biological and cultural integration seen as being essential to forging the postrevolutionary nation.

But while the pageant orchestrators, judges, and readership were parsing through the narrative threads of this nascent identity, Indigenous women were strategically engaging and disengaging on their own terms. Despite the prevailing messages of the pageant that Indigenous women were rural and traditional, the contestant entries and community responses evidence the rich complexity of Indigenous peoples' lives. Seeing this glimpse into narratives that rarely find their way into the archival record is valuable in its own right, but it also does something more. These women were urban, modern, and complex. Their inclusion in the pageant and their responses to it provides a counternarrative to postrevolutionary mythology that positioned Indigenous peoples as being antithetical to modernity. And it shows that these women, especially those who nominated themselves, still considered themselves Indigenous even though Mexican identity politics had rewritten them as being mestiza for their entanglements with urbanity and modern living.

The India Bonita pageant has had a long afterlife. The ideas articulated in the process of finding the nation's "prettiest Indian" influenced popular representations of Indigenous women for decades to come, laid important groundwork for the fledgling postrevolutionary identity projects of Indigenismo and Mestizaje, and reaffirmed racial ideologies and hierarchies that continue to inform Mexican understandings of Indianness today. As with other settler colonial projects, these imposed racial and cultural ideals continue to reproduce a range of romanticized and racialized attitudes about what it looks like and means to be Indigenous. The pageant reinforced the parameters of the conversation about what "authentic" Indigeneity looked like and the people who were authorized to have that conversation. Though non-Indigenous men's voices were the loudest and most visible, the Indigenous women who participated in the India Bonita contest were also critical interlocutors. Their presence serves as an important reminder that in the midst of Indigenismo and Mestizaje projects, the Indigenous experience remained multifaceted and included varying degrees of engagement with—and departure from—efforts to police ever-narrowing parameters of "authentic" Indigeneity.

LA FLOR MÁS BELLA DEL EJIDO

Springtime Maidens, Invented Tradition, and Making
a "Modern" Mexico City

AFTER WENDING YOUR WAY THROUGH the chaotic, crowded streets
of Mexico City's *centro histórico*, the sudden, stark silence inside the
secretary of public education building can be jarring. But this dis-
orientation is quickly forgotten as you're drawn into the world Diego Rivera
painted into being decades ago. His murals sprawl across two courtyards and
three floors of the massive building. Commissioned by Secretary of Education
José Vasconcelos in 1923, they constitute one of the earliest state-sponsored
attempts to visually represent the postrevolutionary social order.[1] The panels
depict everything from pre-Hispanic heroism and caricatures of Wall Street
bourgeoisie to statuesque Indigenous women and the blue-collar mestizo men
tasked with building the modern nation.

One panel, titled "Viernes de Dolores en el Canal de Santa Anita" (Friday of
Sorrows in the Santa Anita Canal), is framed by statuesque women cloaked in
long skirts and rebozos. Behind them, a crowded waterway stretches into the
distance. As with many of his paintings, color has a nearly tangible presence,
from burnt umber skin tones to the meaty reds of the poppy crowns adorning
the heads of many of the women. The panel is saturated in details that would
have signaled "tradition" to viewers in the 1920s: female flower vendors dominate the foreground, and men in stark white cotton *traje* steer boats laden with
revelers through a crowded waterway.

The site depicted in Rivera's mural is Santa Anita Zacatlamanco, a pueblo that had rested on the banks of Lago Texcoco long before invading Spaniards forced their diseases and their god onto the people of Anahuac. It now sits squarely within the central quadrants of the sprawling megalopolis of Mexico City. It's a poor, working-class neighborhood that still holds its traditions dear. On a recent weekend afternoon, residents packed into a small zocalo in boisterous celebration. *Papel picado* flapped in the wind while mariachi music and the sound of *cohetes* (fireworks) filled the air. The waterways that once defined the region exist now only in two dimensions: a tile fresco in the metro station there depicts men steering canoes, and a series of similarly themed murals adorn the concrete pillars of the Calzada de la Viga, a major axis road that traces the path of the now-defunct Canal de la Viga waterway. One mural reads, "The coronation of springtime maidens is the pre-Hispanic heritage of the Santa Ana Pueblo." A neighboring mural depicts one of these maidens as a fair-skinned woman in an embroidered peasant blouse, arms laden with a bounty of corn.

Both Rivera's mural and the more recent murals in Santa Anita invoke a pageant not unlike the India Bonita contest. This pageant had deep roots in the pre-Hispanic past but underwent a postrevolutionary makeover that made it similar enough in form and function that the two are often conflated. What became known as the Flor más Bella del Ejido pageant sought out attractive young Indigenous women and measured their authenticity against a narrow set of cultural signifiers, mannerisms, and phenotypes. And with many of the same men orchestrating and judging the pageants, its revival as a postrevolutionary tradition might well be an extension of sorts of the India Bonita contest.

This chapter traces the postrevolutionary history of this pageant and the Viernes de Flores festivities it was part of, showing how the events were crafted to become a major component of Mexico City's folklife over the course of the Cultural Revolution. In doing so, Mexico City bureaucrats and intellectuals carved out select spaces in which to preserve memories of the Aztec past while also discursively untethering Indigenous claims to autonomy and land in a rapidly urbanizing landscape. In all of this, invented tradition, anthropology, and media coverage worked to delimit popular understandings of Indigenous authenticity to a narrow set of cultural and geographic factors. Ultimately, this invented tradition—and the beauty pageant within it—were made complicit in the settler colonial project of classification, dispossession, and constructed belongings.

RITUAL AND REINVENTION

The roots of the Flor más Bella del Ejido pageant can be found in a pre-Hispanic harvest ritual that involved the selection and sacrifice of young maidens in honor of the goddess Xochiquetzal.[2] Deemed satanic by Catholics, the tradition was appropriated and merged with Viernes de Dolores celebrations, which occurred every year on the Friday before Holy Week. The syncretic festival was firmly rooted in its place of origin—Zacatlamanco Huéhuetl, later known as Santa Anita Zacatlamanco or just Santa Anita, a *pueblo originario* that served as a bucolic reminder of Tenochtitlan's lacustrine origins.

While much of the rest of the city had been reinvented to mirror European cityscapes, Santa Anita remained a semiagrarian space profoundly shaped by its ties to water well into the twentieth century. For centuries it played a critical role as a bridge between Mexico City and the campo as a thoroughfare for food and other goods coming in to the capital. Beginning in the eighteenth century, city dwellers would escape the stresses of city life for tranquil boat rides down the Canal de la Viga. Oil paintings from the era show musicians serenading passersby while women in canoes sell flowers, fruits, and sweets. Alexander von Humboldt as well as other lesser-known explorers wrote romantic homages to Santa Anita.[3] In 1901 the famous Indios Verdes—bronze statues of Aztec emperors Ahuizotl and Izcoatl forged for the Mexican pavilion at the 1889 Paris World's Fair—were relocated from the Paseo de la Reforma to stand at the head of the Canal de la Viga,[4] symbolically demarcating Santa Anita as Indigenous space and setting it apart from Mexico City's insatiable urban sprawl.

By the time Mexico fell under the heavy hand of the Porfiriato, the Viernes de Dolores festival had little to do with its pre-Hispanic origins, but its location in Santa Anita alone suggested an association with the Indigenous past. Renamed Viernes de la Primavera by Díaz himself, the event drew crowds each spring and became a major economic boon to the semiurban enclave.[5] But the fantasy of traveling to a pastoral Mexico Viejo was disrupted by modernist anxieties surrounding safety and cleanliness. An 1884 typhoid outbreak raised public health concerns about the murky waters of the canal, further upsetting its romantic appeal.[6] By 1904 a journalist writing for *El Imparcial* noted that the traditional festivities had been nearly forgotten.[7]

Even so, the event continued for the remainder of the Porfiriato and throughout the decade of revolutionary warfare. Francisco Madero supposedly attended during his short tenure as president, but by then the health concerns and overgrowth of water lilies in the Canal de la Viga had led to depleted crowds and fears that the tradition was soon to be lost altogether.[8] At the same time, Santa Anita's population was beginning to swell with rural-dwelling Indigenous peoples seeking refuge from the devastation of the revolution. The region's Indigenous identity was not simply an elite construction—this semirural space was indeed a pan-Indian mecca, and it became even more so during the 1910s and 1920s.[9]

As the age of postrevolutionary reconstruction dawned, renewed interest in patrimony and tradition once again turned public attention to the event. After an underwhelming turnout for the 1920 festivities, newspaper commentators penned heartfelt lamentations about the lost tradition. Journalist Fernando Ramírez de Aguilar—more commonly known by his pen name Jacobo Dalevuelta—contributed much of this reporting. As with his coverage of the 1921 India Bonita festival and as his chosen name suggests, his writing was infused with nostalgia for a bygone era.[10] In his critiques of Mexican patrimony, Dalevuelta played a role akin to a theater or film critic, evaluating the quality and the production of Indigeneity and *Mexicanidad*. His coverage of the event was no doubt critical to garnering the interest of citizens and bureaucrats alike.

Writing about the March 1920 Viernes de Dolores celebrations, he mourned lost traditions and the waning enthusiasm of festivalgoers. He noted that instead of the sweet smell of flowers, the air in Santa Anita was thick with the unpleasant aroma of burnt oil and pulque.[11] A photo accompanying Dalevuelta's article featured a fair-skinned woman with a dour countenance, identified as "La Reina de Santa Anita."[12] Her stiff pose, pallid complexion, and anachronistically Victorian dress belie nothing of the festival's Aztec origins or its imminent reinvention. Similarly, his coverage of the 1921 festival appeared under the subhead, "Where are the types of yesterday?" and went on to express profound sorrow at the loss of tradition and the unsavory signs of encroaching modernity and urbanization.[13]

Even so, knowledge of the festival's Aztec origins remained alive in public memory. A 1922 article in *Revista de Revistas* paid homage to the legendary festivals of Xochiquetzal, arguing that the Viernes de Dolores festivities were an ideal bridge between the Indigenous past and the modern, mestizo present. While other Indigenous traditions were considered "orgiastic hullabaloos" or "funerary recreation," the author opined that the Viernes de Dolores festival brought together icons of national identity like the "silent *india* with the enigmatic smile" and the "archaic *charro*." He concluded that the legendary "festival of Xochiquetzal" was indeed "one of the foundations of Mexico City's soul."[14] Despite their efforts, the 1922 festival was again a flaccid affair for elite urbanites and, according to hand-wringing journalists, appeared on the verge of being abandoned altogether.[15]

REBIRTH OF THE FIESTA DE FLORES

Journalists' amplification of this "dying" tradition and coinciding interest in rejuvenating the city's folklife brought renewed attention to the festival. In the early 1920s, local government and the cultural elite were keenly interested in fomenting traditions that complemented broader efforts to symbolically incorporate Indigenous peoples. From murals to performances, the Cultural Revolution was blossoming across the city. And the Viernes de Dolores festival, with its pre-Hispanic origins and syncretic symbolism, was ripe for this nationalist project.

Nineteen twenty-three would prove to be a watershed moment for a resurgence of the Fiesta de Flores. That year high-ranking members of the city and municipal governments crafted a major revitalization and reenvisioning of the annual event.[16] They strategized about how to amplify the festival's folkloric nature while also making it more orderly and modern, mandating decorations like *papel picado* and directing dirt roadways to be tarred in order to reduce dust.[17] They also imposed traffic-management plans, banned pulque consumption, upped the military and police presence in order to avoid "scandals and discordant notes," encouraged the trolley company to participate in a new competition of floral decorations, outlined plans to build "Mexican style" pavilions in which bands could perform, and asked the Association of Mexican Charros to organize *jaripeos*. The Department of Diversions granted a sum of 750 pesos so that pamphlets featuring Viernes de Dolores history and poetry could be distributed to attendees.[18] These reforms were all intended to give the event what organizers called an "extremely popular character."[19]

The desire to recraft Viernes de Dolores as a proletarian event only became more pronounced as plans developed. Government officials invited members of the working class to participate, and Secretary of Government Julio Jiménez

Rueda asked that working women be granted leave on the day of the festival in order to facilitate their attendance.[20] Organizers reached out to the municipalities of Santa Anita as well as neighboring Ixtapalapa and Ixtacalco. The planning was being directed by higher-ups in the city government, but they made concerted efforts to engage workers and locals.

At the heart of this revamped tradition would be the election of a queen. A typed planning document initially dictated that a woman from high society should be selected; however, the phrase "high society" was later crossed out and the word *obrera* (female worker) penned in above. Despite the fact that it came as an afterthought, the decision to honor a member of the working class rather than a woman from high society was a deliberate one that would come to define the character of this postrevolutionary reinvention.

This popular reinvention was a success, at least according to some of the city's cultural elite. In his *El Universal* coverage, Dalevuelta delighted over what he deemed an authentic recreation of an ancient tradition.[21] He praised the new contests and noted that cash prizes had been awarded for decorated canoes, floral arches, vendors who dressed in *china poblana* clothing, and original songs.[22]

The working-class Reina de la Fiesta was Carmen Aguilera, a nineteen-year-old employed by the Departamento Establecimientos Fabriles y Militares. Neither Dalevuelta nor anyone else provided information about why Aguilera was selected or by whom, but a photo published in *El Universal* shows her dressed in a black, braided wig, wearing hoop earrings and an embroidered blouse (fig. 4).[23] This photo documents a noticeable transformation in the new queen who, just a few days before, had been pictured in *El Universal* sporting a cropped bob and less ornate clothing.[24] The transformation of the festival, it seems, also necessitated individual participants to transform themselves.

The election of a working-class queen had a precedent in the Obrera Simpática pageant of 1918 in which *El Universal* sought out the "kindest" factory worker at a moment of social discomfort caused by young women supplanting the male workforce.[25] At the time, the pageant helped normalize the idea of female laborers in the revolutionary workforce. The fact that a working-class *china poblana* had replaced high-society queens in the 1923 makeover of an Aztec festival reveals the patchwork of cultural appropriation and proletarian interests at the heart of revolutionary reconstruction. It also signals an attempt to grapple with the influx of women in the city, many of whom arrived without male guardians and threatened to upend the desired social order.[26]

FIGURE 4. Carmen Aguilera, the working-class queen of the Fiesta de Flores the year of the festival's rebirth. *El Universal*, March 24, 1923. Biblioteca Lerdo de Tejada.

There are no *chinas poblanas* in Rivera's SEP (Secretaría de Educación Pública) mural depiction of the 1923 festival, but he did cede some space to the elite consumption of the event: a *chica moderna* with a bob haircut and flapper dress appears in the foreground, the exaggerated whiteness of her face appearing as a glowing orb above the Indigenous vendors kneeling before her. Pudgy, pink-skinned tourists also populate the crowd, an American flag adorning the hat of one, suggesting a subtle critique of the American consumerism of Mexican culture. Overall, the mural is an aspirational portrayal of a vibrant Nahua celebration with women, as in much of Rivera's work, being marked as the primary bearers of tradition.

Rivera's mural also hints at the very real economic benefits of Viernes de Dolores celebrations.[27] It had long been the case that festivalgoers would come to the event to stock up on flowers for their Semana Santa altars, making it a major boon to Santa Anita's economy.[28] And with increased attendance came increased potential to sell flowers, food, and other wares. It also shows the festival to be a grounds for the mingling of different races, classes, and nationalities. But this was no easy melting pot. The boundaries of ideal Indigenous comportment were volubly articulated and enforced in order to make the experience desirable to the well-heeled elites who crowded in for the day.

"AUTHENTIC" INDIANS ON PARADE

The colorful scene crafted by the cultural commission in 1923 established the essence of the Fiesta de Flores as it would come to be known for the next several decades. And Rivera's depiction of the event might have influenced planning in subsequent years. In 1924 the festival was even more elaborate than the previous year, and dignitaries, including President Álvaro Obregón himself, were in attendance.[29] A contest for Indigenous dress was held alongside contests for *chinas poblanas*, *charros*, and regional song and dance. A Juchitecan woman in a classic Tehuana dress won first place in the new Indigenous dress competition, and *El Universal* coverage assured readers of her authenticity. One reporter noted that her handmade costume had "the flavor of La Sandunga" without the flashy qualities of costume props. And while the winner of the contest was never named, coverage of her victory included multiple references to her ethnic purity and even quoted a "Tehuana expert" as saying, "women like that, with Tehuana ardor in their eyes, have until now only been seen in El Espinal" (a village in southwestern Oaxaca).[30] This treatment of the victor as a rare specimen was not part of the newspaper's discussion of any other contest winners.

In addition to the vague but persistent discussion of authenticity that framed the pageant, the victory of the Tehuana woman was notable for a few reasons. First, celebrations of Xochiquetzal and her springtime flower maidens were not part of her cultural heritage. The fact that a Tehuana woman won the first Indigenous dress competition in what was originally an Aztec event underscores the curatorial nature of postrevolutionary identity projects. Under the pretense of revitalizing "authentic" traditions, orchestrators created a cultural cornucopia that at times paid little heed to religion or cultural traditions while at the same time regularly employing the language of authenticity.

Second, it evidences the fact that Tehuana women were icons that had enduring appeal even at the height of the Aztec vogue. Although modernity was often constructed as being antithetical to Indigeneity, popular beliefs that Tehuanas were sexually progressive, aristocratic, and just "exotic" enough helped position them as symbols of Indigenous modernity.[31] As a result, the Tehuana became an established national type often captured in ethnographic photography, film, postcards, and advertisements. Even as the Nahua-inspired *india bonita* came to symbolize the ideal icon of Indigeneity, the Tehuana remained a permanent fixture in the Mexican imaginary.[32]

From 1925 through 1927, the festival became increasingly infused with the flavors of revolutionary reconstruction. Although Jacobo Dalevuelta wrote only occasionally about it for *El Universal*, the paper's coverage continued to praise the rebirth of its traditional components while disparaging less desirable elements, frequent complaints about traffic, excessive pulque consumption, and dusty air. Despite these inconveniences, the newspaper presented the festival as a way to connect with the nation's past and the minor annoyances as a necessary part of the experience. Ironically, headlines in *El Universal* such as "The Resurrection of the Traditional Viernes de Dolores Celebrations" continued to imply that the festival had just been recovered.[33] Each year's organizer, it seemed, wanted to take credit for revitalizing the festival, and *El Universal* capitalized on the supposed novelty to craft attention-grabbing headlines and to praise the event's resurgence with unwavering vigor.

As the festival developed, so, too, did the competitions for *traje*, which were described interchangeably as "regional" or Indigenous dress, and for *chinas poblanas*. While an official Viernes de Dolores queen was rarely named, the victors of these two competitions were always prominently featured in photo spreads accompanying newspaper coverage of the festivities. Despite the fact that they were discussed as separate icons, the styling of the *china poblana* victors often invoked the *india bonita* trope with their long, braided hair and embroidered blouses. Indigenous women were held to stricter codes of authenticity but at times incorporated elements of strappy dance shoes and *pelona* (bob) haircuts into their own styling. For example, the photo of the 1925 winner of the Indigenous dress competition shows a woman with short hair and with notably pale skin. The winner of the *china poblana* competition, in contrast, sported long braids, a huipil, and a rebozo slung across her shoulders. This visual overlap highlights the blurry line between national types and hints at a larger slippage between racial boundaries and icons of national identity.

The Indian Maiden and the *china poblana* were treated as distinct icons, but the differences between the two played out more as a spectrum than as a clear binary and with plenty of crossover between the two tropes (fig. 5). Despite

FIGURE 5. *Indias bonitas* and *chinas poblanas* with almost indistinguishable styling. *El Universal*, April 13, 1935. Biblioteca Lerdo de Tejada.

this ambiguity, terms used to describe the pageant winners varied markedly depending on the contestants' ethnicity. The *china poblana*—a national icon who some trace back to seventeenth-century East Indian slaves, servants, and the visionary Mirrha-Catarina de San Juan[34]—was dubbed the "ideal Mexican Amazon," while diminutive terms were regularly used to describe Indigenous women.[35] In 1926, for example, the winner of the regional dress competition was identified as being Zapotec, but *El Universal* used the words *precious* and *gentle* in the brief identification that accompanied the photo. Although this sort of language might seem benign, it was exclusively employed in discussing the Indigenous candidates and echoed other popular discourses that attempted to cast ideal female Indigeneity as being meek, compliant, and in need of domination. Although there was crossover between the styling of the two types, the Indigenous contestants were treated with a level of racialized scrutiny and assessment that the *chinas poblanas* were not.

As the festival developed over the next several decades, *El Universal* played a particularly important role in hyping the event and in disseminating information about it far beyond the boundaries of the metropolis. For the most part, newspaper photographs of the festival and Indigenous dress pageant winners mirrored ethnographic type photography, providing visual referents for picturing a particular brand of Indigeneity and *Mexicanidad*. The articles that accompanied these photographs provided a widely circulated guide to ideal Indigenous comportment, praising certain traits such as demure behavior and good health and accomplishments such as craft production and the practice of certain traditions. At the same time, they shamed Indigenous people for less desirable behaviors such as excessive drinking, gambling, and fighting.

In his coverage of the event, Dalevuelta condemned the presence of gambling tables and the moral hazards that accompanied them, imploring the government to have more stringent regulations in the future. He closed one otherwise felicitous article by noting that by the end of the day, drunks and gamblers filled the jail cells.[36] Despite his distaste for this "immoral behavior," Dalevuelta also made the case that one of the best things about the celebration was its chaos and disorder. This contradictory attitude—at once condemning and condoning popular celebrations—was in step with other postrevolutionary efforts to craft ideal behavior, selecting aspects of folk traditions to praise while denigrating others as being "backward."

In 1927 festival attendance surpassed previous years, with throngs of people turning out by car, on foot, and on horseback to celebrate. The city raised the water levels in the canal so that the elaborately decorated floats would be more visible to the crowds.[37] The Indigenous dress competition included Tehuanas as well as other groups from Oaxaca, Michoacán, Sinaloa, and the state of Mexico. Silvia Loyo, a florist from Michoacán, was named queen. For the first and only time in the postrevolutionary reconstruction era of the pageant, an Indigenous man, Zapotec Indian Luciano Kubli, was selected to reign alongside the female victor.[38] Although there was no discussion of his dress or behavior, *El Universal* noted that he serenaded the crowd with two songs he had composed: "Tell me yes, Trigueña" (slang meaning "wheat-colored" woman) and "The Illusion of the Rancher." Kubli's inclusion in the festival was an anomaly and highlights how—outside of celebrating of long dead Aztec warriors—celebration of Indigenous masculinity was often left to the periphery of postrevolutionary identity projects.

EVERYTHING OLD IS NEW AGAIN

Beginning in 1928 organizers placed greater emphasis on the festival's historical and performative components. For the first time, the organizing committee established specific contest rules and made them available to the public.[39]

Performances received greater attention with the installation of a permanent platform on the western side of the canal. Those interested in vying for that year's prizes were instructed to bring a letter of intent to the administrative section of the Ayuntamiento, at which point they would receive the details of the competition. While there, they could also view samples of the antique Indigenous dress that contestants would be required to wear. *El Universal* explained to its readers that these new contests and accompanying cash prizes were a way to keep the traditional festival from dying while also capturing some of its original splendor.[40]

In addition to its new historical emphasis, photographs from the 1928 festival illustrate the extent to which it remained an opportunity for cross-cultural and cross-class encounters. In one photo, bourgeois women wearing flower crowns and fashionable jackets sip tea from porcelain saucers while a group of Indigenous women, costumed in frumpy Victorian-era maids uniforms, cluster around a large clay *olla*. In another photograph, Indigenous women sit on the bare earth surrounded by bundles of flowers for sale while upper-class women teeter over them in high heels and fur coats paired with flower crowns and necklaces. The new Fiesta de Flores rendered postrevolutionary invented tradition a consumable entity, allowing social elites to try on other ethnic and social identities for a day and then return to their modern lives in the city. At the same time, this commodification made the festival an even more important economic opportunity for the residents of Santa Anita.

The climax of the 1928 festival was a series of contests in which all participants were required to don historical clothing from the 1870s. Three high-profile men served as judges: historian Nicolas Rangel, labor leader Vicente Lombardo Toledano, and writer Darío Rubio.[41] In addition to the then-standard *charro* and *china poblana* contests, the jury awarded prizes to the best-dressed Indigenous vendors. While *El Universal* provided no clear explanation as to why the contests would be based on the 1870s in particular, the implication was that this older version was somehow more pure and might be read as nostalgia for premodern life, as that decade came just before Porfirio Díaz ushered in his sweeping modernization reforms.

The attempts to inspire historical reenactment through the competitions had mixed results. The contest for the best-dressed male vendor failed to draw any contenders, pointing to the fact that, in this case at least, Indigenous men opted out of the performative creation of national identity. The *china poblana* contest, on the other hand, was so competitive that it sparked a fierce debate among the jurors before they eventually settled on awarding three prizes.[42] Silvia Arroyo won the award for best-dressed Indigenous female vendor with her convincing 1870s dress and display. Arroyo had installed a *puesto de aguas frescas* (vendor station for *aguas frescas*) in her large canoe, going so far as to incorporate utensils and other embellishments from the 1870s. Arroyo's victory highlights the element of performance in the festival and some Indigenous women's willingness to adapt to changing criteria. However, it also points to the irony that contestants and vendors had to invest in costumes and props if they wanted to reap the benefits of a festival that was ostensibly a celebration of some of the city's poorer residents.

Organizers of the 1929 Viernes de Dolores festivities went all in on the historical reenactments, recreating what they said was the first festival held in the canal in 1703.[43] Actors played the Duque de Albuquerque (Viceroy of New Spain from 1702 to 1710) and his wife, Virreina Juana de la Cerda, whom organizers credited with organizing the original colonial-era festival. Organizers went to great lengths to accurately represent the Virrey and Virreina and their court, with artist Carlos González crafting costumes based on the historic paintings that hung in the history wing of the Museo Nacional.

An article in *El Universal* detailed the artistry behind the costumes for the entire court. They reported on the fine brocades and silks, gold and silver embroidery, all rendered in the original colors of the court: violet and black for the male attendants and green, electric blue, and purple for the maids of honor. The costumes for the Indigenous members of the party were also given careful consideration. As court servants, they were to wear a yellow muslin tunic and the "conical hat worn by natives of China and Japan." The women who sold *aguas frescas* at the festival would be costumed in long underskirts with big ruffles, white blouses, and silk scarves.[44]

Jacobo Dalevuelta returned after a seven-year hiatus to report on the 1929 pageant for *El Universal*. He infused his coverage with his signature florid language, and in an unabashedly celebratory tone he wrote about how the class divisions that once plagued the nation had been left behind in the previous century. He also praised this festival for allowing "brother Indians" to open their doors to the outside world to share the fruits of their rich and humid lands as well as to show the charms of their simple, "flower-enveloped" lives.[45] Dalevuelta noted with disgust that in a "disconcerting act of falseness and stupidity," many people arrived at the event wearing hats made of imported multicolor paper instead of buying the traditional fresh poppies that were widely available for sale at the festival. His irritation at the fact that not all attendees were equally committed to accurately recreating previous eras belied the high premium Dalevuelta and the festival organizers placed on what they perceived to be historical authenticity. However, it also marks one of the few times that the scrutinizing gaze was turned toward the festival attendees and not just its Indigenous participants.

In fact the overall focus of the 1929 festival shifted away from Indigenous and popular celebrations. While the accuracy and opulence of the colonial display garnered admiration and awe from the crowds, the Indigenous *traje* contest received less attention than in previous years. Since not a single contestant in the "Inditas Mexicanas" (a diminutive form of Mexican Indian women) contest conformed to the regulations, the prize was instead awarded to a group of female students who wore simple rebozos atop their heads along with cotton blouses and long skirts.[46] This suggests that the standards set for the Indigenous dress competition might have been too specific and too costly or perhaps just seemed too absurd to women who would have otherwise been viable candidates.

In comparison to previous years, the 1929 Viernes de Dolores showed a marked shift toward celebrating a constructed colonial fantasy that reframed the violent past as a tale of racial and class harmony. Neither organizers nor journalists articulated the logic behind this highly produced historical turn, but there are a couple likely explanations. Perhaps it reflected another current of nationalism, *Hispanismo*, which exalted Mexico's European past in hopes of elevating Mexico's status as a cosmopolitan nation. The shift might also have had something to do with the fact that the city was in the midst of a major reorganization in 1929. The newly formed Departamento del Distrito Federal (DDF) centralized governance in the metropolis, effectively removing power from the original delegations. José Manuel Puig Casauranc was the inaugural chief of the DDF and oversaw his department's sponsorship of the 1929 Viernes de Dolores celebrations. Casauranc was an Indigenista but also a known Hispanist, belying his anti-Indigenous sentiments in articles like the one he wrote for *El Universal* about "backward" Indians on the eve of the India Bonita pageant.[47] Perhaps he saw some merit in weaving the colonial past into popular postrevolutionary identity as he and others sought to both modernize the city and preserve some of its original character.

Historical reenactments drove the 1930 competition as well, but that year a more recent past dominated the scene. As part of the festivities, the National

Museum sponsored a float with ten youth dressed in museum-quality replicas of clothing from 1830.[48] *El Universal* coverage noted that because the national museum produced the costumes, they were surely accurate, a sentiment that reflected the widespread belief that museums were proprietors of authentic knowledge about the nation's past. Matilde Urzais "personifying" an Indigenous woman from San Pedro Ixcatlán, Oaxaca, won the Indigenous dress competition by donning a "legitimate" costume from her region that dated to 1870 (fig. 6). In the use of the word *personificar* (personify), *El Universal* implied that the winner might have been an actor performing both the past and Indianness rather than a woman who identified as being Indigenous.[49] This possibility is further supported by the portrait that ran in the paper alongside coverage of the event. The caption referred to Ursaiz as a *dama* (lady) and the photo indicates familiarity with performance: she gingerly holds her dress out as though for display and strikes a dancer's pose with her Mary Jane–clad feet. Regardless of her heritage, Urzais was performing just the type of Indigenous behavior the judges were looking for.

Two sisters from Michoacán, Silvia and Alicia Loyo,[50] were named runners up in the 1930 Indigenous dress competition. In an *El Universal* photo, Alicia appears dressed as an Indigenous man, wearing a simple white cotton suit with a scarf tied around her neck, *huaraches*, a sombrero, and stage makeup including lipstick and eyeliner. Sylvia's stance also reveals an air of theatricality: although she appears in relatively simple dress, she poses expertly with her hand on a playfully jutted-out hip while holding a large bouquet of flowers in the crook of her opposite elbow. This, combined with the fact that Sylvia had also won the 1927 competition by outdoing other performers with her historic *puesto*, illustrates her comfort with costume and performance and raises the possibility that she was a professional or semiprofessional actress.

Despite all these indications of performance, festival organizers and journalists continued to express concern with the authentic reproduction of tradition. Under the subhead "A Note of Bad Taste," an *El Universal* reporter following Jacobo Dalevuelta's lead lamented the widespread use of paper garlands instead of the more traditional flower ones. In the *charro* competition, no one was declared winner because none of the contestants adequately met the contest criteria. Considering the concern with authenticity, it is striking to note the larger role that impersonation played in the festivities. Mestizos regularly wore Indigenous dress, and women performed the roles of Indigenous men. Even so, Indigenous women's authenticity was still highly

FIGURE 6. Matilde Urzais "personifying" an Indigenous woman from San Pedro Ixcatlán, Oaxaca. *El Universal*, April 12, 1930. Biblioteca Lerdo de Tejada.

scrutinized while other groups were permitted to perform and appropriate identities as they pleased.

BOUNTIFUL BEAUTY

In 1931 the festival's historical romanticism transitioned into a new focus on agricultural exposition. As *El Universal* explained, this was part of an effort to motivate those who grew vegetables and flowers and to give visitors an appreciation for all the progress that had been made in agricultural production.[51] The reintroduction of agricultural pageantry in 1931 was the first of several changes that would bring the event closer to its origins as a pre-Hispanic ode to Xochiquetzal. The festivities, which had previously been limited to a single day, lasted a full week in 1931 and included an agricultural exposition. *El Universal* reported that there would be thirty-four different stalls for entrants in various competitions. They also mandated that vendors conform to specific codes of dress and "regional authenticity," though these guidelines were never published in the newspaper. In addition to evaluating *trajes regionales*, judges would also consider the quality of the containers in which they presented products and the use of popular music in the stalls. While the weeklong celebration brought added economic benefit to Santa Anita, the performative demands made on the display of products surely ate into some of the profit for participating vendors.

From 1932 through 1935 public interest in the festival dwindled for reasons that are not made clear in newspaper accounts.[52] Even so, the Federal District's Dirección General de Acción Cívica (DGAC) continued to pour funds and revitalization efforts into the continuation of a festival they saw as being central to the city's folkloric heritage. Despite their efforts, waning enthusiasm and crime dominated coverage of the Fiesta de Flores for several years. More than a hundred men and women were arrested at the 1933 festival, and lurid accounts of spousal abuse and car accidents were more detailed than reports on costuming or competition.[53] After a decade-long resurgence, the festival seemed once again to be on the verge of being lost to history.

In 1934 the DGAC made another valiant effort to revitalize the pageant. Organizers introduced new contests to award *charros* and *chinas poblanas*, but their efforts were met with little enthusiasm from city residents, and attendance was poor.[54] In a new emphasis on *charrería* and competitions for the best-dressed *china poblana*, Aarón Sáenz Garza of DGAC insisted they were celebrating quintessential aspects of Mexican culture "infused with the spirit of love and artistic riches."[55] In 1935 organizers attempted another rebranding, changing the name of the event to Fiesta de Amapolas (Festival of Poppies). Despite their efforts, that year marked a low point for the festival. Journalists lamented that the festival's days of glory were probably not to be recovered.[56]

LA FLOR MÁS BELLA DEL EJIDO

Despite predictions of the festival's impending doom, 1936 marked a new dawn for Santa Anita and its annual celebration. Organizers announced yet another new name—La Flor más Bella del Ejido—and refocused the event on the selection of a *campesina* queen who would reign over the festival and her ejido. Although the narrative coverage of the festival was all but nonexistent in the days leading up to the festival, *El Universal* published photos of the eight finalists for the pageant.[57] Surprisingly, the photos didn't follow conventions established by beauty pageant photography or the ethnographic type photography that had appeared throughout the India Bonita contest and the earlier days of the Viernes de Dolores coverage. Instead, the images—with their borders cropped in close around the women's glowering faces—had more in common with criminal mug shots.[58] Many of the women wore lipstick and pearl earrings rather than the braids and embroidered tops that had become standard signifiers of the *india bonita* trope. *El Universal* announced that they were the finalists for the pageant and supplied their names, but they offered no other information.

Similarly, newspaper accounts of the event included little detail about how or why Ernestina Díaz of Ixtacalco was honored with the inaugural Flor más Bella del Ejido title. The photo of her coronation shows her dressed in more classic Indigenous dress than the clothing featured in her prepageant portrait: she wore an embroidered huipil tucked into a long skirt, and she styled her hair in long, loose waves.[59] New forms of regalia marked her status as queen: a flower crown and a trophy larger than her torso overflowing with flowers and inscribed with the phrase "La Flor más Bella del Ejido." The photograph of her coronation was the only image printed alongside *El Universal*'s coverage of the event that year. This single photograph in lieu of the full photo spreads of previous years was further indication of a new, almost exclusive emphasis on the pageant and election of a single *reina*.

Journalists and organizers of the 1936 pageant did little to explain what motivated the festival's new focus on feting a *campesina* beauty, though this was also likely an attempt to revive the event's "traditional element." Similarly, they spilled no ink in explaining what qualities made Ernestina Díaz the ideal representative of the region's *campesina* population. However, in conjuring the new contest, Cárdenas had specified that the young queen should have characteristics that were both culturally and biologically of "Indigenous extraction" and that she be the daughter of *ejiditarios*.[60]

This, no doubt, was part of the Cárdenas administration's broader campaign to expand the ejido program and lend an air of valor to those who participated in it. It also served to highlight the ejidos' bounty of agricultural products and healthy bodies. But this attempt to promote ejidos through popular culture also signaled yet another state co-optation of Indigenous identity. Referring to the competitors as beautiful flowers, this new "Flor más Bella del Ejido" title equated Indigenous women with rural, agricultural bounty. And the conflation of *ejidotarias*, *Indígenas*, and *campesinas* further coded Indigeneity as being inherently rural.

By 1937 organizers had developed more strategic rhetoric to describe the revamped pageant, adding the phrase "symbol of the emancipation and unification of the workers" to the Flor más Bella del Ejido title.[61] This addition at once appealed to postrevolutionary nationalism and reflected Cárdenas's growing populism. Its inclusion of the proletariat also harkened back to the event's original 1923 reinvention that went to such great lengths to ensure worker attendance, and it marked a rare instance in which the often overlapping identities of *obrera* and *indígena* were acknowledged.

El Universal dutifully repeated this framing and other nationalist messages in their coverage of the pageant. Publishing five articles in the lead-up to the event, *El Universal* journalists extolled the folkloric authenticity and the nationalist pride that the pageant represented. Other changes in the pageant format placed a premium on *Mexicanidad*: foreign music was banned and only *mariachis* were allowed who, according to *El Universal*, were "symbols of our rural musicians who no longer sing the complaints of the campesino because the harvest is so ample."[62] Contests for *trajineras* and *charreria* were revived. There was also an effort to refocus the festivities on the nation's agricultural successes. Organizers changed the name of the event to the Día del Ejido—though it would still be held on the traditional Friday of Sorrows—and women costumed as fruits and vegetables joined in on the parade of *charros* and *chinas poblanas*.[63]

El Universal coverage of the 1937 pageant stated that Señorita Leonor Alonso of Santa María Aztahuacan had been crowned the Flor más Bella del Ejido as a result of "her beauty, of the sort that is genuinely Indigenous, and as a result of her dress."[64] Although the parameters of that "genuinely Indigenous" beauty weren't made explicit, this passage suggests that they existed in some quantifiable way. The same year, organizers banned the sale of hats and paper products in order to avoid the modernization Jacobo Dalevuelta had found to be so deplorable. While "authenticity" may have been ill defined, there were at least unspoken codes and characteristics that differentiated ideal patrimony from some less desirable version of it.

From 1938 onward, the festival became increasingly centered on the pageant. Two oral history testimonies provide rare insights into how these changes were perceived by Indigenous participants. The winner of the 1938 contest, Petra Hernández, was interviewed fifty years after her victory, providing the first extensive account of the pageant from the perspective of an Indigenous woman. Hernández, who was native to Santa Anita, recalled women coming from Milpa Alta, Xochimilco, Mixquic, and Ixtacalco to compete for the title. She also remembered her pueblo coming alive for the event. Starting at 11 p.m. the night before the pageant, she remembered, the canal and a nearby park were filled with salons and kiosks, all brightly lit by little lights. Dances started at midnight, and people arrived in canoes from as far south as Jamaica (a neighborhood in Xochimilco). Santa Anita residents would make *tamales, atole,* and *pulque de apio* to sell to the masses who gathered in their pueblo.[65]

Hernández noted the performative elements of the festival: a *jaripeo* with *charros* and *chinas poblanas* as well as women dressed as *indias* and *Tehuanas* and some dressed in common, contemporary clothes (*común y corriente*). She spoke about how she worked to comply with the established codes of Indigenous performance. In order to compete for the Flor más Bella del Ejido title, she assembled a very specific costume: her father bought her a red and white *chincuete* (a woven belt Hernández said was "like the kind so-called Marías wear now"), a beautifully embroidered belt and blouse, and "a little thing decorated with cords that you put on your head."[66] She wore her hair in braids and carried a tray with what she described as being the most beautiful vegetables: large artichokes, chiles poblanos, bell peppers, and squash. She attributed her victory to having achieved the right look:

I won because of the Indigenous type I was—because I was chubby and had really long braids, because I was dark, well like this except I'm older now, but I was the type, because I wasn't pretty, but I'm telling you this was the type they chose.[67]

When she won, she recalls being crowned by a *charro*, receiving a trophy and a beautiful doll, and taking great pleasure in hearing the crowd applauding for her. "I was really happy," she said, "because my mom was selling that day … and because I won the prize it helped her sell because everyone was coming to congratulate me."[68] After the contest, local dignitaries held a banquet in her honor, and there she was awarded a Singer sewing machine and a plow.

This recollection demonstrates a very keen awareness of the parameters of desired Indigeneity that contestants had to achieve in order to access the material and social benefit that came with victory. In articulating awareness of the hierarchy of Indigenous types, Hernández makes text of what festival organizers and media often left as subtext. And her recollections illustrate that she and her family very deliberately opted in to the desired performance. Thanks to this awareness of the unspoken terms of engagement, Hernández was able to achieve a victory that had very real economic benefits for her family and still spoke about it with pride decades later.

In 1939 new contestant qualifications were implemented, and organizers made greater efforts to assess authenticity by bringing in cultural experts. A letter written to the director of the Museo Nacional in March of that year demonstrated the lengths to which the pageant organizers went to verify the ethnicity of their elected queens. Luciano Kubli, the recipient of the Indigenous men's *traje* award in 1927, reappeared as director of the Department of Civic Action, serving as an organizer and judge of the pageant. In the spring of 1939, he wrote a letter to the director of the Museo Nacional (who remained unnamed in the correspondence), reminding him that they would soon be electing a Flor más Bella del Ejido.[69] He referred to the future queen as a "young *campesina* of greatest kindness and beauty" and echoed the official language by claiming this young woman would be "a symbol of the emancipation and the unification of the workers of the field."[70]

Kubli went on to say that the sponsors of the pageant were committed to selecting a winner who had the "racial characteristics" and "ethnological circumstances" pertaining to the "*masas campesinas.*" He believed it would be prudent to have a representative of the national museum on the jury to authoritatively determine the authenticity of these racial and ethnological characteristics.[71] Professor Rubén M. Campos, head of the museum's Department of Folklore, was determined to be most fit for the task,[72] and he was joined by other jurors from the agriculture department, the office of public health, and the DGAC. Kubli also submitted a call for contestants specifying that all those vying for the title had to be the offspring of *ejiditarios*. Despite the vociferous emphasis placed on racial and ethnic criteria, Kubli refrained from specifying exactly what those criteria were.[73]

The fact that Kubli, who had been identified as Zapotec during the 1927 festivities, was involved at the pageant's organizational level demonstrates that Indigenous peoples were socially mobile despite a public narrative that fixed their identity as being both rural and antimodern. Ironically, Kubli was engaged in enforcing a narrow set of codes associated with authentic Indigenous behavior despite the fact that, as an elected official, he himself had achieved a status that exceeded the commonly understood boundaries of Indigeneity as defined by those codes. Moreover, the fact that he found it necessary to seek guidance from a group of "cultural experts" underscores the extent to which the power to identify Indigenous "authenticity" was reserved for a select group of elite, largely non-Indigenous men.

Despite the lack of stated criteria, the finalists, like Petra Hernández, all seemed to understand the desired parameters of *campesina/india bonita* authenticity. They all wore their hair in braids, kerchiefs tied around their heads, long skirts, and embroidered tops. They invariably held baskets laden with fruits and vegetables. Through beauty pageants and other identity projects, the Indigenized *campesina* trope had become so synthesized by 1939 that the contestants knew not to show up wearing the lacy Tehuana frock or Indigenous dress from other regions. *Campesina* and *india* had become one in the same, demonstrating the extent to which Indigenous peoples had been relegated to being thought of as "country folk" in Nahua-inspired dress despite their diversity and extensive presence as urban citizens.

The 1942 winner of the pageant, María Palma (fig. 7), reflected on what it was like to perform desired codes of Indigeneity under the scrutiny of judges. In the months leading up to the event, the Comité Ejidal de Santa Anita had handpicked Palma to represent her community in the Flor más Bella del Ejido pageant. Though her father initially refused to grant her permission to participate, he eventually came around and even took her all the way to Milpa Alta to get the attire needed for the competition.[74] She recalled the day of the pageant:

When the judges were on the stand we had to pass so that they saw us, so they could evaluate who, according to their criteria, would be the winner. They made me pass three times. First we passed the whole set of participants and they left me behind. Then one of the judges, I think, must have been the one who took me from behind and put me out in front. I was carrying a very heavy tray, but *very* heavy, that made my arms so tired. I felt annoyed because it was a tray full of vegetables. They made me pass by with my tray twice, pose and return, I passed again, then they continued to deliberate and at the end they said my name: MARÍA PALMA is the winner, the Flor Más Bella del Ejido![75]

Muy brillante resultó la fiesta que todos los años se lleva a cabo en Santa Anita, para la elección de la Flor más Bella del Ejido. En este año resultó triunfante en ese concurso la señorita María Palma.

Palma's recollections evidence the tedium and discomfort of participation in the pageant and of the close scrutiny of the judges. She also was aware that it was, as she put it, her "more pronounced Indigenous features" that led to her victory.[76]

Like Petra Hérnandez, Palma also discussed the benefits that came along with winning. Although she didn't get a sewing machine as Hérnandez did—a point she noted with chagrin in her interview—she did receive a set of name-brand

FIGURE 7. Announcement of María Palma's victory. "Las Fiestas del Viernes de Dolores en Sta. Anita." *El Universal*, March 28, 1942. Biblioteca Lerdo de Tejada.

dinnerware. And as the Flor más Bella del Ejido winner, Palma toured around the region as a representative of the Iztacalco Delegation, a rare privilege that she still remembered with pride forty-five years later: "It's emotional," she said. "It's something one could never forget or describe, they're emotions that are felt very deeply, like some sort of dream." Even though this festival had been appropriated and advanced a narrow ideal of what Indigenous women ought to look like and how they ought to behave, the women participated in these activities consciously and strategically and came away with some real material, social, and personal benefits.

Beginning in 1943, *El Universal* coverage of the event became increasingly visually oriented, a fact that probably further contributed to the normalization of the contest's specific *campesina/india bonita* look. The paper began running group photographs of the contestants in the weeks leading up to the event, which was reminiscent of the serialized India Bonita beauty contest of 1921. The women often wore similar attire and held gourd baskets overflowing with fruits and vegetables symbolizing the bounty of the ejido system.

Despite the emphasis on tradition, prizes for pageant winners promoted domestic modernity with items like sewing machines and linen. Children, too, became a more regular part of the festivities. Young girls appeared in many of the contestant photographs and, beginning in 1936, a contest to find the healthiest and strongest children through *niño campesino más sano* or *niño campesino robusto* competitions became a regular part of the event. These competitions gave pageant organizers another opportunity to display some of the benefits of postrevolutionary reform—including advances in education, physical well-being, and discipline—that had been prioritized during the Cárdenas administration.[77] While many identity projects of this era imagined modernity as being antithetical to Indigeneity, this pageant fit with other Indigenista efforts to remake certain Indigenous peoples into modern citizens. By bearing signs of agricultural productivity and healthy children, attractive Indigenous women were made into living testaments to the successes of the revolution and perfect progenitors of a mestizo future.

(DIS)POSSESSING TRADITION

By the late 1930s Santa Anita had begun to undergo a rapid process of urbanization that diminished its visible ties to its pre-Hispanic past and the fertile agrarian present. In 1939 the secretary of health banned the festival's signature poppies because of their narcotic potential,[78] and the Indios Verdes statues were moved from the head of the Calzada de la Viga to the Villa de Guadalupe,[79] symbolically marking a perceived decline of the neighborhood's authentic ties to Mexico Viejo. A 1940 presidential decree officially converted forty hectares of Santa Anita's agricultural land into commercial zoning, and the following year the city began the long process of draining and filling in the famous Canal de la Viga because of concerns that its polluted waters might be a health hazard.[80] By 1951 President Miguel Alemán officially designated the region an urban zone. This transformation was accompanied by rapid population growth, with census numbers rising from 9,261 residents in 1930 to 33,915 residents by the 1950s.[81] In the span of just a few decades, the once semirural Santa Anita was absorbed by Mexico City's insatiable urban expansion.

While these drastic physical changes affected the community and its springtime flower festival, the event remained an important part of life there. But without the canal as its geographic centerpiece and the fabled flower canoes to transport beauty queens and festivalgoers alike, interest in the Flor más Bella del Ejido pageant suffered. Finally, in 1955 organizers relocated the event to Xochimilco, a delegation in the city's far south that had retained its canal system and that had been strategically cultivated as the city's primary site for Indigenous identity.[82] Santa Anita residents "complained bitterly" about the loss and petitioned authorities to help them reclaim an event that was not only core to their community identity but had also become critical to the region's economy and culture, but to no avail.[83]

Tracing the evolution of the festival over the course of the 1920s through 1940s showed us just how an invented tradition evolved as a part of postrevolutionary identity making. As Eric Hobsbawm and Terrence Ranger argue, invented traditions traffic in symbols and practices that are conceived as having some inherent tie to the past and that establish values and behaviors by virtue of repetition.[84] But this particular invented tradition—and others that emerged in the era of postrevolutionary nation building—must also be read as projects of settler colonialism. The Flor más Bella del Ejido pageant helped inculcate beliefs about what being Indigenous really looked like, it established conventions for ideal Indigenous comportment, and it legitimized the institutions like government, media, museums, and the postrevolutionary governing elite.[85] In doing so, this invented tradition normalized mestizo belonging while also erasing the complexities of modern Indigenous life and further disenfranchising Indigenous peoples' rights to land and self-determination.

As Mexico City's DGAC and other civic organizations developed the Fiesta de Santa Anita, they took cues from other public performances and

FIGURE 8. Judges appraise pageant contestants. *El Universal*, April 5, 1941. Biblioteca Lerdo de Tejada.

beauty pageants. They also incorporated shifting ideals surrounding Indigenous female appearance, gender roles, and *Mexicanidad*. The twin premise of beauty and authenticity invited looking, measurement, comparison, and classification of different types by a nation that was in the midst of seeking an identity that could accommodate both the "modern" mestizo and the Indigenous "other"—and draw fine lines of distinction between the two.[86] Judges and journalists alike appraised the contestants as though they were rare specimens, scrutinizing their character, dress, and performance (fig. 8). They were looking for authentic Indians even if they rarely articulated the parameters of that authenticity. While judges didn't talk about authentic Indigeneity as explicitly as the judges of the India Bonita pageant had, their selections reified the codes, categories, and hierarchies established in that earlier pageant.

The centrality of *indias bonitas*, flower maidens, *chinas poblanas*, and *campesinas* to the event reflects the broader tendency to place women at the center of national identity projects. The absence of Indigenous men, meanwhile, speaks to broader attempts to disempower a potentially threatening portion of the population and write them out of the narrative of modern Mexico. In newspaper coverage, they existed only on the fringes of the festival and more often than not as criminals or punch lines. The one award for Indigenous male traditional clothing was awarded to a woman in drag. The only prize granted to an actual Indigenous man was accompanied by a crowd-pleasing musical performance. Indigenous men regularly appeared in photographs with their heads bent low or obscured by shadow—signifying both submission and their status as laborers—as they steered chinampas through crowded canal waters. And graphic depictions showed them as caricatures, variably exaggerating either drunkenness or effeminate qualities.

Aside from the case of Luciano Kubli, no other Indigenous men were named or mentioned in the extensive captions that accompanied the photographs. In the journalistic narratives of the festivities, the famous Indios Verdes statues, which at that time were located in Santa Anita, got far more play than any living Indigenous men. In this celebration of ideal *Mexicanidad*, then, Indigenous men were effectively silenced and relegated to the fringes of that identity. As bell hooks has shown to be the case with historical representations of Black men in the United States, these neutering behaviors discursively and psychologically disempowered a portion of the population whose mere existence was constructed as a threat.[87]

The relocation of the pageant reveals a bitter irony: over the course of three decades Santa Anita residents had adapted to the shifting parameters of authenticity, but in doing so they became signatories to the collective production of a tradition that ultimately rendered their urbanizing community an untenable home for the event. The postrevolutionary construction of the Flor más Bella del Ejido pageant tied it closely to a rural and antimodern version of Indigenous identity, and according to these same logics, it had to be moved once the space that hosted it was no longer easily identifiable as being rural and antimodern. While participation in the collective construction of tradition reveals some degrees of agency, it also shows that playing to elite definitions of Indigeneity could help fix identities in a way that ultimately worked against Indigenous interests.

CONCLUSION

The development of the Flor más Bella del Ejido pageant through the decades of revolutionary reconstruction reveals efforts to rewrite Indigeneity as a primarily female, agrarian identity and discursively erase large portions of the Indigenous population. By setting gendered standards for an Indigenous purity that was both culturally and geographically bound, postrevolutionary leaders effectively reduced the portion of the population that could identify as Indigenous to fractions that only decreased with each generation and with each modernization effort. The evolution of the Flor más Bella del Ejido pageant, then, helped to cement narrow ideas about what Indigeneity looked like and lay the groundwork for the ultimate disavowal of Santa Anita's Indigenous identity as it became increasingly urbanized. At the same time, it determined which aspects of that Indigenous past might be suitably incorporated into the project of imagining mestizo futures.

While Santa Anita is left only with murals and memories, the Flor más Bella del Ejido pageant is still celebrated each spring on the Friday before Semana Santa in Xochimilco. Strict rules govern participant dress and comportment: contestants must be Mexican by birth; they must be single, without children, and be between the ages of sixteen and twenty-three; and they have to prove that they come from a Mexico City delegation with some past or present connection to the ejido system. They are instructed to wear the same specific pieces of Nahua dress popularized during the postrevolutionary period, to leave their nails unpainted, to have feet bare or in sandals, and to carry baskets of fruits and vegetables.[88] The fact that the pageant continues relatively unchanged today demonstrates the power of the identity projects initiated in the 1920s and 1930s. And although the event was an invention of the state and continues to enshrine a narrow version of Indigeneity, it has, to an extent, been reappropriated in order to meet the social desires of the communities that participate in it. It is an opportunity to celebrate Indigenous language, culture, and land—albeit narrow interpretations of each—and it is a source of pride for the candidates who participate each year.[89] In a 2018 interview with the BBC, contestant Itzel Carpio Pavón talked about how in a world that places a premium on tall, light-skinned women, the contest helps reaffirms that other types of beauty matter too: "We're dark women. We're short women," she said. "But this doesn't mean we can't be beautiful."[90]

CINE FOLCLÓRICO

From Racial Fantasy to Cinematic Spectacle

O N SEPTEMBER 26, 1938, PANAMA City's Teatro Cecilia hosted a gala screening of a new film from Mexico, *La india bonita*, a fictionalized retelling of the 1921 beauty pageant that sought the nation's prettiest Indian.[1] The screening was accompanied by a beauty contest that endeavored to find the most attractive Panamanian *india bonita*. The concern with racial and ethnic "authenticity" seen in the original 1921 pageant had been replaced by an attempt to mimic costuming norms that had, by that time, been thoroughly codified as "Indian" in Mexican cinema. Similarly, the fair-skinned contestants whose beauty conformed to European standards looked more like mestiza film stars than the young women featured in the 1921 pageant. To make the dizzying layers of identity politics even more complex, the winners of the contests were awarded traditional *china poblana* dresses[2]—invoking an iconic emblem of Mexican nationhood that was often conflated with Indigeneity. The screenings and contests were the brainchild of Mexican foreign minister Vicente Estrada Cajigal, who was eager to promote his nation's culture and identity abroad. The India Bonita Panameña events demonstrate the potential that both beauty pageants and cinema held for distilling and sharing identity ideals and the fact that, by the late 1930s, postrevolutionary leaders had become increasingly savvy at harnessing that potential.

CINEMATIC NATIONHOOD

As identity negotiations laden with nostalgic romanticism and settler colonial fantasy evolved over the course of the Cultural Revolution, film was also becoming increasingly more popular. This chapter surveys films that spanned the range of Indigenous women's on-screen representations as Mexico's national film industry developed over the 1920s and 1930s. Although these representations didn't fall into a single genre, they were most common in films that centered Indigenous "types" and costuming making up a class of films that I call *cine folclórico*. A close reading of four different kinds of film within this family—drama, documentary, musical, and pornography—reveals themes that remained consistent across genres. Examining these films as text illustrates how messages that advanced postrevolutionary identity politics were strategically encoded within.

Many early Mexican films drew from a long tradition of theatrical performance. But in the transition from stage to screen, directors could employ new techniques for crafting meaning and spectacle. While proscenium theater only allowed one point of view—that of the audience across from the stage—film directors could angle and edit to create complex layers of meaning. The camera could linger on sumptuous close-ups; it could place actors on visual pedestals or diminish them to insignificant parts of a vast landscape. Meanwhile, viewers could enjoy an intimacy and closeness to performers that had never before been possible. Much like beauty pageants, cinematic spectacle captivated viewers with superficial sources of enjoyment while a complex set of identity ideals were being asserted just beneath the surface. It refined and amplified stereotypes while also firmly establishing them as sources of visual pleasure.[3] Familiar Mexican "types" from *charros* to *chinas poblanas* made their way from theater stages to the silver screen during this era.

The *india bonita* trope was included among these cinematic stereotypes. Much like her beauty pageant iterations, this character projected a romanticized, nonthreatening, feminine interpretation of Indigenous culture to national audiences.[4] The trope was characterized by performances of timid, self-sacrificing, pious, and chaste women. *Indias bonitas* almost ubiquitously sported long black braids and were often costumed in embroidered peasant-style blouses, woven belts, long skirts, *huaraches*—or no shoes at all—and their physical attractiveness was highlighted through camera work.[5]

And filmic *indias bonitas* were almost ubiquitously pictured in rural environments. At a moment when urban populations of Indigenous working women were rapidly increasing, envisioning these same women as passive members of the campo would have helped assuage insecurities arising from a shifting social order. As Ageeth Sluis argues, the camposcape imaginary flourished during the Cultural Revolution, forming a sort of uniquely Mexican Orientalism that wed ideas about national identity, "authentic" Indigenous peoples, rural life, and nostalgia for the past.[6]

Variations of the *india bonita* trope appeared in documentaries, dramas, pornography, and the *comedia ranchera* genre that emerged in the late 1930s. While *india bonita* characters were supposed to represent the nation's Indigenous women, they were typically performed by actresses with features that adhered to European or Hollywood-driven beauty norms: fair skin, high cheekbones, and the taller, thinner "deco body" or, later, hourglass silhouettes.[7] These actresses shaped their on-screen performances to conform to a reductive set of idealized "Indian" behaviors. Meanwhile, women with darker skin and features more easily labeled as Indigenous were primarily confined to exoticized roles in documentary films or as extras with no speaking roles.[8]

Collectively, the *cine folclórico* films represented a nationalist logic that teetered between salvation anthropology, Indigenismo, and a brand of social Darwinism that optimistically hoped to solve the "Indian Problem" by replacing the Native-born population with a more modern, mestizo one. They mirrored Mexico's desired racial transformation, combining the best elements of each of the nation's component races, in the manner of *la raza cósmica*.[9] Ultimately, the films featuring this trope allowed viewers to peer into the rural past and remind themselves of just how modern they were and just how good their mestizo futures could look.

CONSUMING CINEMA

In the early days of Mexican cinema, theaters were loud, violent, and predominantly masculine spaces that "decent women" were discouraged from entering for fear that it might threaten their moral sanctity.[10] The more bawdy films of the day were screened in theaters that were explicitly for men only.[11] Different classes of theaters allowed for both wealthy and poor audiences to view films, but since there were typically a limited number of exhibition prints of each of these fragile films, the quality was often so degraded by the time they reached the cheap theaters that film viewing was impaired. If Indigenous working-class women were seeing their on-screen counterparts at all, it was likely in cheaper, crowded theaters with poor viewing quality and the ever-present threat of sexual violence.[12]

The burgeoning film industry became a source of national pride and proved a promising means by which to showcase Mexico's technological modernity and cultural riches on a global stage. Throughout the 1920s and 1930s, nationally made films garnered considerable newspaper coverage. In this, the industry itself became something of a spectacle. While the films themselves were not available to everyone, print media—including newspaper coverage detailing everything from production to plotlines, advertisements, broadsides, and posters—would have been far more visible even to those who could not afford a seat in the theater. The analysis of print media included throughout this chapter, then, offers an important lens for understanding the life of these early films in the day-to-day experience of the broader public.

ANTHROPOLOGY GOES TO THE MOVIES

Some early Mexican movies attempted to emulate successful Hollywood storylines, characters, and narrative tropes, but others adopted decidedly national themes. Documentary films that turned the camera's gaze on the nation's original inhabitants found a niche among a populace thirsting for self-discovery and patrimonial pride. And the emerging field of anthropology and Indigensimo played major roles in shaping how Indigenous peoples would be represented on the silver screen. Manuel Gamio—the Columbia University–trained "father" of Mexican anthropology who helped shape the India Bonita pageant—also used film in the 1910s and 1920s to make his indigenist scholarship widely available to the public. His goal in producing and screening these films, he said, was "to preserve customs, study them, and make them known."[13] Both documentary and narrative in nature, Gamio's films on Indigenous customs, dances, songs, labor practices, archaeological sites at Teotihuacán, and Aztec legends were screened in plazas throughout Mexico City.[14]

Gamio made a film version of his classic study of Teotihuacán—*La población del valle de Teotihuacán* (1922)—that featured the region's prehistory and the customs and dances of its contemporary Indigenous populations.[15] Although the films themselves no longer exist, the surviving stills suggest that they included much of the same racial photography, demographic material, and salvage anthropology seen in the longer, three-volume printed version of the study.[16] Gamio also served as an advisor for several other films: *Tlahuicole* (1925), which screened at a film festival in Los Angeles, and *Quetzalcóatl* (written by Rubén Campos).[17] Another of these films, *Fiestas de Chalma* (1922), was a coproduction of the José Vasconcelos–administered Secretaría de Educación Pública and the Departamento de Bellas Artes.

Gamio's films created new ways of looking at the ethnic other. Movie stills from what was called a "popular scientific film," *Fiestas de Chalma*, show women and men tending to a *temazcal* (a Nahua sweat lodge), mostly in a crouched position facing away from the camera. The camera shots are taken from a medium long distance showing off the full scene and the *traje* of the individuals. In keeping with Gamio's training in cultural materialism, faces are mostly turned away from the camera or obscured so that emphasis is placed on the material elements of the shot rather than the individuals in it. This framing alone would prove to have a major impact on film representations of Indigenous women in particular, with stylized costuming given at least as much on-screen emphasis as the bodies that inhabited the clothing.

The combination of technological novelty and intimate views of Indigenous life on display in Gamio's public screenings would have had a profound impact on the urban individuals who witnessed them.[18] Since these screenings were public, it's likely that urban Indians watched them, too, perhaps with some mix of familiarity, discomfort, and perhaps even laughter at the details these portrayals surely got wrong.[19] For urbanized mestizos, the closeness of these "authentic" others would have heightened the thrill of the cinema experience much in the same way that touristic forays into exoticized "contact zones," like the one afforded by the Fiesta de Santa Anita, delighted those seeking to experience the other from a safe distance in controlled conditions.[20] And because Gamio was an established voice of authority on Indigenous authenticity, his work helped establish a cinematic culture of looking at the anthropological other that had previously been mediated through postcards, pageantry, photography, text, and other stylized renderings.

PLAYING INDIAN ON THE SILVER SCREEN

Other cinematic traditions developed alongside—and drew from—the documentary films and theater traditions. Ernesto Vollrath's 1921 film *En la hacienda*[21] premiered as national interest in *El Universal*'s India Bonita pageant was escalating. One of the earliest *cine folclórico* films that romanticized rural indigenous life, *En la hacienda* melded elements of Gamio's quest for authenticity with other popular representations of *indias bonitas*.[22] In this adaptation of a 1907 *zarzuela* by the same name,[23] American-trained silent film star Elena Sánchez Valenzuela performs the role of a timid Indigenous woman who finds herself caught between two rival suitors.

Although the film itself has been lost, something of its nature can be gleaned from reviews and images that appeared in illustrated newspapers at the time of its debut. Newspaper photographs of Valenzuela in character reveal that even at this early stage of cinema there was a certain behavioral formula for acting "Indian" that signaled submission, suffering, and humility. The images show her in the Nahua-inspired costuming that had already come to be associated with Indigenous authenticity (fig. 9), and she used pigment to darken her face and arms.[24] She poses with a traditional Olinalá-style water jug, yet another symbol that had become a quintessential marker of Indigeneity.[25] In one photo she arches her arm over her head to hold the *olla*; in another she tugs at a braid with one hand while holding the pot in the crook of her other arm.[26] In yet another still that ran in *El Universal*, she clasps her hands politely while holding her head at an extreme side angle, affecting both sweetness and submission.[27] Her attempts to evoke Indianness are even more evident in comparison to a character marked as modern and white who appears next to her in this particular photograph. Following popular photographic conventions of the time, the "modern" woman holds herself in a far more relaxed position and smiles at the camera.

Newspaper reviews reinforced the messages encoded in these images, claiming that Valenzuela's performance captured the "sweet and long-suffering spirit of our Indigenous peoples."[28] At the same time, *El Universal* was running its serialized India Bonita pageant and María Conesa's India Bonita performances were gaining popular appeal. These overlapping events all reinforced one another in their crafting of Indigenous authenticity and the stylized, mestiza performance of the fledgling cinematic *india bonita*.

QUE VIVA MÉXICO

Despite enthusiasm for films like *En la hacienda* and *El automóvil gris*, the Mexican film industry developed at an anemic rate through the 1920s as it struggled to keep up with bigger-budget films imported from Hollywood. In

FIGURE 9. Elena Sánchez Valenzuela in character for the film *En la hacienda*. "La nueva película nacional, 'En la hacienda,'" *Revista de Revistas*, January 22, 1922. Biblioteca Lerdo de Tejada.

the early 1930s, a famed Russian cinematographer played a surprising role in catalyzing development of the flagging national industry. Sergei Eisenstein's *Que viva México* wove together stunning images of land, people, and culture culminating in a heavily symbolic, if distorted, homage to the revolution.

Because of Eisenstein's reputation in his home country and an affinity for all things socialist among many artists of the time, members of the nation's artistic and intellectual vanguard, including Diego Rivera and David Alfaro Siqueiros, advised and traveled with the film crew from 1930 to 1931.[29] Artist Adolfo Best Maguard served as Eisenstein's guide, translator, and authenticity advisor.[30] With the cultural elite as his guides, Eisenstein quickly came to believe that the most authentic Indians and the "real Mexico" could be found in the hinterlands,[31] so much of the making of this "film symphony of Mexico" took place outside of urban centers and reinforced ideas about the storied camposcape.

Under the influence of these artists, Eisenstein depicted the Cultural Revolution as moving picture. In doing so he pioneered new formulas for translating this movement and its accompanying identity discourses into film language. But cinematographers of the time didn't have the opportunity to learn his techniques through the film itself. Although Eisenstein's endeavor garnered a flurry of press and was highly anticipated, customs disputes and inadequate funding prevented him from completing the film before his death in 1948.[32] His now-classic film was eventually stitched together based on his notes and released in 1979. However, the film's influence preceded its final production by decades. Extensive newspaper coverage of its production combined with rumors, stories, and stills meant that *Que viva México* became an influential piece of popular culture even as it was being produced.

A June 1931 series of heavily illustrated articles in *El Universal Ilustrado* by Adolfo Fernández de Bustamante, another cultural advisor to Eisenstein,[33] examined the themes, techniques, and aesthetics that defined Eisenstein's work. Bustamante lauded the film and Eisenstein, arguing that *Que viva México* would "undoubtedly bring glory and prestige" to the nation and show the socialist ideals that undergirded the revolution.[34] Photo spreads that accompanied Bustamante's articles showed the filming process, illustrating how Eisenstein constructed shots and how his director of photography played with light and shadow as well as the juxtaposition of contrasting images to heighten dramatic effect. The photographs also demonstrated how romantic portrayals of Indigenous peoples could be made into suitable material for avant-garde cinema.

FIGURE 10. Sergei Eisenstein (center) directs the filming of *Que viva México*. "Eisenstein, El Magnifico," *El Universal Ilustrado*, June 11, 1931. Biblioteca Lerdo de Tejada.

Bustamante encouraged other filmmakers to follow Eisenstein's lead. He argued that the famous director had uncovered a wealth of cinematographic fodder and that rather than trying to compete with the expensive productions and beautiful actresses of Hollywood, studios ought to take a more nationalist approach by documenting the natural and cultural riches that surrounded them.[35] In doing so, he emphasized two themes that would be repeated throughout *cine folclórico* films: he clearly identified Indians as worthy sources of visual pleasure, and he equated them with nature by indicating that they were essential components of the nation's scenic backdrop, which no studio set could rival.

While Eisenstein's stills also established formulas and techniques for the cinematic viewing of the Indigenous body. Another photo in the same *Universal Ilustrado* spread shows Eisenstein costumed in a full white safari outfit (fig. 10). He is directing a scene as a cameraman shoots a parade of women in full

Tehuana dress from an extremely low angle. This low-angle shot construction was employed throughout *Que viva México* to visually elevate the position of Indigenous women—an influence that can also be seen in later Mexican cinema. Eisenstein was clearly influenced by popular Indigenismo and he, in return, contributed a film language that could be employed to project indigenist ideology on the screen.

Eisenstein's movie stills also created a precedent for the filmic fetishization of the Indigenous face. Although other cinematic traditions the world over had already made a fetish of the female face,[36] Mexican cinema, until that point, had tended toward long shots that gave audiences the same view of the set and its actors that they had in the more familiar live theater scenario. This was especially the case of Indigenous representation on screen, where tableau shots that emphasized traditional dress were favored over close-ups. The published stills from *Que viva México*, on the other hand, illustrate how light and texture could create dramatic contrasts.[37] They also demonstrate that an individual face, when juxtaposed with the craggy surfaces of ancient pyramids or woven fabrics, could convey the same sense of historical and cultural depth that had, until then, been primarily conveyed through costuming and performance.

In the *El Universal Ilustrado* coverage, several movie stills focus solely on Indigenous faces, but one is particularly remarkable. In the first photographic spread published in the magazine, a Juchitecan woman's face rests at the center of a lacy Tehuana headdress as though at the center of a pillow.[38] The light caught and reflected by the white lace and the warmth of the rotogravure print suggest a powerful contrast between the ethereal and terrestrial, the softness and light of the lace amplifying the strong features of the face. This image alone conveys the potency of the "face-object" and justifiably would have given cinematographers new on-screen formulas to consider.[39] Although Eisenstein may have been influenced in this case by the Tina Modotti photographs of Luz Jiménez that Diego Rivera had shared with him during their first meeting in Russia in 1927,[40] Eisenstein was nonetheless forging new ways for depicting a Mexican art movement in the moving image.

The absence of the completed film perhaps gave it even more power at the dawn of Mexico's cinematic tradition. Coverage of the project proposed an approach to inflecting films with elements of Indigenismo and then left an imaginative void for other artists to fill. Rather than providing a specific template, it suggested how films about Mexico might incorporate elements of post-revolutionary discourse. As an internationally acclaimed filmmaker, Eisenstein helped to validate both the exaltation of Native imagery and the cultural elite's claim that Mexico was indeed worthy of contemplation.[41] His stills also asserted that Indigenous beauty had value beyond the folkloric bounty seen in material culture and that there was pleasure to be found in images of the Indigenous body that was stylized and fragmented by close-ups.[42]

THE BIRTH OF NATIONAL CINEMA

The combination of Eisenstein's production, the urgings of Bustamante and other members of the cultural elite, and the overwhelming popularity of Mexico's first sound film, *Santa* (1931), inspired a national film industry that was well established by the mid-1930s. The industry's boom was also fueled in part by President Lázaro Cárdenas (1934–1940), who recognized the potential that film had as a form of soft propaganda to disseminate his populist ideals to the nation. Cárdenas created the Financiadora de Películas to channel funds and institutional support into furthering domestic film production and mandated that theaters screen a certain percentage of domestically produced films.[43] The success of his initiatives is evident in the fact that domestic film production leapt from six films made in 1932 to fifty-seven films produced in 1938.[44]

Allá en el rancho grande was the first film to meet great commercial success following Cárdenas's reforms to the industry. Its rural themes and light-hearted song-and-dance routines drew heavily on the performance components of *zarzuelas* and *revistas*, types of live theater that had been popularized beginning in 1904.[45] The film's success inspired the *comedia ranchera* genre of films in which *india bonita* characters made regular appearances alongside *charros*, *hacendados*, and *chinas poblanas*.[46]

A subset of this fledgling genre placed primary emphasis on romantic reimaginings of Indigeneity with shot construction that encouraged lengthy gazes at the exotic other.[47] These films often repositioned the hacienda system as a quaint emblem of the past and depicted bucolic scenes of a countryside populated by simple Indians who were baffled by modernity but sang and danced their problems away. The Indigenista undertones are undeniable. In addition to regularly casting light-skinned women with European features to play *indias bonitas*, these *cine folclórico* films almost invariably included the promise of racial and social betterment for these "pretty Indians" through marriage or romantic partnership with wealthy urban mestizos.

The 1938 production of *La india bonita* fits neatly into this genre and illustrates the translation of live theater formulas for entertainment and the tentative incorporation of film and editing techniques inspired by Eisenstein. In keeping with the *comedia ranchera* genre and the broader tradition of *cine folclórico* films, the film combined popular notions of Indigeneity, patrimony, and cultural identity in deceptively light-hearted song-and-dance performances, all the while positioning women's bodies as the ideal canvas on which cultural and nationalist ideals could be projected.

As we saw through discussion of the India Bonita Panameña contests at the start of this chapter, the film *La india bonita* recreated the 1921 beauty pageant that sought the most beautiful Indian woman in all of Mexico. The movie opens with a mock cover of the *El Universal* newspaper made to look like an authentic India Bonita contest announcement. The attention to detail in representing the original event establishes a frame of authenticity for the film. Similarly, the 1938 movie uses the concept of Indigenous beauty as a foundation on which to structure more complicated cultural and identity ideals, although the plot deviates drastically from the historical event from that point on.

In the movie, two male city slickers travel to the countryside to visit the lead's familial hacienda. Upon arrival, the men fall in love with two of the local Indigenous women and conspire to bring them back to Mexico City so they can marry them. By insisting that the women must compete in the India Bonita pageant, their urban admirers wrangle them away from their campesino boyfriends and bring them to the city. But as the plot unfolds, the mother of the main *india bonita* character reveals that her daughter and the *hacendado*'s son, who is in love with her, are, in fact, brother and sister. The film barely pauses over this revelation, but the casual allusion to a sexual encounter between a wealthy *hacendado* and an Indigenous employee indicates the commonality of such encounters, many of which were coercive if not explicitly violent.[48] The discovery of shared parentage between the would-be lovers launches a zany series of events that culminates in the *india bonita*'s Indigenous beau interrupting her pageant coronation to woo her back to the ranch for a climactic double wedding that ends the film and resolves all of its narrative conflicts.

As was common in other filmic and staged performances, *La india bonita* featured fair-skinned actors with European features cast in the roles of both the Indigenous and non-Indigenous characters. The lead *india bonita*, Lupe, was played by actress Anita Campillo, whose Hollywood career included the role of a "Spanish" vixen in the John Wayne film, *The Man from Utah*.[49] That

FIGURE 11. Still from the 1938 film *La india bonita*. Printed with permission from the Agrasánchez Film Archive.

film cast Campillo as a saucy coquette with a short bob haircut contemporary to the time. Campillo's performance as an Indigenous woman in *La india bonita*, on the other hand, taps into popular perceptions of Indigenous peoples of the era. Her on-screen behavior is marked by frequently downcast eyes and nervous mannerisms such as constant fidgeting, reflecting common stereotypes of the time that positioned Indigenous people as timid and shy.[50] Costuming included the standard black braided wigs, woven belts, embroidered blouses, and beaded jewelry. While it's not possible or appropriate to identify race based on the appearance of the actors, analysis of how Indigeneity is projected onto this actress, who could slip in and out of on-screen Indianness, provides insight into what film and acting techniques were used to signify Indigeneity.

Throughout the film, Indigenous peoples are consistently portrayed as being backward, rural, simple folk through a series of comedic encounters with modern technology. The characters exhibit fear and confusion when they confront automobiles and other devices common to modern city life. Shots of trains, the ubiquitous symbol of modernity in the late nineteenth and early twentieth centuries, are cut in between shots of ranch and city life as though to signal the movement between the urbanized present and an idyllic past. Through these intercuts, Indigenous peoples are further associated with the campo and, in the scenes that do take place in urban landscapes, the Indigenous characters are consistently characterized as being comically at odds with modern life through their inability to do even the simplest of things, like opening a car door.

A song-and-dance sequence leading up to the crowning of the India Bonita highlights both the extent to which spectacle dominates the film and how costuming was used to establish Indigeneity and gender as a critical part of that spectacle. The sequence spans fifteen minutes, constituting nearly a quarter of the entire film. Men and women perform *ballet folclórico*–inspired routines set to songs celebrating various Mexican regions and types. Musicians perform odes to the women of Oaxaca, the iconic Tehuana, and *chinas poblanas*. Although men and women share on-screen camera time, the women are the subjects of the musical numbers and wear regionally inspired Indigenous costuming. The men are dressed in unremarkable uniforms associated with campesinos: white cotton with straw hats, kerchiefs around their necks, and occasionally ponchos draped over their shoulders. The women's costumes, on the other hand, are far more ornate and vary markedly. They wear different combinations of embroidered huipils, woven belts, Tehuana headdresses, colorful rebozos, and other "traditional" articles of clothing. Despite some attempts at authentically recreating regional dress, the costumes were altered to accentuate the bodies of the female actors. Huipils, for example, were narrowed at the waist and cinched by tight belts as was common practice in Indigenous costuming in films of the time.[51]

The prominence of spectacle and "cinema of attraction" in these dance sequences is notable, especially when conveyed by several pans of an audience that is marked as urban and well-to-do through costuming that included fur coats, top hats, and suits. This display of regional pageantry was consumed by a "modern" mestizo crowd, and Indigenous peoples were further positioned as the exotic other, valuable insofar as they could provide entertainment to spectators. Because the sequence steps out of the narrative arc of the film with no clear explanation as to why, it falls into the realm of cinema of attraction in that it privileges spectacle over narrative.[52] In essence, dance and the performance of Indigeneity functioned as a spectacle within the spectacle of the film itself.

This scene is important, too, for its focus on dancing female bodies, which were particularly evocative sites for the performance of cultural ideals. Scholars from a range of disciplines have illustrated how female performers are uniquely positioned as repositories for and communicators of identity ideals. Jane Desmond, for example, shows how the bodies of female hula dancers performing for tourists in Hawaii "function implicitly as the final authenticators of identity categories."[53] Translating these identity and performance codes into film allowed for the spectacle once seen in theater productions to be enhanced by film language. As Laura Mulvey has argued, "going far beyond highlighting a woman's to-be-looked-at-ness, cinema builds the way she is to be looked at into the spectacle itself."[54] As a result, film drew on and amplified the elements of spectacle and the viewing of "exotic" women's bodies into a potent source of visual pleasure.

In its reimagining of the 1921 pageant, *La india bonita* illustrated how popular thinking about Indigenous people evolved over two decades of postrevolutionary reconstruction. The India Bonita competition had been a project that privileged Aztec ancestry and effectively narrowed the definition of who could legitimately claim Indigeneity. The film, on the other hand, tapped into a growing indigenist ethos of the late 1930s that celebrated select aspects of many different Indigenous cultures. This more expansive—though still highly racialized—view of Indigeneity flourished under the Cárdenas regime and revalued Indigenous peoples as assets in industries like film and tourism. Even so, the centrality of the two Nahua-inspired characters in the film illustrates the fact that Aztec-affiliated groups were still at the top of the hierarchy as far as indigenist identity construction was concerned.

As the India Bonita Panameña screenings demonstrated, the nationalistic race and identity ideals encoded in this film were not just intended for domestic audiences. In addition to the Panamanian screenings, the film was also shown in Latin America and the United States as a form of cultural diplomacy. It screened in New York in conjunction with Mexico's participation in the 1939–1940 World's Fair and the U.S. tour of the state-sponsored "Mexicana," a music and dance revue billed as an amity gesture.[55] A *New York Times* review praised the film and argued that it really ought to be called *Indias bonitas* (plural) because there were so many attractive women to look at in the film.[56] Even so, the author expressed doubt that these *indias bonitas* were "100 percent Indian." The fact that this ethnic performance was called into question by a foreign reporter but never in domestic reviews hints at the extent to which "playing Indian" had become normalized in Mexico.

"CALLADITA TE VES MÁS BONITA"

Not all on-screen representations of Indigenous women were performed by mestiza actresses. In addition to appearances in documentaries, a rare pornography from the silent film era provides a glimpse into another way Indigenous women engaged with the film industry. The film *La campesina* is a complex and challenging piece of popular culture. It's the only film I've encountered from the era that casts a woman with darker skin and clearly Indigenous features in a leading role, and it includes much richer depictions of Indigenous love, joy, and pleasure than other Mexican-produced films from the era. But these nods toward humanizing and empowering Indigenous women are framed by the most graphic scenes of violence and pain seen in any of the sampling of silent pornographic films held at UNAM's Filmoteca. The men in the film display a vexing combination of violence and tenderness, alternately doting on, attempting to pleasure, and abusing the female lead. And the male characters themselves are filmic aberrations, as it was rare to see rural-dwelling Indigenous men depicted as virile in postrevolutionary pop culture—they were more often shown to be either cartoonishly effeminate or drunken buffoons. Untangling the threads of each of these paradoxes lays bare some of the deeply contradictory—and harmful—themes inherent in Mexican identity politics of the day.

La campesina runs just under eight minutes long, and though there are no credits indicating who produced it or when, it can most likely be dated to the 1920s or early 1930s.[57] Shot in grainy 16 mm film on location in what appears to be the rolling hills of the altiplano, perhaps just outside of Mexico City, the film was made hastily with a lot of choppy cuts and seemingly little attention paid to shot construction. The director instead opted to "edit in camera" by trying many different shots and angles in short succession and applied relatively little postproduction refinement. Even so, the film's three unnamed actors are clearly skilled in silent film techniques, and it pays remarkable attention to narrative and character development for a pornographic film of that era.[58] Given the quality of the production and complexity of the on-location set, it is possible it was an outtake from a longer commercial film or a side project made in haste after the feature production had wrapped.[59] While these circumstances will probably never be fully known, what is clear is that this film was made quickly and crudely but that some planning and deliberation clearly went into its production.

In the opening scene of the film, the audience sees two lovers, Pancha and Prudencio, serenade one another amid the rolling hills of the campo. Their love seems innocent enough—she sings and he plays the flute and tenderly places his sombrero on her head in order to shield her from the sun. The scene is periodically interrupted with quick cuts to shots of another campesino, Gregorio, taking an ax to a tree. After the two lovers part, Pancha is taken by surprise by Gregorio, who has finished his day's work and apparently needs to immediately sate his manly desires. Gregorio assaults Pancha while she is squatting to pee in the field, exposed and vulnerable. He sneaks up on her and wrestles her to the ground, and she almost immediately passes out.

He disrobes her and then proceeds to fondle and nibble at her body. She remains unconscious through it all. As this scene unfolds, the camera angle switches to an above shot looking down on her prone body and his abduction of it. It's not a point-of-view (POV) shot, but it's the closest the film comes to including one at all. This is significant in that POV shots allow viewers of a film to experience the film world through the eyes of one of the characters. The fact that this approximation of a POV shot connects viewers to the position of the attacker underscores the film's fetishization of sexual violence.

After a series of close shots that show Gregorio performing cunnilingus on Pancha, the camera slowly tilts up from her abdomen, over her bare breasts, and to her face. Though her eyes remain closed, she has a faint smile on her lips and her mouth is moving. She is apparently now in a state of ecstasy and, moments later, is performing sex acts on him as well. In the world of this film, Gregorio's ability to pleasure Pancha transforms his attack into mutual acts of erotic indulgence. This development is a disturbingly common theme throughout UNAM's pornographic collection, especially when the women are coded as being of a lower class standing than their male counterparts. The message to male viewers is that women might first resist your advances, but proceed with force if necessary, and they will eventually come around to enjoying it. This spurious formula essentially condones acts of sexual violence by positioning resistance as a sort of foreplay.

After the assault is over, the pair gets dressed and then they hold each other closely in an unlikely state of postcoital bliss. All of a sudden Prudencio comes on the scene of these "infieles" (unfaithfuls), as a title card has labeled them. He reacts with rage, chasing Gregorio off into the hills and then comes back to let his woman have it. Pancha pleads forgiveness but he punishes her by pushing her to the ground and then violently raping her. The camera cuts from graphic views of the rape to close shots of her screaming in pain.

There is no mistaking this for pleasure. When Prudencio finishes, Pancha falls to the ground and passes out. He wipes himself clean, then does the same for her as she remains unconscious. The troubling narrative turns of this short film are tied up abruptly with the violent punishment seeming to have made everything right again. The "lovers" get dressed, he puts his arm around her and they walk—or in Pancha's case, limp—into the distance. A title card flashes on the screen assuring viewers that "affection makes *our campesinos* forget everything." The encoded message here is that rape and violence are just normal parts of Indigenous life. The use of the possessive "our" underscores the unrelenting paternalism that imagined Indigenous people to be simple folk requiring the care of their more sophisticated countrymen, and it trivializes the heinous violence that has just unfolded on screen.

There is a lot to unpack in this sordid sex flick, but the centrality of violence must be addressed first and foremost. Though framed by acts of love and tenderness, the female protagonist is repeatedly subjected to violent assault. The film fetishizes both the pain of the victim and the power of her abusers. In the final scene, Pancha's expressions of extreme pain get nearly as much screen time as the sex act itself, suggesting that there was a sadistic market for the suffering of Indigenous women.

The fact that rape and the pain of those victimized by it had become something of a sexual fetish in postrevolutionary popular culture should, sadly, come as little surprise. Such violence had been written into the nation's origin story, with rape being used as a tool of domination that helped engineer the largely mixed-race population. Though there is little data about the extent of sexual violence during the revolution, anecdotal evidence indicates that it was widespread.

The film reflects another major trope of postrevolutionary identity construction: the misconception that Indians were made Indian not by their ancestry or self-determined identities but by their clothing and by the rural places they inhabited. This is underscored by the interchangeability of the terms *indio* and *campesino*, a conflation that we see even in the title of this film. In this sense, the rural setting of *La campesina* is significant, providing a perfect example of Sluis's camposcape: female nudity and Indigeneity are firmly fixed in the campo where they safely belonged according to social codes of the time.[60] The film, then, affirms beliefs about the racial and cultural order of things at a moment of upheaval and change, but then it goes to an even darker place.

Through camerawork and performance, the Indigenous female lead is shown as being a part of the landscape she inhabits and her body as violable as the earth in the settler imaginary. In a series of long shots, Pancha is shown being dwarfed by the landscape that surrounds her, and in other scenes her body mirrors the contours of the land. The male actors, too, are shown to be part of this landscape, but scenes like those of Gregorio chopping down a large tree establish the men as having a certain level of dominion over their environs, while the female character is presented as being more passive. This film language—as rudimentary as it was—reflects and reaffirms a view of Indigenous women as being of the earth and as natural recipients of violation and plunder. The camposcape in this film, then, was imbued with a sort of abject *Mexicanidad* that allowed urban viewers to imagine themselves into that world in a way that ultimately reaffirmed their own dominance and superiority over both the land and the people that lived off of it.[61]

As was common to films of the era, male actors appeared in neutral campesino clothing while Indigenous material cultural was presented as being a fundamental component of female identity. During the initial assault scene, Gregorio struggles to remove Pancha's woven belt, and she ultimately has to do it herself. During the attack, Pancha is nude but her belt remains on screen, artfully splayed beneath her body so that even in her state of undress she is consistently framed by a material signifier of her identity. In the aftermath of this assault, she is shown carefully wrapping the belt around her frame. Given this prominence, the belt is not an incidental costuming piece but rather a key part of the film itself.

La campesina—like so many indigenist films, pageants, and cultural productions of the time—reproduces the idea that Indigenous peoples were defined by the clothes they wore and by the places they inhabited. As demonstrated in chapter 1, this simplistic formula helped narrow popular understandings of the country's large, mobile, and diverse Indigenous population. Wedding that erasure with sexual violence makes this short film a particularly vile presentation of the settler colonial project that was playing out in the years following the revolution.

In order to fully understand the meaning of this film, it is necessary to have a sense of the audiences that might have consumed it. Though it features Indigenous themes, it's highly unlikely it was produced for rural Indigenous audiences since circulation of pornographic films was prohibited and would have been exceedingly difficult outside of cities. Many urban movie houses would screen *cintas prohibidas* at risk of fines and other repercussions, and there were surely other underground movie houses in cities as well. Wealthy urban men had the most access to the equipment and expertise necessary to host private screenings of the films. Anne Rubenstein writes that even President Calles, in his final days in office, hosted private screenings of films with suggestive titles like *La colegiala, La turca, Amor cubana*, and *Novios de repuesto*, at the presidential palace.[62]

The film itself offers further clues about whom it was made for. Though there are few point-of-view shots, the closest that we come to such shots privileges the gaze of the male actors, both of whom are marked as being generically rural and Indigenous. But while both the male actors take turns at dominance, their dishonor is equally as prevalent. Prudencio is shamefully cuckolded and Gregorio comedically chased off into the distance after his assault. Indigenous male power is presented as being a fickle, fragile thing. The point, then, was not to emphasize the virility of Indigenous men but rather to allow audiences an opportunity to imagine themselves into the filmscape. For upper-class urban men, this would have permitted a sort of sexual slumming that let them see themselves as dominant over both the land and the body of the female protagonist without the discomfort of having to imagine Indigenous men as being powerful or threatening in any real way.

Ultimately, the film reinforces the power position of urban mestizo male viewers at a moment when national identity and social structures were in flux. Even though the film centers Indigenous peoples, it fits neatly into a dialogue that positioned urban mestizo men at the top of the social hierarchy, Indigenous men as dishonorable buffoons, and Indigenous women as being sexually violable and inherently frozen in the rural past. Furthermore, it crassly underscores the way in which popular culture that on the surface romanticized Indigenous peoples and cultures could in fact serve to affirm the position of those who held the most power. This rare film offers a pithy distillation of the reductionist, racist, and misogynistic logics that framed popular understandings of Indigenous peoples in the decades following the revolution. Pornography often "celebrate[s] male dominance . . . and glamorize[s] female subordination,"[63] and *La campesina* fully embraced that formula, adding to it elements of identity, race, gender, and class that were specific to the historical moment in which it was produced.

CONCLUSION

Be it through artfully framed close-ups of the face, displays of material culture, dance, or sexual exploitation, film became a highly charged medium for advancing visual dialectics of settler colonialism. It further marked Indigenous women as being inherently located in camposcapes and sexually violable as well as defined by certain clothing and behaviors. Meanwhile, mestiza women performing these Indigenous types were marked as symbols of Mexico's future. And whether it glossed over identity negotiations with spectacle or laid them bare through crude acts of violence, those negotiations were undeniably playing out in *cine folclórico* films of the 1920s and 1930s.

With varying degrees of intentionality, *cine folclórico* reflected and advanced the indigenist ethos of the postrevolutionary era. Identity ideals that melded a romanticized Indigenous past with an idealized mestizo future were projected onto women's bodies. Films like *La campesina* normalized the idea that Indigenous women's bodies were there for the taking. Meanwhile, the many *cine folclórico* films that featured Europeanized *indias bonitas* in ethnic garb were more clearly a project of Mestizaje that quite literally imagined a mestizo populace replacing the Indigenous one.

The frequent positioning of Indigenous peoples as antimodern sustained postrevolutionary national identity discourses that advanced the settler colonial project by arguing that for the good of the nation, Indians had to be assimilated.[64] As seen in other popular culture renditions at the time, the discursive and visual positioning of Indigenous people as being meek and antithetical to modernity was one of the ways that the postrevolutionary regimes could incorporate select aspects of Indigeneity into the mainstream without increasing anxieties about the perceived sociocultural threats Indigenous peoples posed to the minority non-Indigenous elite.[65]

Women marked through costuming and character as Indigenous performed in the frequent dance sequences of *cine folclórico* films and thus further normalized non-Indigenous performance and the appropriation of Indigenous identity. By establishing faux Indian women as "authentic" sites of spectacle, filmmakers trained viewers to indulge in the pleasing visual possibilities of the new racial order. This emphasis on spectacle, visual pleasure, and cinema of attraction encouraged viewers to maintain a soft focus on the fantasy being projected on screen while hierarchies of power, identity, possession, and dispossession were being fabricated just beneath the surface.

VIRGÉN XOCHIMILCO

Pure Women and Waters in Mexico City's Suburban South

A WELL-KNOWN PHOTOGRAPH OF FRIDA KAHLO shows her elegant frame in profile as she leans over the edge of a wooden boat. Her hand, submerged in a placid lake, floats languidly but appears broken, refracted by water and camera lens. She wears a dark, Zapotec style huipil, accented by black clay beads, dangling earrings, and a low braided bun. Behind her the scene blurs: a man in a white cotton shirt and straw hat is bent away from the camera as he steers the boat. The verdant banks, tall spires of *ahuejote* (willow) trees, and open sky above appear out of focus, but they still would have been immediately recognizable to any contemporary viewer as belonging to Mexico City's storied southern enclave, Xochimilco.

By the time Fritz Henle took this photograph in 1937, Xochimilco had firmly secured its status as a tranquil getaway from the chaos of life in Mexico City. Famous for its network of waterways and agricultural chinampas, it marked a living memory of the city's noble Aztec origins. Kahlo, meanwhile, had established an international reputation as the grand dame of Indigenous chic. The fact that her precious hand was submerged in water within city limits at a time when other waterways had been drained, filled in, or declared unsafe for human contact underscores Xochimilco's reputation for being a source of pristine waters. This image weds several prevailing postrevolutionary endeavors: the creation of national types, including the *india bonita*; the framing of

Mexico as a desirable travel destination; and Mexico City's Sisyphean efforts to source potable water for its residents.

Over the course of postrevolutionary reconstruction, Xochimilco served as a portal to the pre-Hispanic past and a critical source of potable water. Mutually constitutive representations of the place, water, and women of Xochimilco all tended to center the concept of purity. Evaluating these overlapping discourses in concert lends insight into the complex construction of settler colonial identity as well as the avenues for Indigenous intervention. In this chapter, I build on previous examinations of the *india bonita* trope, grounding analysis of the ideology as it was deployed in this specific place. Here, popular culture analysis interwoven with regional and environmental history demonstrates that the *india bonita* trope was central to the bridging of the modern (potable water, sanitation, transportation, filmmaking) and the traditional (Indigenous authenticity, living memory of the Aztec) in postrevolutionary nation building.

Long before Kahlo donned her Zapotec costume and posed in a *trajinera* (flat-bottomed boat) on that sunny afternoon, Xochimilco had secured iconic status in art, literature, and visual media. For decades it had been a destination for leisure seekers, a brief escape from the waves of moral panic inundating a modernizing Mexico City. Social clubs for urbanites seeking respite were established during the Porfiriato, and visual records bear witness to the elite consumption of this Edenic atmosphere.[1] Because the region maintained the valley's ancient lacustrine ecosystem and waterways in their "purest" form, it was also seen as a window into the revered Aztec past. For decades, artists and photographers had flocked to the region to record images of Xochimilco. Paul Fischer, José Guadalupe Posada, Saturnino Herrán, and Diego Rivera, among many others, were drawn to the region's verdant landscapes, rustic daily life, and the opportunity to depict romantic views of modern city folk and *indias bonitas* luxuriating in anachronistically pristine environs.[2] Documentary photographers and amateur cinematographers—including Hugo Brehme, C. B. Waite, the Casasola brothers, Franz Mayer, and hordes of amateur cameramen—voyaged to the region looking to capture old Mexico with their modern devices.[3] In early days of the 1921 India Bonita pageant, roving newspapermen turned quickly to Xochimilco in their search for "authentic" Indians. Though as readers might recall, their advances were largely unwelcome.

Photographs and early films of the region tended toward documentary realism with landscapes and waterways providing a scenic backdrop. These images often depicted local women and men at work steering canoes laden with tourists or agricultural goods, selling flowers, or doing laundry in the waters of the canals. Postcards, calendar art images, and narrative films, on the other hand, tended to show romantic interpretations of white-coded women in Indigenous clothing luxuriating amid their flowers rather than working to harvest or sell them. In this imaginary world, Xochimilcan women enjoyed lives of leisure—more prop than laborer or active participant in the place they inhabited.

Visual depictions of Xochimilco invariably centered images of glassy water and, indeed, this was essential to most aspects of life in the region. From its founding in the pre-Hispanic era, Indigenous peoples built their lives around water, mounding plant material and mud atop interlacing networks of willow tree roots to create habitable and arable islands known as chinampas. The *trajineras* like the one that hosted Frida Kahlo in 1937 had been used to navigate the intricate labyrinth of canals for centuries. The long-inhabited waterscape was indeed a storied and beautiful place. But the rosy picture of Xochimilco as it was depicted in art, popular culture, and even in historical narratives obfuscated the fact that the region underwent major environmental and social turmoil that began during the Porfiriato and continued on well into the period of postrevolutionary reconstruction.

CONTESTED PARADISE

Located at the city's far south, Xochimilco's waters and chinampas had long served as an important source of agricultural products coming into Mexico City from the countryside. From the Lago Xochimilco, the Canal Nacional extended north and connected to a series of other canals that traversed the city, a vital artery for food and fuel. Xochimilco was also an essential source of potable water for Mexico City. A multiyear project to pump water from the region's southern springs into the city was finally completed in 1913, with expenses totaling an astronomical US$250 million in today's currency.[4] During the revolution, Xochimilco became a stronghold, with both men and women taking up arms to fight.[5] The Zapatista and Villista armies each set up camps in the region. Zapatistas cut Mexico City's water supply from its source in Xochimilco multiple times, a move that historian Matthew Vitz argues was as strategic as it was symbolic.[6]

With the loss of life and livelihood, the years of revolutionary warfare created a power vacuum that allowed for a period of self-governance and relative autonomy in the region. The land reform laws written into the 1917 constitution allowed Xochimilcans to reclaim territory, but these gains in land and liberty were quickly eroded over the course of reconstruction. In 1918 the government created an ejido in Xochimilco. However, the water-management and land-use needs of this new agrarian model were at odds with those of the well-established *chinamperos*. New tensions among community members emerged and simmered for decades to come. In 1922 Xochimilco remained one of only a few sources of water for most of the city, a poorly managed and tenuous arrangement that resulted in a citizen revolt in November of 1922.[7] Further complicating the situation was the fact that increased demand for wood and charcoal in Mexico City, as well the growth of agriculture and ranching, had led to deforestation of Xochimilco's land base. As a result, sedimentation began filling in the lakes, and rainfall was more likely to cause flooding.[8] The twin torrents of urbanization and revolution had, in essence, set off a series of chain reactions that fundamentally reshaped the region between 1910 and the mid-1940s.

In the meantime, Mexico City was rapidly hurtling toward centralized control of its sprawling network of barrios and municipalities. This trend increasingly limited the ability of individual communities to manage their own futures, a change the largely autonomous, Indigenous Xochimilco did not accept passively. By 1924 protests organized by Xochimilco residents had grown so forceful that President Obregón felt compelled to install a regional advisory council in order to give audience to its disgruntled citizens.[9] In the same year, Xochimilco lost jurisdiction over the neighboring municipality, Tlahuac, motivating members of the ayuntamiento to walk off the job as a way of protesting their growing impotency. In 1929 Mexico City was politically reorganized and power centralized, further decreasing the amount of authority individual municipalities had to govern themselves.

MEXICO'S VENICE

Despite this tumult, Xochimilco managed to retain its reputation as a getaway for both national and foreign tourists. The canals were declared a living reminder of the "old ways" of the Aztec, providing an appealing escape for urbanites immersed in the nostalgia-crazed atmosphere of postrevolutionary reconstruction. Recognition of Xochimilco's status as an essential source of potable water and a cultural treasure was evident in a general atlas of the city that José Manuel Puig Casauranc, newly appointed head of the Departamento del Distrito Federal, wrote in 1929 to aid in managing the newly merged delegations. In describing the system that carried water from "the purest springs" to Condesa, the document detailed a complex system of pumps and canals that brought that water to residents in the city.[10] He acknowledged that this system was in disrepair but promised that no effort nor cost would be spared in maintaining it.

Later in the same tome, Puig Casauranc noted Xochimilco's changing landscape, remarking that the ancient lake was gradually disappearing as it was drained and converted into farmland. He noted that this "Mexican Venice" had great value as a tourist destination, and cast its intricate network of lakes and canals as otherworldly, nourishing the city with sweet waters and serving as a memory of the lagoon that still exists today. He also praised the modern infrastructure that allowed this fledgling tourism industry to thrive: Xochimilco was accessible through modern transport including electric trains and the "magnificent, paved freeway." Even this perfunctory assessment of the city's assets highlighted Xochimilco's curative waters and linked them to modernity in the transport of water and visitors and to the past as a chance to experience "ancient Mexico."[11]

Puig Casauranc's publication arrived at a critical moment in the development of the city and at the dawn of a new tourism industry by setting Xochimilco up to be a mandatory stop on the Mexico City tourist circuit. Although foreign tourism to Mexico had yet to recover fully after diminished interest in travel to the country during the revolution, business leaders initiated new efforts to create a tourist economy beginning in 1928. Recognizing that the industry provided an opportunity to monetize postrevolutionary identity projects, the federal government created the Protourism Commission.[12] By 1929 the fledgling department had been reorganized as the Mixed Protourism Commission, an organization led by prominent businessmen and oil tycoons.

Shortly thereafter, the tourism industry boomed. In 1930 thirty-three thousand visitors came from the United States; that number had risen to 135,000 by 1940.[13] The following decade saw an even more robust growth spurt, with profits increasing from 21.7 million pesos in 1939 to 156.1 million in 1950.[14] For President Lázaro Cárdenas and his administration (1936–1940), tourism provided a golden opportunity to capitalize on identity projects while modernizing infrastructure and improving the nation's image to the outside world. Under his leadership, the government stepped in with funding to help with various programs, ultimately creating the Consejo Nacional de Turismo in 1939.

MAKING "MEXICO'S VENICE"

As this new era of tourism dawned, Xochimilco was perfectly poised to benefit from the industry despite the major environmental and social changes it was weathering. With the foundation of and interest in regional tourism firmly in place, the 1930s saw developments that moved Xochimilco farther along its path to being intractably lodged in the popular imaginary by establishing it as a must-see destination for any visitor. Civic developments helped make the region accessible while also ensuring its vital resources could still be extracted. In 1934 alone, public works projects developed drainage, new infrastructure for transporting potable water to the city, lighting, and the construction of new buildings.[15]

Although Xochimilco had been a destination for decades, the developments of 1934 aligned with both postrevolutionary ideals and capitalist enterprise. The lighting project, for example, was critical to opening access to tourists. These developments, though, struck at the heart of a paradox: the region needed to modernize in order to attract tourists, but it also had to preserve its historic, "exotic" appeal. The tension between development and preservation would remain at the forefront of dialogues about the region for decades to come. As Xochimilco modernized and changed to accommodate tourist demand, it became all the more necessary to sell the idea that it was still an authentic Indigenous center of leisure.

A trilingual (English, Spanish, and French) illustrated book published in 1934 provided a brief history of the region from the pre-Hispanic era to the present.[16] Although this was largely intended to be a tourist publication, the Spanish version included a section warning of impending harm to Xochimilco's pristine waters. The author argued that residents, in their relentless efforts to create more arable land, were destroying the lakes and the canals by importing new soil and expanding the chinampas. He went on to caution that this shameless harm to a Mexican jewel would be detrimental to the nascent tourism industry. Placing blame for environmental destruction on the people who had inhabited that place for centuries can be read as a further attempt to disenfranchise Indigenous stakeholders and cast them as being incompetent stewards of their own homeland.

Despite the tensions that stemmed from this moment of heightened social and environmental change, President Cárdenas saw Xochimilco as being an ideal locale to foster national patrimony. On numerous occasions he traveled there himself for staged photos and ceremonies that bolstered his reputation as a populist president. In 1936 Xochimilco was one of a handful of sites classed a "traditional zone" (*zona típica*) in a presidential decree of protection for monuments, *zonas típicas*, and sites of natural beauty.[17] Cárdenas's interest in the region and his recognition of its economic potential resulted in more funding and support than other delegations in the city received.[18] In the late 1930s, construction began on a massive central market that still stands today and on roadways that further enabled tourist travel, but despite all this beautification and development, poverty remained rampant. The majority of homes were constructed of rustic adobe with dirt floors, and few residences in this region that continued to provide most of Mexico City's water enjoyed the benefits of potable water (only four hundred out of six thousand homes) themselves.[19]

The potential for income from tourist travel to Xochimilco undoubtedly inspired efforts to preserve regional patrimony and to further develop its public facilities. Indeed, tourism seemed to provide a solution to a number of the challenges Xochimilco faced. The Lago Xochimilco had to be preserved as a source of water. Tourism provided a path for preservation while also capitalizing on the lacustrine ecosystem and its history as a leisure spot. However, the "Edenic paradise" narrative had to be crafted and promoted in order to obfuscate the reality of social and environmental turmoil. And that's where *indias bonitas* came in. As tourism imagery is wont to do, the propaganda that emerged in the 1930s developed a specific "image code" for Xochimilco that feminized and exoticized the region while skirting less marketable components of its identity.[20] Efforts to depict Xochimilco as being pristine and impervious to change became increasingly overstated, but the chasm widened between the on-the-ground reality and the sunny image depicted in publicity materials.

XOCHIMILCO'S *INDIAS BONITAS*

The construction of a regional *india bonita* type was central to masking underlying disjunctions, and themes of environmental and aboriginal purity became

FIGURE 12. Mexican Tourist Association poster ca. 1910–1959. Courtesy of Boston Public Library.

crystal clear in advertisements for the region. Images of beautiful young women juxtaposed with crystalline waters became central to regional campaigns, at once affirming the purity of the natural offerings and beckoning leisure seekers with their exotic allure. In the mid-1930s, a spate of Xochimilco calendar art and tourism promotions invariably depicted women ensconced in their environs, glassy water and poplar trees framing voluptuous bodies adorned in colorful Indigenous clothing. Compared to the sexually provocative depictions of women in other calendar art of the time, the Xochimilcan *indias bonitas* were unique in their wholesome prettiness. One such image, printed in 1935, shows a young woman whose body is in profile but whose head is turned back so that her gaze meets the viewer's. She is cloaked in embroidered clothing, with a rebozo draped over her head and a hand placed delicately on her chest. Another image from 1940 shows a woman wearing an embroidered top and a mischievous grin as she steers a canoe laden with flowers.[21] These romantic depictions cast both the natural and Indigenous beauty of the region as being pure and untainted by the ills of modernity, be it urban or sexual in nature. Meanwhile, the images burst with vibrant fuchsias, chartreuses, and teals in an undeniable appeal to the Tropicalist aesthetic.

A poster issued by the Asociacion Mexicana de Turismo (Mexican Tourist Association; fig. 12) with a bold-colored, modernist motif features a canal scene with a man and woman in the foreground and a crystalline waterscape unfolding behind them.[22] Although there are four figures in the scene, only the woman faces forward. Her face is awash in a saintly glow and a halo of palm fronds emerging from the flower basket affixed to her back. Her clothing is somewhat obscured by the flower basket and a rebozo, her pure white dress embellished by an embroidered belt and skirt. Her downcast eyes, demure expression, and tilted head signal the submissive behavior associated with the trope—though the dark coloring of her skin breaks from the tendency to depict *indias bonitas* as light-skinned mestizas. Two other Indigenous men appear in the background, while the man who dominates the image's foreground turns his gaze passively away from the viewer as if to reassure potential visitors that he poses no threat. In all, the image depicts a place and its people frozen in time, gently beckoning visitors to a leisurely float through Mexico Viejo.

A newspaper ad that ran in 1938 drew on this formula and added some modernist elements (fig. 13). The image, broken into three panels, gave equal emphasis to an electric train, a canal flanked by *trajineras* and willow trees, and a woman with her hand placed firmly on her hip. Her makeup connotes the modern *china poblana*: dark, full lips, thin, arched eyebrows, a beauty mark, and theatrically long lashes. Her huipil features geometric and floral Aztec patterning in line with the *india bonita* ideology, but a tricolored bow wrapped around her head and a sombrero resting at the nape of her neck gave a clear nod to the standard *china poblana*. The text encouraged readers to spend their holidays in Xochimilco, the "most traditional place in the capital," and reminded them that at that time of year, the "Mexican Venice" transformed into a "charming orchard." All elements taken together, the advertisement promised the natural and authentic beauty of both the waterways and the women. At the same time, the deployment of *china poblana* characteristics and the centrality of the train in this particular ad underscore an attempt to inflect the pureness of Xochimilco with just enough modern comfort and convenience to make the trip appeal to urbanites and visiting foreigners.

FIGURE 13. Advertisement for Xochimilco featuring modern transport, water, and an *india bonita* in equal measure. "Vaya a Xochimilco," *El Universal*, advertisement, April 14, 1938.

PROJECTING PARADISE

A home movie filmed by an American tourist in 1940 provides a glimpse into what one of those sun-dappled excursions to Xochimilco might have been like.[23] With a shaky hand, Ernest M. Hunt, a rancher from New Mexico, recorded Mexico City street scenes, a bullfight, a trip to Diego Rivera's house, and the obligatory journey down the famous canals of Xochimilco. His footage shows a waterway crowded with *trajineras* carrying other well-to-do visitors and rowdy students. Local women in canoes paddle up to the tourist boats, attempting to sell small bundles of flowers. Unlike the romantic depictions of the women in tourism propaganda, few of those captured in Hunt's footage wear *traje* and braided hair. Instead, they don simple housedresses with aprons and hats to shield their eyes from the sun's glare. Instead of the glossy black braids of the *india bonita* imagery, many wear their hair pulled back away from their faces in practical buns.

As in the promotional pieces, the water is crystalline, but it is far more crowded with tourists and locals than any touristic propaganda would have had you believe. In one shot, Hunt catches two other cameramen on canoes, each steered by one man while another shoots the footage of the passing natural and cultural scenery. For a brief moment, an Indigenous woman passes into the frame; she seems completely impervious to the triangular camera gaze she passes through, indicating that by that point amateur cinematographers were common enough on the canals that sight of them caused little interest. Her disengagement with the cinematic gaze can also be read as a deliberate decision to opt out of the performance these tourists seemed to expect of her. Xochimilco and its residents were keenly adept at working the waves of change and romantic tourist depictions in their favor. Even so, they were able to reap the benefits of tourism without necessarily having to practice "self-commodification" by playing to the image of the *india bonita* that promotional material and popular culture promised.[24]

In contrast to the pristine, carefree world depicted in tourism imagery, concerns about the impact of development weighed heavily on the minds of those who made their living in the region. Xochimilco's patrimonial counterpart, Santa Anita, had recently been urbanized and its iconic Canal de la Viga drained because of concerns that the polluted waters posed a serious public health risk. Since life in Xochimilco was literally built upon its waterways, a similar turn of events would have devastated the community. Residents were able to employ tourism's language of purity and Indigenous beauty for their own interests. In doing so they promoted the constructed narrative that pristine nature and authentic Indigeneity went hand in hand and that both were indispensable for a successful tourist industry.

A petition sent to President Manuel Ávila Camacho in 1941 showed the community's awareness of what was at stake and their savvy engagement in the discourse of the time. Signed by forty-four petitioners from Xochimilco, it claimed:

> Xochimilco's beauty and life are soon to disappear within no more than five years and then in Mexico's Venice visited by tourists and residents of the capital they will find only dry *chinampas* and the desolation and ruin of a beautiful town.[25]

Locals knew that the region's singular assets afforded them a certain political power, and this petition demonstrates how adept they were at wielding it. They drew on patrimonial instincts, the desire for tourism capital, and affinities for European high culture to win support for the preservation of their community.

A 1944 letter printed in *El Nacional* provides another example of how Xochimilcans operated within the imposed power structure to achieve their aims. An article titled "'Mexican Venice' Is Losing Its Originality" consisted of a letter submitted to the paper by Doctor Damián Flores.[26] The letter was intended to draw the attention of authorities to a problem in Xochimilco resulting from the increasing number of motorized *lanchas*, which were polluting the waterways of Xochimilco and causing ecological damage. The letter demonstrated how skilled Xochimilco residents and their allies were at employing popular ideologies to their own advantage and included several references to the heritage value of the region, using the moniker "La Venecia Mexicana" as a reminder that this site helped place Mexico City on par with well-known European cities like Venice. It also employed the phrase "belleza auctotona," or aboriginal beauty, rhetorically invoking the beauty and authenticity of the *india bonita*. Later, it refers to "the sadness that fills the eyes of the Indian" at the thought of modernization—a colonialist fantasy meant to evoke pity for what was cast as a hapless, vanishing race.

Flores went on to compare a modernizing Xochimilco with the motorized boats to the shipyards of modern-day Brooklyn. This disparaging reference to Brooklyn would have surely stoked Mexican anxieties surrounding U.S.

influence in general, thereby inflecting the appeal with some nationalist pride. And in positioning a U.S. version of modernity as a direct threat to Mexican heritage and Indigenous ways of life, the author played on widespread beliefs of the time that imagined Indigenous peoples as being incapable of adapting to modern life. Though the trope was typically used in settler colonial narratives attempting to establish Indigenous existence as being antithetical to modernity, here it is cleverly deployed to protect Indigenous interests.

Finally, this published letter alluded to the possibility of economic loss if tourists—"lovers of poetry, harmony, light, color"—were to become disenchanted by the sudden absence of physical beauty and stop visiting Xochimilco. The author argued that the region would lose its "folkloric interest" and that this "Edenic corner" of the city would degenerate into a generic recreational getaway if the merchants kept utilizing motorized boats. While the changes that Xochimilco weathered were largely out of the hands of the residents, the rhetoric was adapted in order to defend local needs.

CINEMATIC XOCHIMILCO

In the early 1940s Xochimilco became even more firmly lodged in the Mexican imaginary. The 1944 release of the film *María Candelaria* transformed the romantic imagery deployed in tourism propaganda into artfully rendered cinematic expression. Analysis of this film and the circumstances surrounding its production show how Xochimilco was constructed as a source of water, lucrative tourism dollars, and the *india bonita* trope, all of which were mediated through modern technology. Although the audience is led to believe that the film is set on the eve of the Mexican Revolution, its themes were far more reflective of the moment in which it was produced.[27] The film reflected postrevolutionary tensions between a modernizing Mexico and a traditional Xochimilco, with the central drama unfolding on the body of a woman cast as "pure" in both her Indianness and her virtue.

María Candelaria is a significant film to consider here because its life as a cultural artifact extended far beyond the darkened auditoriums of the city's movie houses. Its impact was due in part to its star, Dolores del Río, the Mexican-born actress who had made it big in Hollywood and had just returned to her motherland after a tumultuous affair with Orson Welles.[28] On January 16, 1944, *El Universal* reported on del Río's attendance at the baptism of María Candelaria, a baby born to Emigdio Sánchez Arenas and Petra Flores de Sánchez, "humble horticulturalists of the picturesque pueblo" Xochimilco.[29]

A photograph of the baptism shows del Río affecting a saintly look with her eyes cast to the heavens (fig. 14). She is framed by local Xochimilcans, mostly women swathed in traditional handwoven rebozos. The reporter opined that the people of Xochimilco might have been shocked to see her in such swanky attire as, until then, they'd known her only to wear the humble *traje* that they themselves donned. The reporter surely underestimated the awareness of the Xochimilcans in attendance who undoubtedly knew of Dolores del Río's international stardom and had perhaps even seen some of her films. Even so, this assumed ignorance was yet another instance of the media casting Indigenous peoples as being backward and out of touch even though they'd had direct engagement with this iconic film and its star. As *El Universal* recounted, before being whisked away from a mobbing crowd, del Río promised to be a good godmother and invited the family to visit her in her newly purchased Coyoacán home.

FIGURE 14. Dolorés del Río at a baptism in Xochimilco. *El Universal*, January 16, 1944. Biblioteca Lerdo de Tejada.

Although the baptism occurred well before *María Candelaria* premiered in theaters, the film already had a material presence in the city. A contest sponsored by the production company Filmes Mundiales offered the chance for drivers of hired cars to win a cash prize if they placed a colored promotional sticker featuring Dolores's iconic face on the back windows of their cars.[30] Newspaper ads that ran throughout January 1944 promised greatness in the winning combination of the "best actress of national cinema" and the "most beautiful Mexican countryside." In addition to emphasizing the unparalleled beauty of the film's lead,[31] these promotions—some of which appeared as columns in *El Universal*—promised "shot after shot" of Mexico's Venice.[32] Between Dolores del Río's epic beauty and the beloved waterscapes of Xochimilco, Filmes Mundiales banked on being able to entice viewers to come see the film.

Although it was initially met with criticism and mixed interest, *María Candelaria* would soon secure its place as a treasured addition to the Mexican imaginary.[33] After being lost for decades, a negative was discovered in the United States in the 1990s. In its rediscovery it was billed as a mythical film and was celebrated accordingly with a hero's return.[34] A survey conducted around that same time found that 47 percent of respondents cited *María Candelaria* as being one of the three most important national films ever produced.[35]

The film's director, Emilio "El Indio" Fernández, was a chastened Carrancista who got his start in Hollywood during a brief exile from Mexico. Upon his return, he continued his film career and eventually achieved virtual cinematic sainthood. The son of a mestizo father and Kikapú mother, his heritage earned him the nickname "El Indio." But in keeping with the spirit of Indigenismo, he demonstrated more familiarity and fascination with the Aztec vogue than with his own Native heritage.[36] Fernandez's work with this film in particular illustrates the extent to which mestizos could become agents of settler colonialism.

At the time of the film's production and release, Fernández and del Río were engaged in a tumultuous romance that was widely reported in the press. Even *María Candelaria* itself was a product of their romance. The script was reportedly written by Fernández specifically for the star and delivered on napkins laid dramatically at her feet as he told her, "Here's your saint's day present, a film story. Let's see if you like it, it is your next film and it's called *Xochimilco*. It's yours, it's your property. If someone wants to buy it they have to buy it from you."[37]

Fernández's conservative, nationalist paradigm was clearly on display in *María Candelaria*. The plot intertwines romantic portrayals of pure beauty, race, and landscape. The film's lead character, a young Indigenous woman named María Candelaria, is ostracized by the other *chinamperos* for the sins of her prostitute mother, but her ethereal beauty draws the attention of an artist who repeatedly asks permission to paint her. María is so pure and modest that she declines until she is desperate for his help and has no other choice. After completing the painting of her face, he asks her to disrobe, at which point she flees from his studio at the mere suggestion of such moral disgrace. The painting is finished with the body of another model who does pose in the nude and whose body is appended to María Candelaria's face in the finished painting. When María's nemesis sees the painting, she assumes María has posed in the nude and alerts the community to the immoral behavior of one of their own. A moral panic ensues, ending in María Candelaria's life being taken by her own community.

As in Xochimilcan tourism promotions, Indigenous female beauty and purity took center stage in this classic film. From its opening shots, codes for viewing and evaluating Indigenous beauty are established. The first scene opens to the sound of melancholy flute music and a series of close shots of stone statuary, one fading into the next. The poorly rendered stonework is clearly intended to reference Aztec relics but has the clumsily chiseled quality of cheap tourist knockoffs. The final relic is a stone mask, with narrow, feminine features and a headdress bearing the geometric patterning associated with Aztec design. The shot of the mask fades slowly into a beautiful young woman's face so that the two shots are momentarily superimposed and aligned in such a way that the woman appears to be wearing the stone crown affixed to the mask. The shot then brings the woman's face into clear focus: the light accentuates her high cheekbones and full lips, and a wall of windows provides a backdrop against which her thick black braids of hair are silhouetted. She holds a strong gaze and is as still as the stone statuary of the preceding shots. The camera pulls back to reveal that the woman is posing for a portrait, a painter committing her image to canvas while a crowd of men and women in suits look on.

This series of shots establishes a regime of looking that lays the foundation for the remainder of the film and is pivotal to the story's narrative progression. The artist's gaze and the viewing of his work are paramount to the scene's development. The message here is clear: much as Eisenstein did a decade before in the opening shots of *Que viva México*, Fernández draws a visual link between Mexico's Aztec predecessors and the Indigenous present, anchoring the film in romantic nostalgia for that glorious past and positioning women as the bearers of that heritage.

In the opening scene, a painter talks to journalists about a scandal over a beautiful Indian woman of "pure race" whose beauty was that of the "ancient princesses" who subjugated the conquistadores. This reference invokes popular narratives of La Malinche, the captive Indigenous woman who served as a consort to Cortés and who has a mixed reputation in Mexico as the beloved, but eternally damned, mother of mestizos. The painter's allusion to Malinche foreshadows the film's central tensions, which exist between the polarities of virtue and impurity. It is also a subtle reference to race and racial progression, reminding the audience that Indigenous women were flawed but worthy progenitors of modern Mestizaje.

In keeping with the *india bonita* trope and other *cine folclórico*, a fair-skinned actor adept at on-screen code switching embodied the pinnacle of Indigenous beauty. The message was clear: Indigenous beauty was fine but belonged in the past; mestiza beauty, meanwhile, was the beauty of the future. And this racial fantasy did not promise just any mestiza beauty. At the time, del Río was described as being one of the most beautiful women in the nation. Painting her a few years before the film's production, Diego Rivera had declared her "the most exquisitely beautiful Mexican woman imaginable . . . the ideal Indian or Mestiza beauty."[38] This conflation of *indígena* and mestiza by a major producer of indigenist works illustrates the extent to which mestizo settler colonial belonging had been normalized.

Much of the film's action pivots around del Río's idealized beauty, with countless close-ups drawing the viewer's eye to the delicate lines of her face. While del Río's beauty was an artifact in and of itself, it was presented within other regimes of spectacle and gaze that advanced an idealized melding of traditional Indigenous with modern mestiza. Ultimately, *María Candelaria* reinforces the settler fantasy that mestiza beauties like del Río were the ideal trajectory of Mestizaje. Despite this promotion of racial mixing, the cinematic fantasy was "purified" through emphasis on beauty and virtue.

Del Río's participation in the Xochimilco baptism underscored an element of the film that fortified the star's virtue and undoubtedly contributed to its success: in both plot and shot construction, the film overtly appealed to the Catholic sensibilities that the majority of the nation embraced. A number of scenes reinvent the holy family as two humble Indians caring for their baby pig as though it were their own child. When that piglet is killed by the evil hacendado, María weeps over its limp frame, a visual reference to Michelangelo's *Pietá*. Later, when a cruel twist of fate interrupts the couple's wedding, she threatens to renounce her faith. In a dramatic encounter with the priest and a series of cuts to and close-ups of a statue of the Virgin, she tearfully finds that faith again. As in this close brush with blasphemy, María's virtue is repeatedly confirmed through the specter of sin. Although she is persecuted by her community because of the immoral acts of her mother and ultimately killed because of her own alleged immoral act, the audience knows her to be pure of heart. As film historian Joanne Hershfield has argued, the most successful Mexican films at that time envisioned women on either end of the virgin-prostitute spectrum;[39] the brilliance of *María Candelaria* is that the main character exists within the tension between these extremes. And though viewers might question the purity of her Indigenous heritage, the film leaves no doubt about the pureness of her soul.

Beauty and virtue lie at the heart of this film, but place is more than a simple backdrop. Xochimilco itself plays a major supporting role, underscored by the fact that the film was originally titled *Xochimilco* and that this remained a subtitle in the finished production. Throughout the film, extreme high- and low-angle shots work to alternately elevate and subjugate the lead actors but also to allow for a closer framing of their faces by sky, land, and water. In one dramatic scene, María clutches at the ground and swears she will never leave the rich earth of Xochimilco. "This is our land," she insists. "Look how dark and how smooth." At various points, del Río and costar Pedro Armendáriz are placed in direct relationship with their environment, water framing and reflecting off their faces, their bodies artfully dwarfed by the landscape.

Water also plays a particularly important role, literally and figuratively framing the film from the outset. The opening credits scroll over a track shot of the water. Director of photography Gabriel Figueroa was adroit in his ability to capture the light reflecting off the water in order to illuminate the faces of the actors with an ethereal aura. The primary scene establishing María and Lorenzo Rafael's romance takes place on the water. A full moon hangs over an isolated lagoon with a chorus of frogs and symphonic flute music supplying the score. The scene opens with a long-distance establishing shot of María and her beau traversing the lake while mountains, clouds, and tall spires of trees fill the frame behind them, the image redoubled in the glassy water they traverse. The camera follows the canoe as Lorenzo steers and María reclines at the front in a bed of flowers, her hand languidly running through the water, reminiscent of Frida Kahlo's pose in her 1938 portrait. Twenty-three cuts back and forth between María and Lorenzo ensue, with the framing emphasizing the background as much as the faces of the actors themselves. In one point-of-view shot, the camera follows María's gaze up at the passing sky and trees, a construction that allows audience members to imagine that they themselves are reclined on the boat taking in the paradise around them. The final sequence of the film returns María's placid face to a juxtaposition with the waters of the canal, only this time her lifeless body rests on a bed of flowers in a canoe gliding over glassy water.

Another critical scene gives voice to some of the modernist anxieties surrounding early 1940s life in Xochimilco. María, having contracted malaria, is in a feverish dream state and starts fearfully describing the hallucinations she is having, all of which center around loss of the traditional Xochimilcan land, water, and lifeways: "Oh god! Why! Why is there no water? The canals have been drained and all the animals in the pueblo are dying! The *chinampas* are burning!" Presenting this environmental catastrophe as a nightmare highlights the panic that existed at the threat of actual environmental degradation, the encroachment of modern, urban life, and the very real awareness that Xochimilco was indeed undergoing drastic change.

With Xochimilco cast as the idealized camposcape, those who inhabit it were reduced to antimodern stewards of an ancient land. A copy of the film's script annotated by Fernández himself shows directorial intention in this portrayal. Fernández includes stage directions indicating that the actors playing Indians—movie stars and Indigenous extras alike—mirror movements and behaviors of the natural world. Early in the script he indicates that del Río's embodiment of María Candelaria should be "languid like the stems of the flowers that she lives among."[40] His stage directions instruct "animalistic behaviors" as the stars evade threats posed by their community members, from city folk, and from the auspices of modernity. Later, when the painter approaches María and Lorenzo for the first time in a crowded market, stage directions instructed them to flee from the market "like animals."[41] While the director was supposedly attempting to pay tribute to the original inhabitants of the land, he was clearly informed by racist ideologies that equated Indigenous peoples with animals and the earth. In doing so, the film reinforced ideas that Indigenous peoples were not capable of successfully existing in the modern world.

Other scenes reinforce this backward, animalistic behavior through both content and shot construction. A series of long shots during the "Blessing of the Animals" sequence contains a montage of Indigenous Xochimilcans carrying turkeys, chickens, and ducks on their heads and dragging pigs and dogs and other livestock through the crowded gates of the church grounds. The establishing shot in the sequence—a slow-tilt crane shot—displays Xochimilcans from above and behind so that they appear to be one and the same as the animals that accompany them. This establishing sequence is far more than just B-roll. It fully immerses the viewer in quaint, rural life and constructs life in Xochimilco as being unsophisticated and untouched by modernity.

A scene in the script that would have shown the lead characters in direct contact with modernity was either never filmed or deleted during the editing process. The scene portrays María and Lorenzo at a fair just before their wedding. They eat cotton candy, ride on a Ferris wheel, and pose for a portrait "with their butts comically elevated" in an airplane painted with the slogan "The Spirit of San Luis Potosi" (a play on the famous *Spirit of Saint Louis* piloted by Charles Lindbergh in 1927).[42] These lost scenes evidence the fact that the film was originally written to take place in the 1940s, not on the eve of the revolution as the audience is led to believe from the outset of the film. The scenes were probably cut when Fernández made the decision to set the film at an earlier date rather than the contemporary moment. Even so, their deletion echoes postrevolutionary discourse that imagined Indians as being "traditional" relics of the rural past, incapable of engaging with modern things like Ferris wheels, airplanes, and whimsical portraits.

The film's reflection of postrevolutionary ideals doesn't necessarily prove intentionality. However, other factors indicate that Fernández aligned closely enough with state interests to produce an essentially propagandistic film that buttressed tourism messaging, natural resource management, and ideologies of modern Mestizaje. Fernández's own nationalist fervor and his association with the cultural elite of the time attest to these possibilities. Furthermore, his allegiance to state interests is even more visible in the film's underlying public health message. A conservative nationalist, Fernández enthusiastically adopted the indigenist paradigm that at once celebrated and strove to integrate Indigenous peoples.[43] As a filmmaker he saw it as his duty to "Mexicanize the Mexicans,"[44] and so it was not surprising that his filmography engaged heavily in nationalist identity discourse. In keeping with postrevolutionary identity projects, Fernández saw women as the "alma del pueblo" and felt they had an appealing virtue and vulnerability in them.[45]

Allegiance to state interests plays out in more subtle ways too. The climactic drama is catalyzed by María's lack of access to modern medicine (quinine) and what is portrayed as a foolish reliance on "folk" medicine through engagement with a *huesera*. Indigenous medicine is shown to be antiquated, while modern medicine has miraculous healing qualities. The audience is clearly guided to believe in the merits of Western medicine and the shortcomings of the "backward" ways of Indigenous knowledge systems. This hint that Fernández was aligned with and invested in government interests lends even greater weight to the film's racial and commercial agendas. More than just a whimsical piece of popular culture, *María Candelaria* reflected the logic and reach of postrevolutionary identity and governance. In doing so, it reinforced ideas that Xochimilco was a bastion of Indigenous beauty, pure land and waters, and traditional—if antiquated—lifeways.

Proponents of tourism and preservation in Xochimilco seized on the film's cultural capital, even going so far as to adopt some of the romantic tropes employed in *María Candelaria* for their own purposes. A March 1944 newspaper article imagined a magical Xochimilco, seemingly drawn directly from the reels of *María Candelaria*: "Living there is an Indigenous race as picturesque and as complex as the passages in which they move. Their physical features, dark like the shadows of the chinampas, reflect the discreet happiness of their cleanest springs."[46] This cloying depiction of Xochimilco emphasizes the "clean, crystalline" water in its canals, the clear air, the sensation of "impeccable purity," the fertile land, the "silent drops of tropical poetry," and the place's "miraculous, magical power . . . like a dream of fantastic voyages through the Aztec world." The article is heavily illustrated; one photo in particular reiterates the normalcy of foreign travel to Xochimilco: a sophisticated American couple perches on the front edge of a *trajinera* boat. The man wears a business suit and fedora, and a cigarette casually hangs from his lips. The woman wears stylish heels and leans over the bow of the *trajinera* to accept a small bouquet of flowers from an Indigenous woman kneeling before her in a smaller canoe. This romantic depiction, perhaps emboldened by the success of *María Candelaria*, reflected and reinforced contemporary discourses about Xochimilco. It also illustrated the extent to which touristic consumption of the region's supposed riches had been normalized by 1944.

As testament to the success of Xochimilco's enduring reputation, the Flor más Bella del Ejido pageant was relocated from Santa Anita's desiccated canals to the verdant banks of Xochimilco in 1955.[47] With a crowd of ten thousand in attendance at the first Xochimilco celebration, Evangelina Romero of the Tláhuac delegation was crowned queen of the ejido. Photos from the festival show Romero posing with a rebozo full of palm fronds and flowers tied to her back, echoing a memorable market scene from *María Candelaria*.

CONCLUSION

By the mid-1940s, Xochimilco's reputation as a destination for pristine waterscapes and Indigenous authenticity was as secure as it had been during the Porfiriato, and it was further bolstered by layers of postrevolutionary zeal and commercialism. As Mexico City heaved its way through modernization reforms and urban expansion, Xochimilco served as a counterweight to the waves of moral panic that accompanied that growth. This southern enclave played an essential role as a source of potable water, but it was also reimagined as a *lieu de memoire*, a living monument—equal parts authentic and invented—of pre-Hispanic glory.[48] Despite the fact that it was undergoing major changes, postrevolutionary identity discourse sold it as, in the words of travel writer Frances Toor, "primitive and quite untouched by civilization."[49] Paradoxically, modernization was required to enjoy the offerings of this memento: the Xochimilco that came of age after the revolution was necessarily mediated through film, photography, transportation, and urban development. But that, too, came with a new set of tensions and competing interests.

India bonita imagery allowed proponents of tourism and the city's cultural elite to, quite literally, put a pretty face on tensions that emerged from modern enjoyment of this "pristine" enclave. The Xochimilcan *indias bonitas* at once symbolized purity, modernization, and "old Mexico" through mutually reinforcing discourses. Linking water to Indigenous women and the pre-Hispanic era made a vital natural resource appear to be more natural and pure while also helping to brand a unique and inviting destination for tourists and moviemakers alike. The virtuous and demure *india bonita* figure was positioned as a cure-all to a competing set of interests in Xochimilco. This icon of Mestizaje was used at once to entice tourists and demonstrate idealized racial futures that excluded the complexities of actual Indigenous inhabitance. Through her, an emblem of the past became a roadmap for the future.

But these representations came at a cost to the place and people they symbolized. Images of Europeanized *indias bonitas* as situated in pristine Xochimilco with impeccable Indigenous *traje* masked the reality that Indigenous women were laborers negotiating a new set of social and environmental scenarios that had been introduced by urbanization and revolution. Further, binding Indigeneity to a specific place had the adverse consequence of disavowing the possibility of Indigenous existence outside of that space.[50] Indigenous women who didn't conform to the place-based *india bonita* ideal were subject to accusations of inauthenticity. As seen in the Flor más Bella del Ejido pageant, establishing the *india bonita* type as an ethnic ideal was a thinly veiled project of erasure that limited the parameters of "legitimate" Indigeneity to a specific place-gender-material culture formula.

Beneath the crystalline surface of this romantic reimagining, Indigenous Xochimilcans also faced the double bind of coping with environmental degradation and repeated attempts to show that they weren't capable of being stewards of their own homeland. This rhetorical fettering of Indigenous self-governance was visible everywhere from official complaints that locals were destroying the treasured land to *María Candelaria*'s themes of Indigenous incompetence through their failure to engage with modernity. It was part of broader settler colonial efforts to disempower Indigenous peoples in order to more completely assimilate them into the nation and to disavow any future claims to autonomy they might make.

Despite these assimilative efforts, citizen participation in the form of letter writing, petitions, and involvement in tourism and movie making demonstrates multifaceted Indigenous engagement and disengagement with this settler colonial project. Embracing this discourse reinforced ideas that Indigenous peoples were "of the past," but doing so could also be employed as a strategy for survival. Just as Gabriela Spears-Rico argues that contemporary P'urhepechas perform certain "commodified personas" for tourists, so, too, did some Xochimilcans strategically engage with a romanticized identity that those in power became invested in preserving.[51] However, as home movie footage revealed, Indigenous Xochimilcans didn't always have to play to the *india bonita* ideology in order to gain a foothold in the emerging tourist economy. Instead, their refusal to do so can be read as small acts of resistance to imposed ideologies and engagement with settler colonial encroachment on their own terms.

DOÑA LUZ JIMÉNEZ

"The Most Painted Woman in All of Mexico"

F YOU HAVE EVER BEEN to Mexico City you have probably encountered Luz Jiménez, though chances are you don't know it. Considered by many of the nation's great postrevolutionary artists to be the "archetype of the Indigenous Mexican woman,"[1] her face and body grace famous works of art throughout the city. She is Orozco's Malinche, she appears repeatedly in Rivera's murals, she has been photographed by Edward Weston and Tina Modotti, and a life-size statue of her likeness reigns over Parque México (fig. 15), among countless other representations. In a career that spanned most of her lifetime, this Nahua woman modeled for some of the best-known artists of Mexico's postrevolutionary vanguard and has been called "the most painted woman in all of Mexico."[2] She was also a gifted storyteller, teacher, and intellectual who imparted knowledge that helped shape the work of artists and scholars alike. Jiménez's life story illustrates the kinds of interventions Indigenous women could make into the postrevolutionary identity-making process but also the ways in which that engagement was restricted by the limitations of the settler colonial imagination.

Many of Jiménez's artistic collaborators saw her at once as a dear friend and as someone who could give them access to invaluable cultural knowledge. They forged rich and, in several cases, lifelong relationships, but few gave her adequate credit for her contributions to their art and scholarship. Despite her visibility and decades of meaningful engagement with members of the postrevolutionary cultural elite, she lived in poverty, and her legacy is largely obscured from the historical record. Her pay for teaching and modeling in some of the city's most prestigious institutions was so meager—and the needs of her family and community so great—that she continued intermittent work as a street vendor, a nanny, and a housemaid for the duration of her life. While her image graced the walls of the National Palace, she temporarily had to live in a crate on the streets of the capitol.[3] Her name is often absent from the famous works of art she posed for and from the books she helped to author. Scholars

FIGURE 15. José María Fernández Urbina, *El fuente de los cántaros* (1927), a statue for which Luz Jiménez modeled, that stands at the entrance to Mexico City's Parque México. Photo by the author.

like Frances Karttunen, Kelly McDonough, Adriana Zavala, Jiménez's grandson Jesús Villanueva Hernández, plus a handful of others have made critical contributions to help correct this historical erasure, but Jiménez's name and story remain relatively obscure in comparison to the artists and intellectuals with whom she worked so closely.

Jiménez's story strikes at the inherent contradictions in Mexico's Cultural Revolution. For a movement that circled obsessively around the question of how to handle the nation's so-called Indian Problem, Indigenous peoples were rarely afforded opportunities to voice their own thoughts on issues of identity, representation, and nation making. Yet Jiménez relentlessly showed that one could assert that voice and live a dignified life even when entangled in settler colonial matrices of violence, poverty, and erasure. Jiménez leaves behind a remarkable legacy, having influenced the work of some of Mexico's greatest artists and working within—but also challenging—the boundaries of her proscribed station in the postrevolutionary cultural order. This chapter traces the making of that legacy while also critically examining the more intimate side of settler colonialism as it played out in the paradoxical personal relationships that Jiménez forged with members of the postrevolutionary cultural and intellectual vanguard.

"SOY DE MILPA ALTA"

Born to Emilio Jiménez and Manuela Gonzalez Jiménez in 1897, Julia Jiménez González was the second of six children in this family of Nahua subsistence farmers. They lived in Milpa Alta (Momochco Malacatepec in Nahuatl), a small pueblo situated in the rolling hills that extend south from Mexico City between the mountains of Cuauhtzin and Teuhtli. Jiménez's early life was profoundly influenced by her Porfirian education, which focused on regimen and indoctrination. She and other Indigenous students were forced not only to attend school but to conform to dress and hygiene codes that reflected Western values. Noncompliance could result in jail time for adult members of the family and humiliating corporal punishments for children.[4]

In recounting her school years, Jiménez recalled that after initially resisting these changes, her community finally came around to what she referred to as "the good path."[5] This phrasing indicates she internalized the supposed superiority of Porfirian values, but she also held her Indigenous heritage close to her heart, covertly teaching herself Nahuatl against her family's wishes. "My whole family spoke Nahuatl, but they didn't teach me because I was in school and my aunt didn't want me to know it, so I studied it in secret," she later told an *El Universal* reporter.[6] This pursuit of a dual education illustrates Jiménez's ability to harness multiple knowledge systems, a skill that would prove essential to her later success as a model and teacher.[7]

When Jiménez was thirteen years old, violence erupted across the country. The ensuing decade of revolutionary warfare would lead to displacement and turmoil that disrupted millions of lives, including those of Jiménez and her family. In a memoir she later narrated to anthropologist Fernando Horcasitas, she recalled, "The heavens did not thunder to warn us that the tempest was coming. We knew nothing about the storms nor about the owlish wickedness of men."[8] Since Milpa Alta was close to Mexico City, it was a strategic location for warring armies and was occupied alternately by the troops of Carranza and Zapata. Starvation, sexual violence, death, and displacement became common facts of life in the once-tranquil community. In 1916 a massacre at the hands of Carranza's troops took her father's life as well as the lives of most other men in the village.

Jiménez and her surviving family, along with most of the remaining Milpateñas, were forced to relocate to the Mexico City enclave of Santa Anita. Jiménez's memoir abruptly ends there, but other remarkable details of her life were just beginning to materialize. Away from their home and traditional support network, Jiménez and her family struggled to make ends meet alongside scores of other refugees of revolutionary violence. Jiménez was the eldest of several daughters, and, in the absence of male family members, responsibility for earning money fell on her shoulders.[9] She initially worked as a street vendor, but soon new opportunities opened up for her.

MODEL CITIZEN

In 1919 Jiménez is rumored to have competed in and won Santa Anita's Viernes de Dolores pageant, the annual contest that awarded women both for their looks and for their "authenticity" as determined by an evolving and arbitrary set of factors.[10] The following year, she happened on an ad calling for models at La Pintura al Aire Libre de Chimalistac, one of a string of new open-air art schools that played a pivotal role in cultivating a new nationalist aesthetic.[11]

Her grandson Jesús Villanueva Hernández notes that Jiménez's mother was adamantly opposed to her work as a model, but Jiménez forged ahead on that path anyway, highlighting the level of individual agency that Jiménez practiced in becoming a model.[12] Responding to the ad for models, Jiménez soon found herself at the epicenter of a new movement.

As Mexico struggled to rebuild and redefine itself in the aftermath of the revolution, a parallel artistic movement took shape. Indigenous art, culture, and people became increasingly common themes as artists worked to paint the ideals of the revolution into being. This trend wasn't unique to Mexico but rather was part of a global movement that featured exoticized Indigenous peoples surrounded by their natural and cultural environs. The impressionist Paul Gauguin and then cubist, expressionist, and surrealist painters in Europe popularized this primitivism, as it was called, and soon a generation of Latin American artists began producing regionally specific renditions of the genre.[13] Peruvian Indigenismo found early expression in the "Incaism" of painter José Sabogal, whose paintings featured robust and romantic depictions of his country's Indigenous peoples. In Mexico City, meanwhile, this global trend and the fervor of postrevolutionary nationalism influenced a new generation of artists.

A photo of Jiménez modeling at an art school in Coyoacán provides a glimpse into the world she had stepped into. In the photo, she is wearing a blouse and belt embroidered in a style unique to Milpa Alta,[14] a tattered skirt, and hair plaited into long braids. She stands firmly between the intersecting gazes of five observers—Fernando Leal, Ramón Avila de la Canal, Francisco Díaz de Léon, an unknown artist, and the photographer. The men have paused their work to pose for the photograph and stare directly at the camera, but it is clear they have only momentarily diverted their attention from Jiménez. Defying the common depiction of Indigenous women as being meek and humble, she appears confident and strong, her gaze firmly fixed on a point in the middle distance.

The Coyoacán art school photograph makes clear that Jiménez was indeed an exquisite model, invoking a dancerly grace even in her stillness. She soon became a favorite model and muse for Fernando Leal.[15] In 1922 she posed for his *Zapatista Encampment*,[16] a pioneering image in the Mexican school. The painting is a romantic depiction of the revolution that stands in direct opposition to Jiménez's own memories of the era.[17] The "owlish wickedness of men" has been reimagined here as a sort of diffident camaraderie, with Jiménez appearing just outside of a semicircle of Indigenous men dressed in ceremonial attire.[18] Though she is not an immediate part of the group, she still dominates the tableau with a gaze that meets viewers and invites them into the scene, presaging the role she would soon come to play as a bridge for outsiders into Nahua language and culture.

Leal depicted Jiménez so frequently and they grew so close that rumors circulated they were having an affair, though their families are quick to refute the notion that their affection was anything but platonic.[19] Some interpret the relationship from the same patronizing perspective often applied to Indigenous Mexicans, as evidenced by a family member of Leal's who claims that Leal "discovered" Jiménez and that "she would be nothing without him."[20] The same relative also asserted that it was Leal that dubbed her "Luz" instead of her given name, "Juliana," suggesting he had gifted her with her artistic identity. While these narratives might hold at least grains of the truth, they strip Jiménez of agency and instead replicate narratives that posit settlers as benevolent benefactors and Indigenous peoples as helpless charity cases.

Writing in 1946 Leal mentions "Luciana" somewhat offhandedly as "an Indian girl" who modeled for him those many years ago.[21] Despite the fact that Leal publicly downplayed the depth of their connection, it was clearly meaningful enough for both of them that they chose to maintain the friendship for decades. In 1964 Jiménez wrote to Charlot of the shock she felt when she was told of Leal's death. According to her daughter Concha, the light went out of her mother's life when he passed away. From that day on to her own death the following year, Jiménez "went through the motions of daily life, but her heart was no longer in it."[22]

Through Leal, Jiménez met other artists. Diego Rivera had been a student of cubism in Paris but returned home after the revolution, eager to merge his European training and socialist political leanings with his newfound appreciation for Aztec history and culture. Jiménez proved to be an ideal conduit into that world. By 1922 she was posing regularly for Rivera in murals like *La creación* (1921–1922) and in many of those he was commissioned to paint at the secretary of public education building (1923–28) and at the national palace (1929–1935).[23] Rivera's daughter, Guadalupe Rivera Marín, noted that "for my father she symbolized what we were before the Conquest."[24]

But Jiménez was more than a model to Rivera. They, too, forged a friendship that lasted for decades. After she had moved back to her home village, he and Frida would drive out to Milpa Alta to pick her up when he needed her to model. She had her own apartment at the famous Blue House, stocked full of books and other comforts.[25] And when her daughter Concha was young, she would accompany her mother on those trips. Concha told her son that Frida's pet monkey would express its affection by wrapping its tail around her leg, though the monkey's fondness for her was not reciprocated.[26] Even after their artistic collaboration had ended, the bond between the two remained, and Rivera occasionally helped Jiménez out financially when major life events and illnesses exceeded her meager budget. Although there is no record of Jiménez sharing cultural knowledge with Rivera, her relationship with another artist lends insight into the sort of collaboration they might have shared.

Jean Charlot was another mainstay in the canon of postrevolutionary artists. An expat Frenchman, Charlot had grown up hearing stories of his great-grandmother, a Nahua woman who had married a Parisian in the nineteenth century. His childhood home was full of handcrafted dolls, trinkets, and other small relics of Mexican life, and he grew up romanticizing this distant land.[27] In his early twenties, Charlot moved to Mexico to establish himself as an artist and connect more fully with his Aztec heritage. Trained in the French tradition and with a minimalist aesthetic, everyday expressions of Indigenous identity appealed more to his tastes than festivals and ceremonial dress. To Charlot, Jiménez was a "woman of deep compelling mystery" and an archetype of the Native Mexican woman.[28] He saw her as embodying the everyday Aztec and as a conduit of traditional knowledge and culture. Years later he recalled,

> There is a whole image there that she projected. Now many of the other girls *could* put their village clothes on and pose with a pot on their shoulders, but they didn't do it, so to speak, to the manor born. And Luz had one thing that was important: she could do it both naturally, as the Indian girl that she was, and know enough so that she could imagine from the outside, so to speak, what the painters or the writers saw in her, and she helped both see things because of that sort of double outlook she could have on herself and her tradition.[29]

From all accounts, Jiménez was intimately familiar with her own culture and adept at explaining it in a way that made sense to outsiders. She told Charlot stories about her life and taught him Nahuatl, which they would practice during her modeling sessions. Pablo O'Higgins recalled walking in on one modeling session in which Jiménez was posing on a *petate* (woven mat) in the nude and speaking to Charlot in Nahuatl while he painted her.[30] In an artistic era that valued authenticity, Jiménez's access to cultural knowledge and her willingness to teach it were enormously valuable to the artists for whom she modeled. Charlot later acknowledged that in addition to providing access to Nahua language and culture, Luz advised him on how to represent that world in paintings. In an interview later in his life, he said, "Of course one of the great influences on me at the time is Luciana, who was my Indian model. I would ask her what she thought about the things I did, and she would correct them very carefully."[31] She was not a passive muse but rather a cocreator who helped shape how she and her culture were depicted.

What began as an artistic collaboration morphed into a lifelong friendship that is well documented through letters, photos, and remembrances. That friendship and Jiménez's talent for teaching Nahua language and culture led to opportunities with others in Charlot's milieu. In the early 1920s, Charlot was dating Anita Brenner, a Mexican-born Jewish woman who grew up in both Mexico and the United States. A writer and intellectual, Brenner documented Mexican history, culture, and art for English-speaking audiences. She, too, valued Jiménez's knowledge and considered her a valuable "informant." As early as 1925 Brenner was recording Jiménez's stories, a fact that she noted alongside meandering reflections and introspective ruminations in her personal diaries.[32] The two grew close enough that when Jiménez's daughter Concha was born, she named Anita Brenner—still a practicing Jew—as her baby's baptismal godmother in the Catholic Church. Yet even as they forged these intimate and intellectual bonds, Brenner continued to employ Jiménez as a domestic servant, suggesting that an unequal power dynamic persisted in their relationship. And as Jiménez later noted in letters to Charlot, communication and pay from Brenner were unreliable. The friendships Jiménez shared with the artists were clearly meaningful to her, but they were ultimately shaped by existing hierarchies of race, class, and gender. Read within the broader landscape of postrevolutionary identity politics, these complex relationships can be seen as everyday expressions of settler colonialism.

BODY OF ART

By the early 1920s, members of Jiménez's family were able to move back to Milpa Alta. She began inviting artists and intellectuals like Charlot, Rivera, Leal, Brenner, and others there, introducing them to her family as well as demonstrating Nahua practices like backstrap weaving and how to use plants to prepare herbal remedies.[33] Like Xochimilco and Santa Anita, the once war-ravaged pueblo of Milpa Alta came to be seen by nationalist artists and thinkers of the time as a place where México Viejo lived on, even gaining a reputation as being home to the purest form of Nahuatl language. Charlot later recalled that the access Jiménez provided to Milpa Alta was an "important contribution to the new nationalist movement."[34] Indeed, Charlot, Pablo O'Higgins, and dozens of anthropologists and linguists—including the famed Benjamin Lee Whorf—built their careers on work in the community.

In 1925 Charlot, Brenner, and travel guide author Frances Toor accompanied Jiménez and her family on a pilgrimage from Milpa Alta to Chalma. This semiannual pilgrimage is a crucial part of the Milpateña religious cycle, and it had already caught the interest of the postrevolutionary elite. One of Manuel Gamio's early films, *Fiestas de Chalma* (1922), chronicled this journey and was later screened in Mexico City's Olympic Theater with dignitaries like José Vasconcelos in attendance.[35] Still, Jiménez's willingness to let artists accompany her and her family on this sacred journey showed the extent to which she was willing to bring outsiders into her world. In Chalma the group witnessed community blessings and bathing in a sacred spring, inspiring Charlot's first painting of Jiménez in the nude.[36]

In *Nude of Chalma*, Charlot depicts Jiménez's body using deep sienna tones and long brush strokes more common in landscape painting than in classic portraiture. She holds a cloth around her waist but her torso is naked, with swollen belly and breasts filling the center frame. Jiménez's grandson Jesús Villanueva Hernández maintains that there was nothing vulgar about *Nude of Chalma*, or other nude portraits she posed for. "Charlot saw Luz as something of a mother earth," Villanueva Hernández said in an interview; "The first nude he did of her was the nude of Chalma, and when people go to Chalma they bathe in the nude. So when he first saw Luz in the nude, it was part of this profound embodiment of Aztec culture."[37]

Indeed, the image is deific and reverential, but it also presents Jiménez as being one with the landscape that surrounds her. This conflation fixes Indigenous women in a sort of Edenic utopia and, as the film *La campesina* illustrates so crassly, this logic can be used to justify exploitations of both land and body.[38] While it's unlikely that Charlot's intentions were so nefarious, his work still contributed to broader settler colonial ways of viewing Indigenous women.

American photographer Edward Weston met Jiménez through Charlot and Rivera and also published images of her in the nude. In a pair of photographs, Jiménez stands with her back to the camera and face just inches from a wall. The use of lighting and the straight-on framing of her entire body are more akin to ethnographic photography than other portraiture produced by Weston, who typically depicted his female nudes in contorted positions and often only showed a portion of their bodies. And although Jiménez is naked, material culture—braided hair, a woven mat, and a rebozo crumpled around her feet—is used to underscore the fact of her Indigeneity. Weston's ethnographic gaze is also an objectifying one, with the inclusion of the crumpled rebozo adding a sexually suggestive subtext to Jiménez's state of undress. In his Mexico City diaries, Weston openly admitted to having exploited his Indigenous servants sexually and financially.[39] While Jiménez left no indication that she suffered such overt abuse, understanding Weston's misogynistic behavior toward Indigenous women lends a crucial interpretive lens to her naked vulnerability in this pair of photographs. Images like these underscore the tendency to couple representations of Indigenous womanhood with allusions to sexual violability, and they serve as a reminder that Jiménez might not have always had the opportunity to exercise agency over how she was depicted.

Perhaps the most famous depiction of Jiménez in the nude can be found in José Clemente Orozco's *Cortés and Malinche* (1926; fig. 16). In that painting, which still looms over a stairwell in Mexico City's Colegio del San Idelfonso, Jiménez's bronze skin contrasts sharply with the flat alabaster of Cortes's. Her downward, passive gaze plays into tropes of the docile Indian woman that had been well established by beauty pageants and popular culture alike. Meanwhile, Cortes is domineering and statuesque, extending a protective—or perhaps restrictive—arm across Jiménez's body and casting a strong gaze to the distance. At his feet lies the naked, crumpled body of an Indigenous man. As art historian Mary Coffey notes, the scene recasts the conquest as a bloodless and a loveless one, accomplished not through violence but through an indifferent union of white European men and Indigenous Mexican men.[40] Jiménez's embodiment of the controversial Malinche places this painting, and her career, within larger discourses of Mestizaje. She wasn't just the ideal Indigenous woman—she was an idealized representative of *la raza* and, in the matrix of postrevolutionary identity politics, fit for passively producing a more perfect mestizo future.

While Orozco's *Cortes and Malinche* would go on to become one of the most celebrated murals of the era, a Fernando Leal tableau featuring a partially nude Luz Jiménez produced at the same time was received quite differently. In 1925 Leal was commissioned to paint a mural in the office of the secretary of health and public assistance.[41] In *La Escala de la Vida* he rendered a couple as

FIGURE 16. José Clemente Orozco's *Cortés and Malinche* in the Colegio del San Idelfonso featuring a depiction of Luz Jiménez. Photo by the author.

they moved through phases of life together from childhood into early adulthood. It was the last panel that caused a scandal. In the controversial image, the couple appears in an amorous embrace, and Luz is partially disrobed. Her face is hidden, but her bare breast is featured prominently, and her woven belt is partially unraveled. The mural was completed in 1927, then deemed immoral and destroyed by the Comisión de Orden y Decoro in 1928.[42]

While the hand-wringing about public representations of female nudity largely classed nude images of Indigenous women as being ethnographic in nature, this depiction of lovemaking—and *Indigenous* lovemaking at that—upset the postrevolutionary sense of proper decorum. And while the painting's rural setting and elements of tradition ought to have safely placed its subjects in a distant camposcape, the focus on Indigenous love clearly threatened the desired progression toward Mestizaje. The scandal surrounding the mural underscores the genocidal underpinnings of postrevolutionary indigenist popular culture: Indigenous female bodies could be depicted as ethnographic specimens, as objects of sexual desire, or as agents of Mestizaje, but *not* in a state of enraptured love with Indigenous men.

Despite extensive evidence to the contrary, Jiménez publicly denied having ever modeled in the nude. In a 1961 interview about her modeling career, she told a reporter, "They always painted me while dressed."[43] Jiménez's denial of her nude modeling was probably an attempt to safeguard her reputation and protect her family. In a real-life parallel to the fictional *María Candelaria* film, Jiménez's nude modeling would have been highly taboo and could have imperiled herself and her family. Because she didn't talk about her nude modeling, it's difficult to understand her feelings about it with any nuance, but her grandson Jesús thinks her decision to model in the nude was just another part of her desire to be a teacher. He argues that it wasn't her body that was on display but rather the body of all Indigenous women.[44] By this interpretation, her nude modeling was an embodied way of declaring "we're still here, we still matter" and a counternarrative to the pervasive vanishing Indian trope. It also shows that contrary to postrevolutionary identity norms, Jiménez did not see her own Indigenous womanhood as being inextricably coupled with her *traje* or other elements of material culture. And practically speaking, the work also provided a much-needed source of income even if it was a meager one.[45]

While reading the nudes as a testament to Indigenous survivance is a provocative and empowering interpretation, the fact remains that they were received by an audience primed to objectify Indigenous women as disappearing relics of the past. Their similarity in form and style to ethnographic primitivism and their allegiance to the mores of settler colonialism places the images within a larger context of colonizing male gazes. Further indication of this imagined erasure can be found in the fact that as depictions of nude Indigenous women became more frequent in postrevolutionary portraiture, light-skinned mestiza women were increasingly depicted in *traje*. In these popular representations, Indigenous women were literally stripped of their material culture while mestiza bodies were deemed the ideal bearers of that culture. Thus, even as Jiménez had her own motivations for modeling, the nudes she posed for existed within a cultural landscape that fetishized Indigenous women as the disappearing, exotic other.

MADRE LUZ

A white marble statue of Jiménez—*El fuente de los cántaros* (1927)—silently greets visitors to Parque México in Mexico City's posh Condesa neighborhood (see fig. 15). When the fountain is running, water pours from two pots that she holds alongside her bare breasts, evocative of the milk that she once produced as a nursing mother. In its allusion to female fecundity, José María Fernández Urbina's rendition of Jiménez hints at another common theme in depictions of her: Luz as mother.

At the time of that first nude painting in Chalma, Jiménez was pregnant with her only daughter, Concha, whom she raised as a single parent while still providing for her own mother and siblings. There has been speculation that Fernando Leal was Concha's father, but their offspring strongly refute this idea. Instead, Jiménez's family names a man from Ixtacalco, Manuel Hernández Chaparro, as the father. Jiménez left scant record of her relationship with Chaparro, so we have little information about the nature of their union, but letters to Charlot make clear that he had very little to do with Concha's upbringing.[46]

Jiménez never let herself be painted in the nude while visibly pregnant, but her early motherhood was thoroughly documented in photos and paintings. She granted artists access to some of her most intimate experience as a Nahua woman. An undated photograph that, according to Villanueva Hernández, is sometimes wrongly identified as being of Concha's birth shows Jiménez with infant Concha in a dimly lit enclosure. The sweaty glow of Jiménez's skin and the positioning of her body coupled with the presence of an elderly woman make it easy to see why people have interpreted this as a birthing photo. Villanueva Hernández explains that in reality the tightly framed image depicts a blessing ceremony in a *temazcal* (a Nahua sweat lodge) shortly after Concha's birth. Although the photo doesn't document an actual birth, this religious rite was still a profoundly intimate and private moment. And even though there is no evidence that the photo was published or widely shared, the mere presence of a camera at such an event evidences the extent to which Jiménez allowed this outside gaze into her life.

A 1928 issue of Frances Toor's bilingual *Folkways* magazine features Jiménez nursing an infant Concha in photographs taken by Tina Modotti. In one photo, she appears with Concha sitting on her lap, but in the second photo, which was later reprinted more widely, a nursing Concha and Jiménez's naked breast dominate the frame. The images ran alongside an article that tells of Nahua birthing practices, postpartum remedies, and early infant care.[47] Diego Rivera captured a similarly intimate moment in *Flower Seller* (1926), an image in which Jiménez's bare breast and nursing child are only partially screened by a basket of flowers in the foreground of the image. But even with the more discreet portrayal, her body is still treated as something exotic and other—no artist of the time would even think to depict an upper-class mestiza woman in this way.

These ethnographic representations of Jiménez fit into popular narratives propagated by Gamio and others about the urgent need to document "vanishing" ways of Indigenous life. They also fit into contemporary conversations about childhood wellness, much like those seen in the *niño más sano* competitions seeking robust and healthy children. Mothers and their children, after all, were critical to the reproduction of a new postrevolutionary nation. And Jiménez's motherhood also fit into the desired postrevolutionary racial progression because Concha was consistently marked as mestiza in paintings, photographs, and remembrances. Villanueva Hernández also recalled that his mother, Concha, tried to distance herself from her Indigenous identity,[48] a not uncommon pattern in a society where Indigenous peoples were typically relegated to the lowest rung of the social hierarchy. Viewed within the larger scope of the settler colonial project, Concha's embrace of her mestiza identity reinforced Jiménez's position as the ideal icon of female Indigeneity: she embodied the traditional but did not replicate it. In other words, this perfect paragon of Indigeneity had fulfilled her postrevolutionary duty by contributing to the project of Mestizaje.

"WOMEN WHO WORK"

Throughout the 1920s and 1930s, Jiménez and her daughter became frequent fixtures in the artists' milieu, though the social and economic disparities were undeniable. A photo taken sometime in the late 1920s showing Jiménez and

Concha standing on a rooftop with a group of these artists illustrates some of those disparities (fig. 17). While both Jiménez and Concha wear house clothes frayed from use and age, the remainder of their party sport much finer apparel, including pinstriped suits and smart black dresses. But despite the chasms that existed between their lived experiences, Jiménez formed deep friendships with many of the artists. She and Charlot were particularly close, with their Catholicism and love for Nahua culture, language, and spirituality forming the foundation of a profound but, according to their offspring, strictly platonic friendship.[49]

After Charlot left Mexico, the two maintained a written correspondence for decades. Charlot kept many of these letters, particularly those sent between the 1940s and the end of Jiménez's life. Though sporadic, the letters conveyed a deep friendship through well wishes, updates on life events, and intimate news about themselves and their family members. Their correspondence also included frequent requests from Jiménez for small loans to pay for medicine, food, and other basic expenses. She made it clear that she was not proud of having to seek support from Charlot and that she was anxious he would grow sick of her requests. In a March 1942 letter to Charlot, she asked for twenty

FIGURE 17. Luz Jiménez and her daughter Concha with a group of well-to-do compatriots. Photo courtesy of The Jean Charlot Collection, University of Hawaiʻi at Mānoa Library.

pesos to help her out after an extended illness and wedding expenses for her daughter Concha. She signed the letter, "su desgraciada comadre" (your miserable comadre).[50] Other letters include litanies of illness, misfortune, and expenses that far exceeded her family's meager budget. Villanueva Hernández notes that indeed his grandmother's life was "very difficult. She had so many hardships: first because of the revolution, then as an Indigenous person, as a woman, as a woman who had a baby outside of marriage, as a single mother, as a woman who posed in the nude."[51]

"We can think it was all adversity, no?" Villanueva Hernández asks. But he quickly urges a more nuanced view of her life. He argues that her modeling work and the relationships she forged with artists allowed her to thrive in an urban environment that she was forced into as a refugee of revolutionary warfare, and that these relationships led to opportunities that few Indigenous peoples were afforded at that time. Jiménez used her position to improve her family's well-being and to access financial support when it was most sorely needed. In addition to the small sums of money she was paid to model, gifts and loans from Charlot and other artists elevated her family slightly above the poverty that plagued many in her community. Diego Rivera, for example, contributed one hundred pesos to her daughter Concha's wedding, a gift that helped them to hold a church ceremony rather than just a civil one.[52] When Jiménez's mother died, the students and professors of a school where she modeled pooled their money together to help with the funeral expenses.[53] And Charlot often sent the small sums of money she requested, though their correspondence suggests that his financial support stemmed from their friendship rather than from a sense that he was financially beholden to her for the years she spent helping him develop the aesthetic and intellectual foundation that informed his work.

While Jiménez balanced motherhood with a rotating cycle of itinerant labor, the work that she most desired eluded her in any formal sense. What she really wanted was to teach, but state bureaucracy prevented her from doing so. In May of 1936 Jiménez wrote to the head of the Secretary of Public Education's (Secretaría de Educación Pública [SEP]) Department of Rural Teachers (Departamento de Maestros Rurales) asking that she be considered for a rural teaching position through the Maestro Rural program.[54] In the letter, she explained that she lacked the records indicating she had completed her fifth year of education in 1912 but hoped that documentation of her sixth year would prove she had completed all the necessary schooling. In August of the same year, she wrote again, reiterating her desire for a Maestro Rural position and her willingness to be stationed wherever she was most needed.[55] She included a letter from Joaquin Jara Díaz, head of the department of primary and "normal" education, attesting to the fact that she completed fifth grade.[56] A photo of Jiménez that also appeared on a *tarjeta sanitaria* identification card was stapled to the certification so that there would be no confusion about her identity in the semiofficial document. Her attempts were futile. There is no evidence of an official response from the SEP, and she never secured the desired teaching role. Jiménez found many other ways to teach, but the fact that she was barred from formal teaching in the Maestro Rural program illustrates the institutional barriers that made it nearly impossible for her to formally pursue a role for which she was clearly quite gifted.

Even though she was treated as an "informant" rather than credited—or compensated—as the knowledge producer that she was, Jiménez's body of work illustrates the depths of her talents as a teacher and an intellectual.[57] Although she did not have the opportunity to teach in a formal classroom setting, her success as a model largely rested on the fact that she played the role of a teacher. She also used her modeling connections to gain work as a teacher of Nahuatl language and as a cultural informant with anthropologists, linguists, and writers. She advised linguist Benjamin Lee Whorf, narrated folktales to anthropologist Robert Barlow, and recounted her life story in a series of *testimonios* to Fernando Horcasitas. She worked closely with Anita Brenner and Frances Toor as an advisor and collaborator in their popular works about Mexican history and culture. In 1942 Jiménez and Brenner published a children's book together, *The Boy Who Could Do Anything and Other Mexican Folk Tales*. The collection of Nahua stories was illustrated by Charlot, and all the content was derived from Luz's narrations. Even so, Jiménez was not given authorial credit, and there is no indication she received any of the royalties.[58] Recognizing both her contributions and the injustice of the situation, Jiménez wrote to Charlot, "If my comadre were good she would send me something of my part for the books, but I have little hope of this."[59]

Though Brenner was notorious for neglecting her financial commitments to many of her collaborators, she failed her *comadre* in other ways during what was a particularly difficult year for Jiménez. In August of 1942 Jiménez wrote to Charlot, who was then pursuing a teaching career in the United States, "I am absolutely wretched, more so than in other years, so sad and sick." She relayed a litany of illnesses she'd suffered: pneumonia, rheumatism, and states of paralysis.[60] She complained that her pay from Brenner was inconsistent, that she was promised work that didn't come through, and that Brenner would disappear for months on end, leaving Jiménez without access to the work she loved and the income she needed.[61] Another 1942 letter from Jiménez to Charlot says that her *comadre* had offered to give her a regular salary of twenty-five pesos per month but that she hadn't seen any of that work or income. She reports that she'd had no response to a letter written to Brenner twenty days before and then implores Charlot to intervene.[62] The same year that Jiménez became a published author she requested a letter of recommendation from a former employer, indicating that she was having to look for more work as a domestic servant.[63] The letter attests that Jiménez was good at chores and washing, was honorable and loyal, and would make a good servant. It's worn and water stained, as though Jiménez had carried that letter with her for years and shared it with many prospective employers. While her collaborators built careers out of their work together, Jiménez had to keep returning to sources of income that postrevolutionary society deemed befitting of Indigenous women.

Despite repeatedly encountering barriers, Jiménez persisted. By the end of the 1940s, she had secured more work that drew on her cultural knowledge. On April 20, 1948, she wrote to Charlot about working in the National Museum with Professor Barlow and Stanley Newman, who was working on a Nahuatl grammar at the time. Jiménez served as his "informant" and was paid ten pesos to work from four to seven at night one day a week. Jiménez loved this work. "It's really sad," she wrote to Charlot, "because I only work one time per week."[64] She continued in this capacity for the remainder of her life, and she became a beloved fixture at educational institutions across Mexico City. But she was never compensated or employed at a rate that would allow her to fully devote herself to education, which meant that she also had to continue working as a street vendor, domestic servant, and model. Even so, her intellectual labor was a critical part of her identity, and she clearly relished being able to work in this capacity.[65]

The power imbalances were undeniable, but was Jiménez's relationship with artists and intellectuals a fundamentally exploitative one? Villanueva Hernández, who still maintains friendly contact with the descendants of Charlot and other artists, denies that there was anything exploitative about Charlot's relationship to Jiménez.[66] He argues that Charlot and his contemporaries were not well off themselves, and that they paid the models what they could. He points to all the residual benefits that Jiménez received for her modeling work and suggests that it helped her thrive in the urban environment into which she was forced. "Modeling let her integrate not just into the city but into the highest class," Villanueva Hernández observed.[67] Alongside this charitable interpretation, it is instructive to note that this "integration" fits within larger efforts to Mexicanize Indigenous peoples and that firm social boundaries meant there were limits to Jiménez's capacity to thrive at the same level as her collaborators.

Villanueva Hernández's favorite photograph of his grandmother captures her selling crafts in the streets of Cuernavaca. He says this is his favorite because it shows who she really was: a worker. In the photo she has several woven belts on one shoulder and an array of woven bags hanging from her wrist. Jiménez looks to be in her mid- to late fifties in the photo and wears a worn-looking apron with a heavy satchel tied around her back, perhaps more crafts to sell or her personal belongings. Villanueva Hernández reported that she frequently made such trips in order to sell crafts to tourists.[68] Her daughter Concha also remembered her selling her wares on the streets of Mexico City, calling out in English, "Lady, lady, Mexican curiosities."[69]

Despite the scores of images that depict Doña Luz as a mother, as a traditional Indigenous woman, or in the nude, her life as a teacher and working woman is largely absent from the pictorial record. Indeed, in spite of the fact that the postrevolutionary avant-garde eagerly championed proletarian causes, representations of female factory workers, domestic servants, and street vendors are surprisingly absent from this canon. Instead, Indigenous women stood for tradition and domesticity while men with raised fists in denim coveralls represented the working class. In reality, factory work in Mexico City in the aftermath of the revolution was predominantly the charge of women.[70] But working Indigenous women did not have the same "exotic" appeal as Indigenous women in *traje* or in the nude. Even in their vast representations of Jiménez as an iconic Indigenous woman, artists were erasing a major part of her experience. In doing so they reinforced narrow interpretations of female Indigeneity and stripped her of key components of her identity.

Even though artists did not depict Jiménez as a working woman, she cultivated this image of herself when given the opportunity. The letters she sent to Charlot occasionally included keepsake images for him. In these, she presented herself predominantly as an educator, a laborer, and a mother. One pair of photos sent to Charlot shows her in a work setting she loved, in the courtyard of a school with the painter Manuel Rodríguez Lozano (fig. 18). She doesn't

FIGURE 18. Luz Jiménez with the painter Manuel Rodríguez Lozano in the courtyard of a school where they worked together. Courtesy of The Jean Charlot Collection, University of Hawai'i at Mānoa Library.

note this on the back of the photos, but she was visiting the school in order to model and teach Nahuatl language learners.[71] Instead, she wrote a warm New Year's greeting to Charlot on the back of the photos and included a lengthy poem about the joys of friendship. In the images, she is kneeling on the ground on a blanket, hands folded in her lap, and gaze directed downward. Lozano stands behind her smiling at the camera in one photo, and in the other he appears in profile, gazing almost directly down at Jiménez. Their positioning is a not subtle reminder of the uneven power dynamics at play in this image.

Still, Jiménez took pride in the fact that she was working at the school, and this photograph is an important memento of that work.

Media representations of Jiménez reinforced the image of her as a traditional culture bearer. In January 1962 she wrote to Charlot letting him know that she had been interviewed about the work she had done with him, Leal, Orozco, and Rivera.[72] "I had to go in traditional clothing, *chincuete* and embroidered blouse," she said. "For this reason I didn't write, I wanted to see the result." She explains that what precipitated the interview was a chance encounter with the director of Chapultepec galleries, Guadalupe Solórzano, who recognized her from her early days as a model. Jiménez told Charlot about the encounter, which occurred when she went to work with the students of one of the painting schools. "All of a sudden the director was there, and she gave me a kiss and a hug." Jiménez relayed her surprise to Charlot and said that the director had to remind her she had once painted her portrait. She reported that Solórzano insisted, "Now I want to send you to *Excelsior*." Though Jiménez says she didn't want to do it, Solórzano pushed her by saying, "I don't want history to pass you by." Jiménez reports to Charlot that she eventually relented, saying, "Well if you want it, I will accept it."

As a result of this encounter, Jiménez was featured in a television show called *Mujeres que trabajan* and the following month in the pages of *Excelsior*.[73]

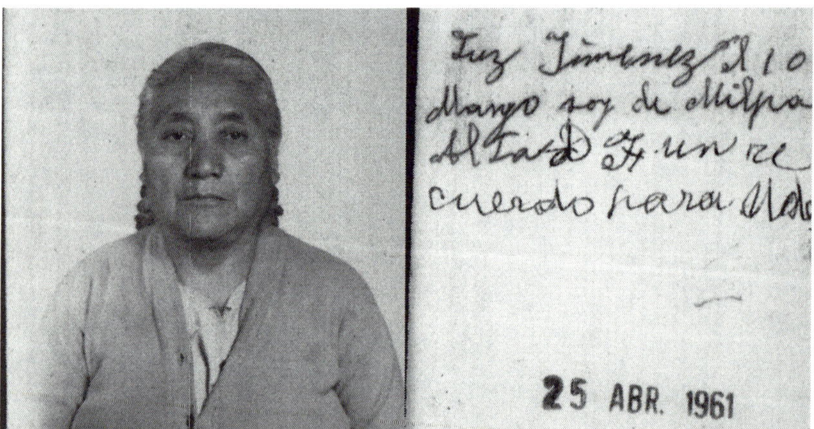

FIGURE 19. (a) Photograph of Luz Jiménez sent to Jean Charlot in 1962. (b) On the back she wrote, "Luz Jiménez May 10 I am from Milpa Alta. A memento for you." Courtesy of The Jean Charlot Collection, University of Hawaiʻi at Mānoa Library.

But her reluctance to receive media attention and the fact that she didn't want to write until after seeing the "result" of how she was represented in *traje* suggests a certain level of fatigue with being in the spotlight and having to performing a specific Indigenous type. This was visible, too, in the letter she wrote to Charlot about the interviews. Instead of enclosing the newspaper clipping or a photo of herself in *traje*, Luz sent what looked like a simple identification photo (fig. 19). In it she is wearing an old cardigan and simple top clasped together at the neck with a safety pin, and she looks tiredly into the camera. On the back she wrote, "Luz Jiménez May 10 I am from Milpa Alta. A memento for you." Nothing is put on or posed in this image. Even so, her grandson says this photo also represented success to her because it was taken when she went to be interviewed for *Mujeres que trabajan*. Villanueva Hernández says she sent it to Charlot to show "I'm not just a flowerpot sitting in the hall."[74] She wanted him to know that she was active, even thriving. In her view of herself she was neither a static icon nor a rarified relic of a bygone era but rather a modern woman navigating between disparate social circles.

THE DEATH OF DOÑA LUZ JIMÉNEZ

Jiménez's sudden death highlights the paradoxes of privilege and disprivilege that characterized much of her life. On the morning of January 25, 1965, she went into her daughter Concha's room and blessed her, a rare act that struck Concha as odd. She then set out to teach Nahuatl classes at the Universidad de las Americas.[75] She was eager for this work and was hoping to use the income to buy school clothes for her nieces and nephews. But when Jiménez arrived at the school, she was told there was no work that day. With the extra time, she paid a visit to Anita Brenner, and shortly after she left Brenner's Lomas de Chapultepec home, she was struck by a car. Jiménez suffered a fractured skull, cerebral bleeding, and a fractured leg. She'd had close calls before due to the fact that her failing vision made it hard to see oncoming traffic.[76] But on this particular day, her family was convinced she knew death was near. "I believe she sensed the approach of her death and so did we," Concha later wrote to Charlot. For weeks she had "suffered from cold and seemed as fragile as a bubble blowing in the wind."[77]

Jiménez was checked into the nearby Red Cross Hospital at 2:35 in the afternoon and would remain there alone for more than twenty-four hours while her friends and family searched for her. When her daughter and grandsons eventually found their beloved matriarch, they were allowed to be with her only long enough to identify her, then they were quickly ushered out of the room on the insistence that the injured woman must not be disturbed or talked to. Only Susannah Glusker, Anita Brenner's daughter, was allowed to stay in the room, and she was the only one present at the time of her death. Luz Jiménez passed away at 9:00 a.m. on the morning of January 27, which happened to be her sixty-eighth birthday.

After her death, Brenner covered all the immediate costs and conscripted the secretary of public education to pay for the transportation of her body back home and contribute to the costs of the funeral. Diego Rivera's children attended the funeral, as did staff and students of Universidad de las Americas and other notable artists and scholars. *Excélsior* also memorialized Jiménez, noting that the "model of Rivera, Orozco, and Siqueiros" had been killed but that "her image lives on in the murals of the national palace and the secretary of public education."[78] Neither of these tributes mentioned Jiménez's work as a linguist, intellectual, domestic worker, or street vendor. Instead, they secured her legacy as a pretty Indian woman who "made it" by modeling for the greats.

An article in *Mexico This Month*, most likely authored by Anita Brenner, extoled the "primeval serenity" of Jiménez's face and talked about the many great artists who painted her. It depicted Jiménez as being economically secure, wrongly claiming that she "bought a lot, built a home, furnished it cleanly with fair comfort." It also depicted her as being strong and independent, stating that she had refused to marry the father of her child because she didn't want to be pinned down.[79] The article is illustrated with a 1926 Jean Charlot painting of Jiménez as a young mother rather than a more contemporary photograph of the woman herself. This final tribute to Jiménez presents a relatively nuanced—if not entirely accurate—view of her life but underscores the reality that her story was often mediated through the words and work of her collaborators.

CONCLUSION

Jiménez's death highlighted the paradoxical hypervisibility, erasure, proximity to wealth, and poverty that followed her throughout her life. As well-known as her face, body, and words were, she herself did not share the fame or the relative material comfort enjoyed by the artists and intellectuals who relied so heavily on her image and cultural knowledge. Jiménez's life story stands as evidence that Indigenous women were agents in the postrevolutionary identity-making process but that agency was limited by deeply entrenched social hierarchies. She lent her knowledge, artistry, skills as a teacher, and even her own body to refine representations of Nahua culture and womanhood. Even so, major parts of her life and her own desired representation of herself were obscured.

Because the works of art she modeled for only capture certain aspects of her life, and because her name was largely left out of the works of scholarship to which she contributed, the official narrative of postrevolutionary Mexico contains only a thin trace of who she was. Even in her hypervisibility and in her relative agency in influencing the work of her artistic collaborators, she was rarely depicted as the dynamic and complex women that she was, a fact that underscores the inevitable erasures that settler colonial projects leave in their wake. Meanwhile, upper-class mestiza women like Frida Kahlo and Dolores del Río gained celebrity for their personal and artistic interpretations of Indigenous culture and identity. As in other instances of the *india bonita* trope, Mestizaje was ultimately privileged over the complex realities of Indigenous womanhood. Women like Luz Jiménez were constructed as being of the past and poorly suited for inclusion in the modern world despite abundant evidence that they were as much a part of that world as anyone else. Even so, Jiménez used that position to fulfill her lifelong goal of being an educator and, to some degree, influenced how Indigenous women were represented in postrevolutionary art and scholarship. Acknowledging the paradoxes that framed Jiménez's life allows us to see her beyond the two-dimensionality to which she is too often confined and to begin to untangle the complexities of the most intimate expressions of settler colonialism.

CONCLUSION

A 2018 EXHIBITION AT THE MUSEO Nacional de Antropología illustrated just how pervasive the narratives crafted in the era of postrevolutionary reconstruction still are. The exhibit *La flor en la cultura mexicana* featured several rooms filled with stone artifacts from the pre-Hispanic era and others brimming with postconquest Catholic reliquary.[1] It concluded with displays of contemporary floral-themed textiles, folk art, and works by famous painters of the twentieth century. Explanatory text in the Modern Mexico rooms acknowledged José Vasconcelos, Dr. Atl, and other members of the mestizo cultural elite for their roles in the national revaluing of Mexican folk art but failed to mention any of the Indigenous artists who actually produced the work.

The exhibit's erasures were most blatantly enshrined in its final section, a tribute to the clothing and art of Indigenous women in which not a single Indigenous woman could be found. Instead, grey mannequins were dressed in elaborate floral *traje* from various regions across Mexico. These faceless figures where Indigenous bodies belonged invoked the disappearance of Indigenous peoples that orchestrators of Mestizaje imagined. The clothing displays were interspersed with paintings of white-coded mestiza women wearing Indigenous *traje* as if to underscore the narrative of Indigenous disappearance. In one painting by Xavier Machada (1938), a blonde woman wearing an embroidered top identified as "*traje* de Mestiza" stared placidly at the viewer, the pyramids of Teotihuacán rising majestically behind her. Another painting, *Alma Tehuana* (Demetrio, ca.1950–1975) featured a woman with European features and pale skin adorned in a Tehuana headdress. Throughout the exhibit, the absence of Indigenous women was answered by a persistent reproduction of mestiza bodies in their stead.

As this exhibit so clearly illustrated, the formulas for Indigenous erasure and appropriation manufactured in postrevolutionary popular culture are still

FIGURE 20. Display in the Museo Nacional de Antropología exhibit *La flor en la cultura mexicana* (2018) featured faceless mannequins in *traje* and artwork featuring mestiza women in Indigenous dress. Photo by the author.

being actively reproduced in present-day Mexico. Indigenous peoples are still largely associated with the campo, sometimes rendered as buffoonish caricatures and at other times invoked to lend folkloric "color" to visual presentations of Mexico's unique cultural riches. Light-skinned *indias bonitas* populate *telenovelas*, postcards, tourism commercials, and public celebrations of Mexico's past. Meanwhile, Aztecs are largely heralded as the predecessors to modern Mexico. Reminders of this heritage are visible across Mexico City from metro station names and beverage branding to the Aztec dancers who flank the Zócalo and politicians who rhetorically invoke this regal legacy.

Despite the ongoing erasures and cloying stereotypes, Indigenous women continue to interrupt this settler colonial project. Though Indigenous peoples are cast as inherently of the campo, they're locked into a seemingly endless struggle for basic land and water rights that would make life in the campo tenable. Mexico City's chronic water shortages have led to such encroachments on Indigenous sovereignty. But there, too, is resistance. The Cutzamala reservoir system—the largest single source of the city's drinking water—is situated in the homeland of the Mazahua Indians who have seen their land and water usurped by Mexico City's unquenchable thirst. Mazahua have ample water in their own backyard, but they only have direct access to that water about once a week. And their territorial homeland is now scored by intersecting barbed wire barriers and military boundaries established to protect the reservoir.[2] On December 11, 2006, members of the Mazahua Women's Army in Defense of Water occupied the Los Berros plant and shut off six of the main valves that carried water to Mexico City, suspending water service to approximately six million Mexico City residents.[3] Dressed in brightly colored *traje* and armed with tools and wooden rifles, the women's statement was as symbolic as it was strategic. Examples like this unfold daily across the country, and they serve as a testament to Indigenous women's ongoing resistance.

Even so, the patterns of erasure, appropriation, strategic engagement, and disengagement testify to the fact that the identity projects initiated in the 1920s continue to mold understandings of race, class, and gender today. The formulas for establishing Mestizaje as the race of the future while also managing the so-called Indian Problem were effective enough that they continue to inform policy and pop culture alike. This longevity is at least partially due to the interplay between social constructs bolstered by scientific knowledge and the mass production of popular culture that allowed these ideals to reach wide audiences. And its staying power can also be understood by viewing Indigenismo,

Mestizaje, and postrevolutionary nation building as forms of settler colonialism, which, by its nature, is a self-reproducing construct.

Settler belonging is a fragile thing, as was Mexican national identity in the years following the armed conflicts of the revolution. Much in the same way that imperial nations constantly work to define and expand their boundaries, so, too, do settlers feel compelled to constantly delineate the boundaries that separate them from the Native population while also claiming ownership and attempting to prove their superiority over those they've settled. Because of the inherently blurry lines between mestizo and Indigenous, those boundaries were continuously defined and reproduced in order to elevate the former over the latter.

In the attempt to fix the parameters of Indigenous identity, Mexico's cultural elite applied the classificatory logics of race science to the cultural realm. They sought to create distinct identities in order to assign hierarchical roles more clearly within an extremely fluid cultural and racial landscape. Following Patrick Wolfe's assertion that "racializing practices seek to maintain population-specific modes of colonial domination through time," postrevolutionary cultural production fit neatly within the classificatory matrices that often undergird the settler colonial social order.[4]

The obsession with authenticity further proves this project's complicity with settler colonialism. As historian Jean O'Brien writes, the "penchant for Indian purity" reflected settler inability—or unwillingness—to imagine Native New Englanders as being adaptable and capable of coexisting in the modern world as justification for non-Native inheritance of Native land.[5] The idea that only those Indians who dressed and performed a certain way were "real" Indians laid the foundation for narratives of Native extinction, since relatively few actually conformed to those specific standards. In Mexico this manifested in the form of simultaneous lamentations over the loss of tradition and the appropriation of select symbols of a glorified Aztec past. Similarly, the narrowing boundaries of Indigenous authenticity meant that more people were seen as mestizo and fewer and fewer seen as Indigenous. In effect this engineered a state of extinction in the sense that Indigeneity was subverted and Mestizaje was fashioned as the natural heir to the future of the nation.

The centrality of women to this project was not incidental. Indigenous women had long been conceptualized as the intermediaries between Indigenous and European in part because the physical burden was on them to birth a new mestizo nation. The pornographic film *La campesina* made a spectacle of the sexual fetishization of Indigenous women and further normalized acts of rape and violence. While messages encouraging brief sexual trysts between Indigenous women and mestizo men were refracted throughout postrevolutionary popular culture, these encounters were meant only to be fleeting and for the express purpose of producing the new nation. In keeping, Indigenous motherhood was celebrated when, as with Luz Jiménez, it led to mestizo offspring but condemned if it threatened to reproduce Indigenous citizenry, as with María Bibiana Uribe's pregnancy and Francisco Leal's scandalous mural.

While popular understandings of what it meant to be an Indigenous woman became increasingly narrow, mestiza appropriation of Indigenous dress became increasingly more common. The *india bonita* trope that filled cinema screens, calendar art, and postcards alike allowed Mexicans to celebrate a romanticized version of their rural past and imagine just how good their mestizo futures could look. In doing so, film and other modern technologies helped advance the visual dialectics of settler colonialism by marking Indigenous women as being inherently located in camposcapes and sexually violable, while mestiza women were positioned as the nation's future.

Place was also paramount to this project. The construction of Indigenous peoples as being quintessentially rural and "old fashioned" elided the possibility that they could exist in modern, urban spaces and thereby fixed them as romanticized icons of the past. Ever fewer spaces were deemed appropriate for Indigenous life. As with Santa Anita and Xochimilco, Indigenous spaces within or near Mexico City were constructed as getaways that "modern" Mexicans and foreign tourists might visit in order to sate their desire for a romanticized past. But because Indigenous space and identity were so intricately connected in the postrevolutionary imaginary, the urbanization or modernization of a geographic locale could pose an immediate threat to the perceived authenticity of its Indigenous inhabitants. This pattern marked one of the many ways that abstract identity constructs were translated into actual dispossession and disenfranchisement, but not without Indigenous resistance. As in the case of Xochimilco, letter writing, petitions, and involvement in tourism and movie-making endeavors illustrate how Indigenous people strategically employed postrevolutionary discursive and visual tropes to protect the lands and waters that were rightfully theirs.

The new ways of viewing these nascent postrevolutionary identities were critical too. Photographers captured pageants and other events, then newspapers mass produced and circulated those images. New visual dialectics of race and gender were born. Filmmakers of the 1920s and 1930s established new ways to encode postrevolutionary values in their work and brought visual culture to life. In film there was an intimacy and a sense of truthfulness that photographs and postcards simply couldn't capture. *Cine folclórico* focused viewers' attention on surface-level sources of pleasure, while narratives condoning violence, Indigenous dispossession, and racial betterment through Mestizaje played out just beneath this polished surface.

Luz Jiménez's life stands as a testament to the sort of complex, nuanced existence Indigenous women had within the matrices of settler colonialism. In some ways she helped shape how Indigenous women were seen. At the same time, depictions of her often fell prey to the limiting stereotypes that were so widely employed at the time. Though Jiménez formed close bonds with some of the artists and intellectuals who reproduced her image, the terms of their relationships were still informed by the dictates of the settler colonial imaginary. In her case, too, it became evident that class worked alongside race and gender in structuring the hierarchies of power.

Just as these mechanisms of settler colonialism continue to play out in popular culture, so, too, have they been encoded into law. A series of constitutional reforms introduced beginning in 1992 formally recognized Mexico as having a "pluricultural composition with an Indigenous base."[6] By enshrining Mestizaje as the official Mexican identity, Indigeneity was relegated to a past "foundation" rather than an autonomous identity in its own right. And though the reforms guaranteed the right to self-determination, there was no institutional mechanism in place for Indigenous people to claim or benefit from that right.

The 1992 constitutional reforms were part of a broader move across Latin America to affirm cultural difference while sweeping in market-driven neoliberal policies that placed an especially heavy burden on Indigenous peoples and other marginalized groups. Under this neoliberal governance, nations projected the illusion of inclusivity through the selective allotment of rights and recognition while ultimately imposing hegemonic terms of engagement that consolidated power and further disenfranchised Indigenous peoples.[7] This, too, was settler colonialism at work.

As Shannon Speed argues, settler colonialism helped clear the path for capitalist encroachment throughout the hemispheres by establishing systems of dispossession and exploitation. Today, she argues, "the logics of the settler state conjunct with neoliberalism in the current moment in ways that generate ongoing violence and render Indigenous women particularly vulnerable."[8] In its current form, neoliberal settler colonialism benefits from the structures of race, gender, and class that were refined and mass produced during the post-revolutionary culture boom.

But despite centuries of erasure, displacement, exploitation, and disenfranchisement, reminders of Indigenous women's perseverance can be found everywhere in Mexico. They are engaging and disengaging with the tourism economy. They are running for president and other elected offices. They are starring in mainstream movies. They are leading movements, uprisings, and sit-ins. They are protesting the disappearance of their sons and husbands. They are creating, teaching, mothering, working, worshipping, reading, laughing, and dancing. They are also suffering rape, abduction, and murder. They are immigrating and they are staying put. And in all the complexity of Indigenous women's lives today, there is one thing that is undeniably true: They're still here. They're still here. *They're still here.*

NOTES

INTRODUCTION

1. "México elige su candidata a Miss Universo," *Telemetro*, April 22, 2009.

2. Ibid.

3. "Miss Mexico Is Crowned Miss Universe," *Telegraph*, August 24, 2010 (accessed October 2015), http://www.telegraph.co.uk/news/worldnews/northamerica/usa/7961274/Miss-Mexico-is-crowned-Miss-Universe.html.

4. "El presidente Calderón recibe en Los Pinos a la nueva Miss Universo," CNN.com, September 14, 2010 (accessed November 2018; no longer posted), http://mexico.cnn.com/entretenimiento/2010/09/14/el-presidente-calderon-recibe-en-los-pinos-a-la-nueva-miss-universo.

5. This book encompasses the decades following the Mexican revolution from the early 1920s through the late 1940s as well as some precedents and antecedents. Since these decades also include the waning years of revolutionary warfare and the regimes of revolutionary leaders who maintained power until 1946, some scholars argue that the revolution continued until 1946. While I agree there is merit to those arguments, the Cultural Revolution and era of nation building that followed the height of the armed conflict were distinct in many ways. For the purposes of clarity, I refer to this book's primary era of study as "postrevolutionary."

6. María Josefina Saldaña-Portillo, *Indian Given: Racial Geographies across Mexico and the United States*, (Durham, N.C.: Duke University Press, 2016), 27.

7. See Eric Hobsbawm and Terence Ranger, eds., *The Invention of Tradition*, Canto Classics (Cambridge: Cambridge University Press, 1983).

8.   Alexander Dawson, *Indian and Nation in Revolutionary Mexico* (Tucson: University of Arizona Press, 2004), 3.

9.   The term *Aztec* refers to Nahuatl-speaking peoples who historically inhabited the land on which Mexico City now sits. They more commonly refer to themselves as Mexica. Barbara E. Mundy, *Death of Aztec Tenochtitlan, the Life of Mexico City* (Austin: University of Texas Press, 2015), 2.

10.   Christina Bueno, "Excavating Identity: Archaeology and Nation in Mexico, 1876–1911" (PhD diss., University of California Davis, 2004), 34.

11.   Paul Vanderwood, "Betterment for Whom? The Reform Period, 1855–75," in *The Oxford History of Mexico*, ed. William Beezley and Michael C. Meyer (New York: Oxford University Press, 2010), 368.

12.   In particular, volume 1's section on Indigenous history written by Alfredo Chavero: "The Aztecs are the most important to our history, and they are the closest to us." As quoted in Christina Bueno, "Forjando Patrimonio: The Making of Archaeological Patrimony in Porfirian Mexico," *Hispanic American Historical Review* 90, no. 2 (2009): 215–45, 221.

13.   Bueno, 219.

14.   Mauricio Tenorio Trillo, *Mexico at the World's Fairs: Crafting a Modern Nation* (Berkeley: University of California Press, 1996), 81–95.

15.   Mary Kay Vaughn and Stephen Lewis, eds. *The Eagle and the Virgin: Nation and Cultural Revolution in Mexico, 1920–1940* (Durham, N.C.: Duke University Press, 2006), 8.

16.   Dawson, *Indian and Nation*, 7. Manuel Gamio, *Forjando Patria: Pro-Nacionalismo*, trans. Fernando Armstrong-Fumero (Boulder: University Press of Colorado, 2010), 7.

17.   Ricardo Pérez Montfort, *Estampas de nacionalismo popular mexicano: Diez ensayos sobre cultural popular y nacionalismo*, 2nd ed. (Mexico City: Centro de Investigaciones y Estudios Superiores en Antropología Social, 2003), 163.

18.   Pérez Montfort, 162.

19.   Edward Said, *Orientalism* (New York: Vintage Books, 1979).

20.   For example, Dawson claims that Indigenismo "departed from the exclusionary past, endeavored to empower Indians as individuals, and reflected a willingness to grant rights to those who were willing to assimilate." Dawson, *Indian and Nation*, 20.

21.   Saldaña-Portillo, *Indian Given*, 116.

22.   Kelly S. McDonough, *The Learned Ones: Nahua Intellectuals in Postconquest Mexico* (Tucson: University of Arizona Press, 2014), 126.

23.   Adriana Zavala, *Becoming Modern, Becoming Tradition: Women, Gender, and Representation in Mexican Art* (University Park: Pennsylvania State University Press, 2010), 159.

24.   Rick López, *Crafting Mexico: Intellectuals, Artisans, and the State after the Revolution* (Durham, N.C.: Duke University Press, 2010), 134.

25.   Dawson, *Indian and Nation*, 43.

26.   Dawson, 73.

27.   Dawson, 19.

28. The Casa del Estudiante Indigena, for example, was a boarding school in Mexico where Indigenous male students were educated and "civilized" (Dawson, 24).

29. Zavala, *Becoming Modern, Becoming Tradition*, 154.

30. Dawson, *Indian and Nation*, 21.

31. Diane Nelson, *A Finger in the Wound: Body Politics in Quincentennial Guatemala* (Berkeley: University of California Press, 1999), 221.

32. Jason Ruiz, *Americans in the Treasure House: Travel to Porfirian Mexico and the Cultural Politics of Empire* (Austin: University of Texas Press, 2014), 173.

33. As viewed from Mexico City, Tehuana women were also considered to have a certain cachet and sexual appeal, but they were seen as the exotic other more than viable components of the social project at hand.

34. This phrase was frequently used to describe living Nahuatl speakers in newspaper coverage of the India Bonita pageant. See, for example, Jacobo Dalevuelta, "María Bibiana Uribe de la Sierra de Puebla, proclamada la India Bonita de Mexico," *El Universal*, August 2, 1921.

35. Zavala argues that Tehuanas were "the most iconic rendition of the Mexican woman" during the postrevolutionary era, an assertion with which I respectfully disagree. Zavala, *Becoming Modern, Becoming Tradition*, 3.

36. This follows Diane Nelson's argument that "race is gendered and gender is raced in particular ways in Guatemala." Nelson, *Finger in the Wound*, 222.

37. Rosa Casanova, Alberto del Castillo Troncoso, Rebeca Monroy Nasr, and Alfonso Morales, *Imaginarios y fotografía en México, 1839–1970* (Madrid: Lunwerg Editores, 2005), 127.

38. Casanova et al., 124. See also John Mraz, *Looking for Mexico: Modern Visual Culture and National Identity* (Durham, D.C.: Duke University Press, 2009).

39. Visual economy following Deborah Poole's conceptualization of the term. Deborah Poole, *Vision, Race, and Modernity: A Visual Economy of the Andean Image World* (Princeton, N.J.: Princeton University Press, 1997), 8.

40. López, *Crafting Mexico*, 14–17. Here, López makes a compelling case that visual aesthetics were a core part of national identity formation in the aftermath of the Mexican Revolution.

41. López, 122.

42. Deborah Poole, "An Image of 'Our Indian': Type Photographs and Racial Sentiments in Oaxaca, 1920–1940," *Hispanic American Historical Review* 84, no. 1 (2004): 37–82.

43. Vaughn and Lewis, *Eagle and the Virgin*.

44. "El Sr. Ing. Félix F. Palavicini abandona la gerencia de 'El Universal,'" *El Universal*, April 3, 1923.

45. López, *Crafting Mexico*, 33.

46. Several chapters of this book trace *El Universal* and *El Universal Ilustrado* coverage more closely than that of other publications because I found it more instructive to follow the trajectory of the publication that had deliberately aligned itself with the interests of the revolution, rather than to do a broader, comparative study of postrevolutionary publications.

47. See, for example, Anne Rubenstein, "The War on Las Pelonas: Modern Women and Their Enemies, Mexico City, 1924," in *Sex in Revolution: Gender, Politics, and Power in Modern Mexico*, ed. Jocelyn H. Olcott, Mary Kay Vaughn, and Gabriela Cano (Durham, N.C.: Duke University Press, 2006); Joanne Hershfield, *Imagining* la chica moderna*: Women, Nation, and Visual Culture in Mexico, 1917–1936*, (Durham, N.C.: Duke University Press, 2008).

48. Zavala, *Becoming Modern, Becoming Tradition*.

49. Jean M. O'Brien, *Firsting and Lasting: Writing Indians out of Existence in New England* (Minneapolis: University of Minnesota Press, 2010), xxi–xxii; Shannon Speed, "Structures of Settler Capitalism in Abya Yala," *American Quarterly* 69, no. 4 (2017): 787.

50. Lisa Kahaleole Hall, "Navigating Our Own 'Sea of Islands': Remapping a Theoretical Space for Hawaiian Women and Indigenous Feminism," *Wicazo Sa Review* 24, no. 2 (2009), 21.

51. Ageeth Sluis coins the term *camposcape* to describe "a constellation of spatial imaginaries imbued with pastoral qualities rendered as timeless, static in geographic, physical, and human features." Ageeth Sluis, *Deco Body, Deco City: Female Spectacle and Modernity in Mexico City, 1900–1939* (Lincoln: University of Nebraska Press, 2016), 18.

52. Ardis Cameron, ed., *Looking for America: The Visual Production of Nation and People* (Malden, Mass.: Blackwell, 2005), 11.

53. Patrick Wolfe, "Settler Colonialism and the Elimination of the Native," *Journal of Genocide Research* 8, no. 4 (December 2006): 388.

54. Scott Morgensen, *Spaces between Us: Queer Settler Colonialism and Indigenous Decolonization*, (Minneapolis: University of Minnesota Press, 2011), 36.

55. "Settler Colonialism in Latin America" ed. M. Bianet Castellanos, special issue, *American Quarterly* 69, no. 4 (December 2017): 777–81; Maylei Blackwell, Floridalma Boj Lopez, and Luis Urrieta Jr., "Introduction," in "Critical Latinx Indigeneities," ed. Maylei Blackwell, Floridalma Boj Lopez, Luis Urrieta Jr., special issue, *Latino Studies* 15 (2017):126–37; M. Bianet Castellanos, Lourdes Gutiérrez Nájera, and Alturo J. Aldama, eds., *Comparative Indigeneities of the Américas: Toward a Hemispheric Approach* (Tucson: University of Arizona Press 2012); and Gabriela Spears Rico and Evelyn Nakano Glenn, "Settler Colonialism as Structure: A Framework for Comparative Studies of U.S. Race and Gender Formation," *Sociology of Race and Ethnicity* 1, no. 1 (2015): 52–72.

56. In *Traces of History: Elementary Structures of Race* (London: Verso Books, 2016), he illustrates how Brazilian history conforms to this model, but other works exclude the possibility.

57. In "Structures of Settler Capitalism," 786, Speed goes on to argue that concepts like "coloniality" and "internalized colonialism" aren't adequate theoretical frameworks because they assume that the settlers are now from the place they settled while settler colonialism provides a framework for understanding how that very idea of settler "from here-edness" is constructed.

58. Shannon Speed, "Indigenous Women Migrants: Embodying Transnational Settler Capitalist Vulnerability," conference presentation, Native American and Indigenous Studies Association, Los Angeles, May 17, 2018.

59. Speed, "Indigenous Women Migrants."

60. Scholars like Shannon Speed, Richard Gott, and Bianet Castellanos argue that in myriad ways, mestizos became settlers in Latin America after independence. M. Bianet Castellanos, introduction to "Settler Colonialism in Latin America," special issue, *American Quarterly* 69, no. 4 (December 2017), 778.

61. Shona N. Jackson, *Creole Indigeneity: Between Myth and Nation in the Caribbean* (Minneapolis: University of Minnesota Press, 2012), 3.

62. See Castellanos, introduction to "Settler Colonialism in Latin America," 778; Jackson, *Creole Indigeneity: Between Myth and Nation in the Caribbean* (Minneapolis: University of Minnesota Press, 2012); Saldaña-Portillo, *Indian Given*; Gabriela Spears-Rico, "Consuming the Native Other: Mestiza/o Melancholia and the Performance of Indigeneity in Michoacán" (PhD diss., University of California, Berkeley, 2015); and Speed, "Structures of Settler Capitalism," 783–90.

63. This logic follows the work of Patrick Wolfe, *Traces of History*, 4.

64. J. Kēhaulani Kauanui, "'A Structure, Not an Event': Settler Colonialism and Enduring Indigeneity," *Forum: Emergent Critical Analytics for Alternative Humanities* 5.1 (Spring 2016).

65. Maylei Blackwell, Floridalma Boj Lopez, and Luis Urrieta Jr., "Introduction," in "Critical Latinx Indigeneities," 126.

66. Speed, "Indigenous Women Migrants." Speed is also credited with positing that encomienda, repartimiento, and hacienda were systems of settler colonialism. Adam Warren is credited with the notion that casta paintings were part of this system as well, personal communication, May 2017.

67. Philip J. Deloria, *Playing Indian* (New Haven, Conn.: Yale University Press, 1998); *Indians in Unexpected Places* (Lawrence: University of Kansas, 2004); O'Brien, *Firsting and Lasting*.

68. Ruiz, *Americans in the Treasure House*.

69. Deloria, *Indians in Unexpected Places*, 9–11.

70. Poole, *Vision, Race, and Modernity*, 7.

71. Jennifer Jolly, *Creating Pátzcuaro, Creating Mexico: Art, Tourism, and Nation Building under Lázaro Cárdenas* (Austin: University of Texas Press, 2018), 12.

72. Jolly, *Creating Pátzcuaro, Creating Mexico*; Spears Rico, "Consuming the Native Other"; Poole, "An Image of 'Our Indian.'"

73. López, *Crafting Mexico*; Zavala, *Becoming Modern, Becoming Tradition*.

CHAPTER 1

1. These events are gleaned from newspaper headlines in *El Universal*, 1920.

2. "Cual es la india más bonita," *El Universal*, January 15, 1921.

3.   References to the Mexicana más Bella contest (1920) and the Obrera Simpatica contest (1918).

4.   Emilio Rabasa, "El problema del indio mexicano," *El Universal*, January 8, 1921.

5.   J. M. Puig Casauranc, "El indio americano y el de México," *El Universal*, January 10, 1921.

6.   "El Concurso de la India Bonita abarcara todo la república," *El Universal*, January 25, 1921.

7.   "El Concurso de la India Bonita abarcara todo la república," *El Universal*, January 26, 1921.

8.   "El Concurso de la India Bonita abarcara todo la república," *El Universal*, January 27, 1921.

9.   "El concurso de la india bonita," *El Universal*, January 28, 1921.

10.   "El concurso de la india bonita," *El Universal*, January 28, 1921.

11.   "El Concurso de la India Bonita," *El Universal*, February 1, 1921.

12.   "El Concurso de la India Bonita," *El Universal*, March 18, 1921.

13.   As Susie Porter shows in *Working Women in Mexico City: Public Discourses and Material Conditions, 1879–1931* (Tucson: University of Arizona Press, 1995), the decade-long revolutionary war had resulted in about two million casualties, severely depleting the men active in the labor pool. As a result, more of the burden of bringing money into a family fell on the shoulders of young women. Wartime destruction of crops and villages had driven many rural dwellers into urban centers and, as a result migratory labor became increasingly common among young Indigenous women.

14.   "El Concurso de la India Bonita," *El Universal*, April 22, 1921.

15.   "El Concurso de la India Bonita," *El Universal*, May 8, 1921.

16.   Term coined by Ageeth Sluis, *Deco Body, Deco City: Female Spectacle and Modernity in Mexico City, 1900–1939* (Lincoln: University of Nebraska Press, 2016).

17.   Fernando Mota, "Una charla con la mujer mas bella de México," *El Universal*, May 4, 1921.

18.   "Tipos de belleza," *El Universal*, March 20, 1920.

19.   Deborah Poole, "An Image of 'Our Indian': Type Photographs and Racial Sentiments in Oaxaca, 1920–1940," *Hispanic American Historical Review* 84, no. 1 (2004): 37–82.

20.   "El Concurso de la India Bonita," *El Universal*, March 1, 1921.

21.   "El Concurso de la India Bonita," *El Universal*, April 28 and May 27, 1921.

22.   "El Concurso de la India Bonita," *El Universal*, June 17, 1921.

23.   "El Concurso de la India Bonita," *El Universal*, April 16, 1921.

24.   "El Concurso de la India Bonita," *El Universal*, April 28, 1921.

25.   "El Concurso de la India Bonita," *El Universal*, March 21, 1921.

26.   "El Concurso de la India Bonita," *El Universal*, February 28, 1921.

27.   "El Concurso de la India Bonita," *El Universal*, March 25, 1921.

28.   "El Concurso de la India Bonita," *El Universal*, March 25, 1921.

29.   Aurelio de los Reyes, *Manuel Gamio y el cine* (Mexico City: Universidad Nacional Autónoma de México, Instituto de Investigaciones Estéticas, 1991).

30. Jacobo Dalevuelta, "La representante de la raza: La princesa de ojos de obsidian que reinara en las fiestas de septiembre," *El Universal*, August 2, 1921.

31. J. Sorel, "Porque triunfo María Bibiana," *El Universal*, August 4, 1921.

32. Manuel Gamio, "La raza indigena," *El Universal*, July 23, 1921.

33. Dalevuelta, "La representante de la raza."

34. López also notes the fact that the finalists conformed to a very narrow version of the Indigenous "authentic." López, *Crafting Mexico*, 40.

35. López, 40.

36. Dalevuelta, "Mi entrevista con la india bonita," *El Universal*, August 2, 1921.

37. Jacobo Dalevuelta, "María Bibiana Uribe de la Sierra de Puebla, proclamada la India Bonita de Mexico," *El Universal*, August 2, 1921.

38. Dalevuelta, "Mi entrevista con la india bonita," *El Universal*, August 2, 1921.

39. Dalevuelta, "Mi entrevista con la india bonita," *El Universal*, August 2, 1921.

40. Dalevuelta, "Mi entrevista con la india bonita," *El Universal*, August 2, 1921.

41. J. Sorel, "Porque triunfo María Bibiana," *El Universal*, August 4, 1921.

42. Adriana Zavala also discusses how the pageant "mobilized an 'economy of desire,' wherein the 'Indian' lower class, and in this case a particular Indigenous woman, were situated as objects of (sexual) consumption for middle- and upper-class men." Adriana Zavala, *Becoming Modern, Becoming Tradition: Women, Gender, and Representation in Mexican Art* (University Park: Pennsylvania State University Press, 2010), 182.

43. "D. Andres Fernandez y su distinguida esposa ofrecieron ayer una fiesta a la india bonita," *El Universal*, August 24, 1921.

44. "D. Andres Fernandez y su distinguida esposa ofrecieron ayer una fiesta a la india bonita," *El Universal*, August 24, 1921.

45. "D. Andres Fernandez y su distinguida esposa ofrecieron ayer una fiesta a la india bonita," *El Universal*, August 24, 1921.

46. "Lo que tiene en efectivo María Bibiana Uribe," *El Universal*, August 19, 1921.

47. "La gran fiesta de la india bonita en el colon," *El Universal*, August 25, 1921.

48. "Palavacini esta loco / Y perez Taylor no escribe / Por pensar a todas horas en María Bibiana Uribe," in "La gran fiesta de la india bonita en el colon," *El Universal*, August 25, 1921.

49. "La gran fiesta de la india bonita en el colon," *El Universal*, August 25, 1921. Note the rare instance of the more respectful *indígena* and the reference to beauty (*belleza*) instead of prettiness or racial characteristics.

50. "La gran fiesta de la india bonita en el colon," *El Universal*, August 25, 1921.

51. "La gran fiesta de la india bonita en el colon," *El Universal*, August 25, 1921.

52. López, *Crafting Mexico*, 47.

53. "Lo que tiene en efectivo María Bibiana Uribe," *El Universal*, August 19, 1921.

54. "La apoteosis de la india bonita: Historia del concurso en que triunfo María Bibiana Uribe," *El Universal*, September 25, 1921.

55. José Albuerne, "Belleza mexicana," *Revista de Revistas*, January 8, 1922.

56. "La india bonita," *El Informador*, August 18, 1921.

57.   "La india bonita," *El Informador*, August 18, 1921.

58.   "Los indigenas de Ixtacalco y Santa Anita Agasajaron ayer a María Bibiana Uribe," *El Universal*, September 11, 1921.

59.   See chapter 2. The Fiesta de Santa Anita, now the Flor Más Bella del Ejido pageant, has deep roots in the Santa Anita neighborhood and is sometimes conflated with the India Bonita contest.

60.   See chapter 2.

61.   "Los caracteres de raza de María Bibiana," *El Universal*, April 12, 1922.

62.   *Memorias de un mexicano*, directed by Silvio Toscano (1950), https://www.youtube .com/watch?v=g8bZt9QbesY.

63.   López, *Crafting Mexico*, 58.

64.   "En la suntuosa velada de anoche en el 'Iris' la india bonita lució su belleza y fue aclamada por la multitud que invadió el coliseo," *El Universal*, September 26, 1921.

65.   "En la suntuosa velada de anoche en el 'Iris' la india bonita lució su belleza y fue aclamada por la multitud que invadió el coliseo," *El Universal*, September 26, 1921.

66.   "La india bonita es una abnegada madre de familia," *Excelsior*, April 10, 1922.

67.   "La india bonita es una abnegada madre de familia," *Excelsior*, April 10, 1922.

68.   "La india bonita es una abnegada madre de familia," *Excelsior*, April 10, 1922.

69.   Ricardo Pérez Montfort, *Estampas de nacionalismo popular mexicano: Diez ensayos sobre cultural popular y nacionalismo*, 2nd ed. (Mexico City: Centro de Investigaciones y Estudios Superiores en Antropología Social, 2003), 162.

70.   "Vive de la renta de su capital Bibiana Uribe," *El Universal*, April 11, 1922.

71.   "Vive de la renta de su capital Bibiana Uribe," *El Universal*, April 11, 1922. *Mexicano* and *Nahuatl* are used interchangeably.

72.   "Los caracteres de raza de María Bibiana," *El Universal*, April 12, 1922.

73.   Manuel Gamio, "Condiciones fisicos-biologicos," in *La poblacion del Valle de Teotihuacan* (Mexico City: Imprenta de la Dirección de Estudios Geográficos y Climatologicos, 1924).

74.   Zavala, *Becoming Modern, Becoming Tradition*, 161.

75.   Zavala, 154.

CHAPTER 2

1.   Mary K. Coffey, *How a Revolutionary Art Became Official Culture: Murals, Museums, and the Mexican State* (Durham, N.C.: Duke University Press, 2012), 6.

2.   Noemí Quezada, *Amor y magia amorosa entre los Aztecas*, 3rd ed. (Mexico City: Universidad Nacional Autónoma de México, 1996), 39.

3.   Departamento del Distrito Federal, "Iztacalco 1992," Government, June 1992, Biblioteca Nacional de Antropologia e Historia, 18.

4.   Seth Dixon, "Mexico City's Indios Verdes: Exploring Cultural Processes Using Public Memorials," *Journal of Geography* 109, no. 2 (2010): 54–60.

5.   Anna M. Fernandez Poncela and Lilia Venegas Aguilera, *La Flor Más Bella Del Ejido* (Mexico City: INAH, 2002), 82.

6. Dixon, "Mexico City's Indios Verdes."

7. Dixon.

8. Fernandez Poncela and Venegas Aguilera, *La Flor Más Bella del Ejido*, 83.

9. Gleaned from the accounts of Luz Jiménez, who moved with her Nahua family and neighbors to Santa Anita after their home community succumbed to revolutionary violence.

10. "Dale vuelta" is a command to reverse or return to something.

11. Jacobo Dalevuelta, "De las antiguas fiestas de Santa Anita solo queda el recuerdo," *El Universal*, March 26, 1920.

12. Although it's not clear how long a beauty contest had been part of this post-conquest version of the festival, the tradition was very clearly in practice by the Revolutionary Era. The first documentation of this practice I encountered was in 1917. It's likely it predates that, but I haven't seen sources to verify.

13. Jacobo Dalevuelta, "La nota popular del Viernes de Dolores," *El Universal*, March 19, 1921.

14. "El Viernes Florido," *Revista de Revistas*, April 9, 1922.

15. "El Paseo de Santa Anita," *Revista de Revistas*, April 16, 1922.

16. Archivo Histórico del Distrito Federal (AHDF), Secretaria general, Gobernación, vol. 3935, exp. 389, fojas 20, año 1923. Although the document's author was not identified, it was probably composed by well-known artist and cultural savant Adolfo Best Maugard, who served as the head of the cultural commission responsible for the festival's revitalization. Jacobo Dalevuelta, no title, *El Universal*, March 24, 1923. Fernandez Poncela and Venegas Aguilera cite Arturo Saracho as the head of the Ayuntamiento de la Ciudad de Mexico's efforts to revitalize the pageant, saying he "led a commission of people who loved Mexican traditions." Fernandez Poncela and Venegas Aguilera, *La Flor Más Bella del Ejido*, 86.

17. AHDF, Secretaria general, Gobernación, vol. 3935, exp. 389, fojas 20, año 1923.

18. AHDF, Secretaria general, Gobernación, vol. 3935, exp. 389, fojas 20, año 1923.

19. AHDF, Secretaria general, Gobernación, vol. 3935, exp. 389, fojas 20, año 1923.

20. AHDF, Secretaria general, Gobernación, vol. 3935, exp. 389, fojas 20, año 1923, telegram from Secretary of Government Julio Jimenez Rueda to subsecretary Licenciado Gilberto Valenzuela.

21. Jacobo Dalevuelta, *El Universal*, March 24, 1923.

22. AHDF, Secretaria general, Gobernación, vol. 3935, exp. 389, fojas 20, año 1923

23. Jacobo Dalevuelta, *El Universal*, March 24, 1923.

24. "Srta. Carmen Aguilaera, electa reina de las flores que presidirá la fiesta popular de hoy en el paseo de la viga," *El Universal*, March 23, 1923.

25. Susie S. Porter, *Working Women in Mexico City: Public Discourses and Material Conditions, 1879–1931* (Tucson: University of Arizona Press, 2003).

26. Ageeth Sluis, *Deco Body, Deco City: Female Spectacle and Modernity in Mexico City, 1900–1939* (Lincoln: University of Nebraska Press, 2016), 13.

27. Fernandez Poncela and Venegas Aguilera, *La Flor Más Bella del Ejido*, 75.

28. Ibid. 80.

29. "Fiesta del Viernes de Dolores en Santa Anita," *El Universal*, April 12, 1924.

30. "Fiesta del Viernes de Dolores en Santa Anita," *El Universal*, April 12, 1924.

31. This identification was not new to the postrevolutionary era but rather had been circulating since the arrival of early French, American, and British travelers, as noted in Deborah Poole, "An Image of 'Our Indian': Type Photographs and Racial Sentiments in Oaxaca, 1920–1940," *Hispanic American Historical Review* 84, no. 1 (2004), 53.

32. Adriana Zavala, *Becoming Modern, Becoming Tradition: Women, Gender, and Representation in Mexican Art*, (University Park: Pennsylvania State University Press, 2010), 3.

33. "La resurrección de las tradicionales fiestas del Viernes de Dolores," *El Universal*, March 27, 1926.

34. Roshni Rustomji-Kerns, "Mirrha-Catarina de San Juan: From India to New Spain," *Amerasia Journal* 28, no. 2 (2002): 29–36.

35. "Fiesta del Viernes de Dolors en Santa Anita," *El Universal*, April 11, 1924.

36. Jacobo Dalevuelta, *El Universal*, March 24, 1923.

37. "Quienes fueron los premiados en los diversos concursos organizados," *El Universal*, April 9, 1927.

38. "Quienes fueron los premiados en los diversos concursos organizados," *El Universal*, April 9, 1927.

39. "Entusiasmo para celebrar el Viernes de Dolores," *El Universal*, March 28, 1928.

40. "Entusiasmo para celebrar el Viernes de Dolores," *El Universal*, March 28, 1928.

41. "Entusiasmo para celebrar el Viernes de Dolores," *El Universal*, March 28, 1928.

42. "Entusiasmo para celebrar el Viernes de Dolores," *El Universal*, March 28, 1928.

43. "Fiesta típica en el Canal de la Viga," *El Universal*, March 5, 1929. Note that this date contradicts the 1785 date quoted by Fernandez Poncela and Venegas Aguilera in *La Flor Más Bella del Ejido*. I have not found any evidence that clarifies which date is accurate.

44. "Trajes de la Virreina y el Virrey se Terminaron," *El Universal*, March 20, 1929.

45. Jacobo Dalevuelta, "Llena de color fue la Verbena de Dolores," *El Universal*, March 23, 1929.

46. Ibid.

47. J. M. Puig Casauranc, "El indio americano y el de México," *El Universal*, January 10, 1921.

48. "Las tradicionales fiestas de primavera, se iniciaron," *El Universal*, April 12, 1930.

49. "Las tradicionales fiestas de primavera, se iniciaron," *El Universal*, April 12, 1930.

50. Silvia Loyo had also won the Indigenous dress competition in 1927.

51. "Las Fiestas del Viernes de Dolores en Santa Anita," *El Universal*, March 19, 1931.

52. This may have been a result of the Great Depression or sanctions placed on religious celebrations.

53. "Las Fiestas del Viernes de Dolores muy lucidas," *El Universal*, April 8, 1933.

54. "Estuvo desanimada la Fiesta de las Flores," *El Universal*, March 24, 1934.

55. "Un concurso de chinas, de charros, y de trajineras," *El Universal*, March 17, 1934.

56. "Dos escenas de la fiesta de Amapolas, celebrada ayer en Santa Anita, que no tuvo el lucimento de otros años," *El Universal*, April 13, 1935.

57. "Candidatos a ser la 'Flor Más Bella del Ejido,'" *El Universal*, April 3, 1936.

58. Ibid.

59. "La 'Flor Más Bell del Ejido,' Srita. Ernestina Díaz, de Ixtacalco," *El Universal*, April 4, 1936.

60. Fernandez Poncela and Venegas Aguilera, *La Flor Más Bella del Ejido*, 88–89. The authors cite Cordero Espinosa, saying that these changes were made in 1935, but that contradicts evidence I found in newspaper archives.

61. "Esplendor de las Fiestas de Santa Anita," *El Universal*, March 6, 1937.

62. "La gran fiesta popular del día 19 en Sta. Anita concursos florales," *El Universal*, March 17, 1937.

63. "El paseo de Sta. Anita se vió ayer muy concurrido . . . Eleccion de la reina del ejido," *El Universal*, March 20, 1937.

64. "El paseo de Sta. Anita se vió ayer muy concurrido . . . Eleccion de la reina del ejido," *El Universal*, March 20, 1937.

65. Rosario Robles Berlanga, *Mujeres de Xochimilco* (Mexico City: Gobierno del Distrito Federal, 2000), 47–46.

66. Hernandez is likely referring to a *tocochimitl*.

67. Robles Berlanga, *Mujeres de Xochimilco*, 47.

68. Robles Berlanga, *Mujeres de Xochimilco*, 47.

69. Luciano Kubli, "Se solicita un representante del museo nacional para el jurado calificador del concurso que se indica," March 15, 1939.

70. Kubli.

71. Kubli.

72. Luciano Kubli, "Su Oficio #180 Exp. VIII-3/003.1/-8 de fecha 24 del actual," March 29, 1939, Museo Nacional de Antropologia Archivo Historico.

73. Luciano Kubli, "Convocatoria para la designacion de la 'Flor Más Bella del Ejido' y del 'Nino Campesino más Sano,'" March 1939, Museo Nacional de Antropologia Archivo Historico.

74. Robles Berlanga, *Mujeres de Xochimilco* 49.

75. Ibid.

76. Ibid., 50.

77. Ann Blum. *Domestic Economies: Family, Work, and Welfare in Mexico City, 1884–1943* (Lincoln: University of Nebraska Press, 2009), 127.

78. Fernandez Poncela and Venegas Aguilera, *La Flor Más Bella del Ejido*, 90.

79. Seth Dixon, "Mexico City's Indios Verdes: Exploring Cultural Processes Using Public Memorials." *Journal of Geography* 109, no. 2 (2010), 54–60.

80. Departamento del Distrito Federal, "Iztacalco 1992," government report, June 1992, Biblioteca Nacional de Antropología e Historia, 36.

81. Ibid.

82. María Eugenia Terrones López, *A la orilla del agua: Política, urbanización y medio ambiente; Historia de Xochimilco en el siglo XX* (Mexico City: Instituto Mora, 2004).

83. Fernandez Poncela and Venegas Aguilera, *La Flor Más Bella del Ejido*, 91.

84. Eric Hobsbawm and Terrence Ranger, eds., *The Invention of Tradition*, Canto Classics (Cambridge: Cambridge University Press, 1983), 1.

85. Hobsbawm and Ranger, 9. The authors established three main types of invented tradition: ones that create social cohesion, ones that legitimize institutions, and ones that are primarily concerned with socialization. The invented *fiesta de Santa Anita* traditions fit into all three of these categories.

86. Ardis Cameron, "Sleuthing Towards America: Visual Detection in Everyday Life," in *Looking for America: The Visual Production of Nation and People*, ed. Ardis Cameron (Malden, Mass.: Blackwell, 2005), 27.

87. bell hooks, *We Real Cool: Black Men and Masculinity* (New York, Routledge, 2004).

88. "Fiesta de la Flor Más Bella del Ejido 2014, Edición CCXXIX: Convocatoria," poster published by Delegación Xochimilco, 2014.

89. Fernandez Poncela and Venegas Aguilera, *La Flor Más Bella del Ejido*.

90. Natasha Pizzey-Siegert and James Fredrick, "Somos mujeres morenas, bajitas pero eso no significa que no seamos bellas," *BBC Mundo*, April 6, 2018, http://www.bbc.com/mundo/media-43673735.

CHAPTER 3

1. Antonio Helú, *La india bonita* (Mexico City: Aztla Films, 1938). Amelia M. Kiddle, "Cabaretistas and Indias Bonitas: Gender and Representations of Mexico in the Americas during the Cárdenas Era," *Journal of Latin American Studies* 42, no. 2 (May 2010): 263–91.

2. Kiddle.

3. Laura Mulvey, "Visual Pleasure and Narrative Cinema," in *Film Theory and Criticism: Introductory Readings*, ed. Leo Braudy and Marshall Cohen (New York: Oxford University Press, 2009), 712.

4. This follows an argument made by Philip Deloria about performance of Native American identity in U.S. popular culture in *Playing Indian* (New Haven, Conn.: Yale University Press, 1998), 190.

5. Nahua-inspired dress was the most popular, but the formula also included other iconic Indigenous types like the Tehuana.

6. Ageeth Sluis, *Deco Body, Deco City: Female Spectacle and Modernity in Mexico City, 1900–1939* (Lincoln: University of Nebraska Press, 2016), 18.

7. Ageeth Sluis, "City of Spectacles: Gender Performance, Revolutionary Reform, and the Creation of Public Space in Mexico City, 1915–1939" (PhD diss., University of Arizona, 2006), 28.

8. Ricardo Pérez Montfort, *Estampas de nacionalismo popular mexicano: Diez ensayos sobre cultura popular y nacionalismo*, 2nd ed. (Mexico City: Centro de Investigaciones y Estudios Superiores en Antropología Social, 2003), 166.

9. José Vasconcelos, *La raza cósmica: Misión de la raza iberoamericana; Notas de viajes a la América de Sur* (Madrid: Agencia Mundial de Librería, 1925).

10. Anne Rubenstein, "Theaters of Masculinity," in *Masculinity and Sexuality in Modern Mexico*, ed. Víctor M. Macías-González and Anne Rubenstein (Albuquerque: University of New Mexico Press, 2012), 143. In fact, concerns about the immoral acts that might be performed in dark theaters resulted in the creation of ordinances requiring that green lights be installed throughout theaters (Macías-Gonzalez and Rubenstein, 137).

11. Ageeth Sluis, "Projecting Pornography and Mapping Modernity in Mexico City." *Journal of Urban History* 38, no. 3 (2012): 476.

12. Anne Rubenstein, unpublished book chapter draft shared with author via personal correspondence, February 8, 2018.

13. Ibid.

14. Aurelio de los Reyes, *Manuel Gamio y el cine* (Mexico City: Universidad Nacional Autónoma de México, Instituto de Investigciones Estéticas, 1991), 89.

15. Ibid.

16. Manuel Gamio, *La población del valle de Teotihuacán* (Mexico City: Secretary of Public Education, 1922).

17. Campos went on to serve as the head of the Department of Folklore and a judge of the 1937 Flor más Bella del Ejido pageant.

18. John Fullerton, "Creating an Audience for the Cinématographe: Two Lumière Agents in Mexico, 1896." *Film History* 20, no. 1 (2008): 95–114.

19. I have not found any documentation of Indigenous viewing experiences from this time period, so this is based purely on contemporary writing about what it's like for Indigenous people to encounter such portrayals.

20. Mary Louise Pratt, *Imperial Eyes: Travel Writing and Transculturation*, 2nd ed. (New York: Routledge, 2007).

21. Ernesto Vollrath, *En la hacienda* (Mexico City: Estudios Camus, 1921).

22. de los Reyes, *Manual Gamio y el cine*, 225.

23. A zarzuela is a type of theater performance featuring song and dance.

24. Pérez Montfort, *Estampas de nacionalismo popular mexicano*, 167.

25. Bill Hart, "Las próximas peliculas nacionales," *El Universal Ilustrado*, September 9, 1921.

26. *Revista de Revistas*, February 12, 1922.

27. Aristripo, "La nueva película nacional 'En la Hacienda,'" *Revista de Revistas*, January 22, 1922.

28. Hart, "Las próximas peliculas nacionales."

29. Masha Salazkina, *In Excess: Sergei Eisenstein's Mexico* (Chicago: University of Chicago Press, 2009), 29.

30. Salazkina.

31. Adolfo Fernández de Bustamante, "Los indios del Señor Eisenstein," *El Universal Ilustrado*, June 23, 1931.

32. Grigory Alexandrov, introduction to *Que viva México*, directed by Sergei Eisenstein (1979).

33. *Tehuana*, Artes de México 49 (Mexico City: Artes de México, 2000).

34. Adolfo Fernández de Bustamante, "Eisenstein, El Magnífico," *El Universal Ilustrado*, June 11, 1931.

35. Ibid.

36. Roland Barthes, "The Face of Garbo," in *Film Theory and Criticism: Introductory Readings*, ed. Leo Braudy and Marshall Cohen (New York: Oxford University Press, 2009), 471.

37. This was a signature way in which Eisenstein constructed meaning in film, creating "a sense of meaning [that] is not proper to the images themselves but derived exclusively from their juxtaposition." André Bazin, "The Evolution of the Language of Cinema," in *Film Theory and Criticism: Introductory Readings*, ed. Leo Braudy and Marshall Cohen (New York: Oxford University Press, 2009), 44.

38. Adolfo Fernández de Bustamante, "Eisenstein, El Magnífico," *El Universal Ilustrado*, June 11, 1931.

39. Barthes, "The Face of Garbo," 473.

40. Salazkina, *In Excess*, 22.

41. Joanne Hershfield, "Screening the Nation," in *The Eagle and the Virgin: Nation and Cultural Revolution in Mexico, 1920–1940*, ed. Mary Kay Vaughn and Stephen Lewis (Durham, N.C.: Duke University Press, 2006), 259–78. Andrea Noble, *Mexican National Cinema* (London: Routledge, 2005), 133.

42. Mulvey, "Visual Pleasure and Narrative Cinema," 719.

43. Hershfield, "Screening the Nation," 264.

44. Hershfield, 265.

45. Sluis, "City of Spectacles," 87.

46. Sluis, 267.

47. Tom Gunning, "An Aesthetic of Astonishment: Early Film and the (In)credulous Spectator," in *Film Theory and Criticism: Introductory Readings*, ed. Leo Braudy and Marshall Cohen (New York: Oxford University Press, 2009), 743.

48. The uneven power dynamic in hacendado-Indigenous love suggest that consent was questionable and violence or coercion likely.

49. *The Man from Utah*, directed by Robert Bradbury (Lone Star Productions, 1934).

50. Analysis of the several hundred entries to the India Bonita pageant illustrated that these words were frequently used to describe contestants in the original contest. See chapter 1.

51. Julia Tuñón, "Femininity, 'Indigenismo,' and Nation: Film Representation by Emilio 'El Indio' Fernández," in *Sex in Revolution: Gender, Politics, and Power in Modern Mexico*, ed. Jocelyn Olcott, Mary Kay Vaughn, and Gabriela Cano (Durham, N.C.: Duke University Press, 2006), 92.

52. Tom Gunning, "The Cinema of Attraction: Early Film, Its Spectator and the Avant-Garde," in *Film and Theory: An Anthology*, ed. Robert Stam and Toby Miller (Malden, Mass.: Blackwell, 2000), 64–66.

53. Jane Desmond, *Staging Tourism: Bodies on Display from Waikiki to Sea World* (Chicago: University of Chicago Press, 1999), xiv.

54. Mulvey, "Visual Pleasure and Narrative Cinema," 271.

55. Kiddle, "Cabaretistas and Indias Bonitas," 267–68.

56. H. T. S., "At the Teatro Latino," *New York Times*, April 15, 1939.

57. Mexico's first sound film, *Santa*, was produced in 1931, but it's possible that silent film technology would have still been used for lower budget movies like *La campesina* well into the decade.

58. By comparison, it wasn't until the 1970s that U.S.-produced pornographic films started to be inflected with such narrative arcs. Jennifer C. Nash, *The Black Body in Ecstasy: Reading Race, Reading Pornography* (Durham, N.C.: Duke University Press, 2014), 63.

59. Anne Rubenstein first suggested this possibility in email correspondence with the author, February 7, 2018.

60. Sluis, *Deco Body, Deco City*.

61. Ibid., 18.

62. Anne Rubenstein, unpublished book chapter draft shared with author via personal correspondence, February 8, 2018. Rubenstein's citation: Archivo Plutarco Elías Calles, Fondo PEC, Exp. 38: Peliculas, Leg. 1/2, Inv. 4381. (Junio-Agosto 1928.)

63. "Pornography, then, celebrates male dominance, it eroticizes sexual assault, it glamorizes female subordination, and it 'sexualizes women's inequality'—quite simply, it is the linchpin of male control over female bodies." Nash, *Black Body in Ecstasy*, 9–10.

64. Julia Tuñón, "Femininity, 'Indigenismo,' and Nation," 85.

65. Rick López, *Crafting Mexico: Intellectuals, Artisans, and the State after the Revolution* (Durham, N.C.: Duke University Press, 2010), 9–12.

CHAPTER 4

1. María Eugenia Terrones López, *A la orilla del agua: Política, urbanización y medio ambiente; Historia de Xochimilco en el siglo XX* (Instituto Mora, 2004), 169–170.

2. *Xochimilco*, Artes de México 20 (Mexico City: Artes de Mexico, 2008).

3. Terrones López, *A la orilla del agua*, 168.

4. Jeffrey M. Bannister and Stephanie G. Widdifield "The Debut of 'Modern Water' in Early 20th Centruy Mexico City: The Xochimilco Potable Waterworks." *Journal of Historical Geography* 46 (2014): 39.

5. Alejandro Ortiz, "Xochimilco y sus mujeres," in *Mujeres de Xochimilco*, ed. Estafania Chávez Barragán and Carol de Swan (Mexico City: Gobierno del Distrito Federal, Delegación Xochimilco, 2000), 28.

6. Matthew Vitz, *A City on a Lake: Urban Political Ecology and the Growth of Mexico City* (Durham, N.C.: Duke University Press, 2018), 72.

7. Vitz, 94–100.

8. Vitz, 114–15, 138.

9.   Terrones López, *A la orilla del agua*, 56.

10.   José Manuel Puig Casauranc, *Atlas general del Distrito Federal (1929)*, 2nd ed.(Mexico City: Grupo Condumex, 1991), 110.

11.   Puig Casauranc, 243.

12.   Dina Berger, *The Development of Mexico's Tourism Industry: Pyramids by Day, Martinis by Night* (New York: Palgrave Macmillan, 2006), 3.

13.   Andrea Boardman, *Destination México: "A Foreign Land a Step Away"; U.S. Tourism to Mexico, 1880s to 1950s* (Dallas, Tex.: DeGoyler Library, Southern Methodist University, 2001), 84.

14.   Boardman, 69.

15.   Terrones López, *A la orilla del agua*, 60.

16.   Rafael García Granados, *Xochimilco: 75 Illustraciones* (Mexico City: Talleres Gráficos de la Nación, 1934).

17.   Terrones López, *A la orilla del agua*.

18.   In 1940, DDF spent 852,407.18 pesos on Xochimilco (out of a total of 2,987,786.16 spent on small public works in all twelve of the delegations), Terrones López, *A la orilla del agua*, 35.

19.   Terrones López, *A la orilla del agua*, 69.

20.   Hershfield, *Imagining* la chica moderna*: Women, Nation, and Visual Culture in Mexico, 1917–1936*, (Durham, N.C.: Duke University Press, 2008), 143.

21.   Angela Villalba, *Mexican Calendar Girls* (San Francisco: Chronicle Books, 2006), 54–55.

22.   Although the poster is dated circa 1910–1959, it is stylistically aligned with other work produced in the 1930s and 1940s. "Mexico. Xochimilco," poster (Mexico: Asociación Mexicana de Turismo [printed at offset galas]), https://ark.digitalcommonwealth.org/ark:/50959/5999n380s.

23.   Ernest M. Hunt, "Old Mexico Trip, 1940," https://www.texasarchive.org/2010_02120?b=0.

24.   Alexis Celeste Bunten, "Indigenous Tourism: The Paradox of Gaze and Resistance," *La ricera folklorica: Indigenous Tourism, Performance, and Cross-Cultural Understanding in the Pacific*, no. 61 (2010): 51.

25.   Vitz, *A City on a Lake*, 150.

26.   Damián Flores, "La 'Venecia Mexicana' está perdiendo su originalidad," *El Nacional*, January 14, 1944.

27.   An original script of the film contains a scene that includes a type of airplane that very clearly positioned the film in the 1940s, so it was originally written to be a contemporary view of the region. Emilio Fernández, *María Candelaria* (Mexico City: Filmes Mundiales, 1943).

28.   Linda B. Hall, *Dolores del Río: Beauty in Light and Shade* (Stanford, Calif.: Stanford University Press, 2013), 257.

29.   "Dolores del Río, Madrina," *El Universal*, January 16, 1944.

30.   "Las calcomanias de 'María Candelaria': Los choferes estan de suerte y desde hoy el fotógrafo de la suerte les ayudara," *El Universal*, January 18, 1944.

31. "Cuando María Candelaria va a pedirle a Dios que dejen libre a su Lorenzo Rafael," *El Universal*, January 18, 1944.

32. "Las ilusiones de los dos enamorados están cifradas en una pequeña marranita," *El Universal*, January 19, 1944.

33. Hall, *Dolores del Río*, 219–20.

34. Francisco Gaytan Fernández, *Historias recuperadas: El rescate* (Mexico City: Filmoteca UNAM, 2004).

35. Andrea Noble, *Mexican National Cinema* (London: Routledge, 2005), 79.

36. A July 2015 tour of his home, for example, revealed an impressive collection of Aztec statuary and symbols but no relics of his Kikapu heritage.

37. The original title of the film was *Xochimilco*; the final version retained this title in parenthesis beneath the final title in the film's opening credits. Hall, *Dolores del Río*, 217.

38. Hall, 264.

39. Joanne Hershfield, *Mexican Cinema/Mexican Woman, 1940–1950* (Tucson: University of Arizona Press, 1996).

40. Emilio "El Indio" Fernández, interview by Julia Tuñon, August 8, 1980, transcript, 7.

41. Fernández, interview, 27.

42. Fernández, interview, 62–63.

43. Fernández, interview, 281.

44. Fernández, interview, 280.

45. Fernández, interview, 279.

46. Salvador Piñeda, "El alma fragrante y misteriosa de Xochimilco," *Revista de Revistas*, March 5, 1944.

47. "10,000 personas en el fiesta de Xochimilco," *El Universal*, April 1, 1955.

48. Pierre Nora, "Between Memory and History: Les lieux de mémoire," *Representations*, no. 26 (1989): 17–24.

49. Frances Toor, *Frances Toor's Motorist Guide to Mexico* (Mexico City, 1938), 132.

50. Diane Nelson, *A Finger in the Wound: Body Politics in Quincentennial Guatemala* (Berkeley: University of California Press, 1999), 131.

51. Gabriela Spears-Rico, "Consuming the Native Other: Mestiza/o Melancholia and the Performance of Indigeneity in Michoacán" (PhD diss., University of California, Berkeley, 2015). Spears-Rico credits anthropologist Alexis Bunten for the concept of "commodified persona." Alexis Celeste Bunten, "Sharing Culture or Selling Out? Developing the Commodified Persona in the Heritage Industry," *American Ethnologist* 35, no. 3 (2008): 380–95.

CHAPTER 5

1. Jesús Villanueva Hérnandez, "Tecualnezyolehua: La que sublima cosas bellas a la gente," in *Luz Jiménez, símbolo de un pueblo milenario 1897–1965* (Mexico City, Instituto Nacional de Bellas Artes y Literatura, 2000), 26.

2.   Merry MacMasters, "Luz Jiménez es 'la mujer más pintada de México,' sostiene Blanca Garduño," *La Jornada* (Mexico City), November 24, 1999.

3.   Frances Karttunen, *Between Worlds: Interpreters, Guides, and Survivors* (New Brunswick, N.J.: Rutgers University Press, 1996), 198. "When Charlot and his family were in Mexico City in the mid-1940s, Luz showed Charlot's wife how she and her family had once lived in Mexico City in packing boxes."

4.   Luz Jiménez as quoted in Fernando Horcasitas, ed., *Life and Death in Milpa Alta: A Nahuatl Chronicle of Díaz and Zapata* (Norman: University of Oklahoma Press, 1972), 33.

5.   Horcasitas, 99.

6.   Maruxa Villalta, "Modelo de Rivera," *El Universal* (Mexico City), May 10, 1961.

7.   Kelly S. McDonough, *The Learned Ones: Nahua Intellectuals in Postconquest Mexico* (Tucson: University of Arizona Press, 2014), 129.

8.   Horcasitas, *Life and Death in Milpa Alta*, 125.

9.   Jesús Villanueva Hérnandez (grandson of Luz Jiménez and family historian) interview with the author, June 2017.

10. See chapter 2. Jiménez's victory in this pageant is noted in the tribute penned by Anita Brenner, who ahistorically refers to the pre-1920s event as the Flor más Bella del Ejido pageant, and is part of family lore about Jiménez. I was unable to find newspaper evidence of this victory, but it is possible that it simply wasn't recorded.

11. Villanueva Hérnandez, "Tecualnezyolehua."

12. Villanueva Hérnandez.

13. Erik Camayd-Freixas and José Eduardo González, eds., *Primitivism and Identity in Latin America: Essays on Art, Literature, and Culture*, 2nd ed. (Tucson: University of Arizona Press, 2000), xiii.

14. Villanueve Hérnandez, interview.

15. John Charlot, "Jean Charlot and Luz Jiménez," *Crónicas*, no. 13 (2010): 6–30, 10.

16. Also known as "Camapento de un coronel Zapatista," or "Zapatistas at Rest."

17. Karttunen, *Between Worlds*, 201.

18. Mary K. Coffey, *How a Revolutionary Art Became Official Culture: Murals, Museums, and the Mexican State* (Durham, N.C.: Duke University Press, 2012), 9.

19. Villanueva Hernández, interview, and Fernando Leal Audirac (son of Fernando Leal, the painter) in discussion with the author, March 2018.

20. Villanueva Hernández, interview, and Fernando Leal Audirac (son of Fernando Leal, the painter) in discussion with the author, March 2018.

21. Karttunen, *Between Worlds*, 44.

22. Karttunen, 44.

23. Alma Lilia Roura Fuentes, *Olor a tierra en los muros* (Mexico City: Instituto Nacional de Bellas Artes y Literatura, 2012), 162. According to Roura Fuentes, Luz modeled for five of the ten female figures in this mural, representing wisdom, faith, tradition, justice, and fable. *Luz Jiménez, símbolo de un pueblo milenario 1897–1965*, 146. Luz appears in six murals: *La maestra rural, La cosecha del maíz, El reparto de la tierra, Mítines 1 de Mayo, El tianguis,* and *Viernes de Dolores en al Canal de Santa Anita.*

24.   "Revelan obra sobre modelo de Rivera," *El Vigia*, February 22, 2012. https://www
.elvigia.net/espectaculos/2012/2/22/revelan-obra-sobre-modelo-rivera-72728.html.

25.   Villalta, "Modelo de Rivera."

26.   Villanueva Hernández, interview.

27.   Many of these artifacts are preserved to this day in the Jean Charlot Collection,
University of Hawaiʻi at Mānoa Library.

28.   Charlot, "Jean Charlot and Luz Jiménez," 10.

29.   Jean Charlot quoted in McDonough, *The Learned Ones*, 132.

30.   Charlot, "Jean Charlot and Luz Jiménez," 16–17.

31.   Charlot, 27.

32.   Anita Brenner, *Avant-Garde Art and Artists in Mexico: Anita Brenner's Journals of
the Roaring Twenties*, ed. Susannah Joel Glusker (Austin: University of Texas Press,
2010), 15.

33.   Charlot, "Jean Charlot and Luz Jiménez," 18.

34.   Charlot, 18.

35.   Auerelio de los Reyes, *Manuel Gamio y el cine* (Mexico City: Universidad Nacional
Autónoma de México, Instituto de Investigaciones Estéticas, 1991), 72.

36.   Jesús Villanueva Hernández states that this is the first nude of a Mexican Indigenous woman.

37.   Villanueva Hernández, interview.

38.   See chapter 3.

39.   Karttunen, *Between Worlds*, 5. According to Frances Karttunen, Edward Weston
writes in his published Mexico City diaries that his household had young Indigenous maids and that "he used them sexually and grew irritated with them when
they became emotionally dependent. Nor did he have any scruples about pilfering
their savings to pay his utility bills."

40.   Coffey, *How a Revolutionary Art Became Official Culture*, 7–8.

41.   Fernando Leal, personal correspondence, "Chalma Notes," unpublished document
emailed to author, March 2018, 27.

42.   Leal, 27.

43.   "Siempre me pintaron vestida." Villalta, "Modelo de Rivera."

44.   Jesús Villanueva Hernández, *Una Luz en Milpa Alta* (2012), DVD.

45.   I haven't found any documentation indicating how much she was paid to model
during this phase of her life or whether modeling in the nude earned Luz more
money than other types of modeling. However, given that she continued to live
in poverty and had to hold other jobs simultaneously, it's clear that her modeling
income was not substantial.

46.   Luz Jiménez letter to Jean Charlot, undated, but context places it in 1942.

47.   Margaret Park Redfield, "A Child Is Born in Tepoztlan," *Mexican Folkways* 4
(1928): 102–8. Although the author references an informant, it does not make
clear whether Luz was interviewed for the article or whether she just modeled
for it.

48.   Villanueva Hernández, interview.

49. John Charlot, email to Frances Karttunen, March, 18, 2006, and Villanueva Hérnandez, interview.

50. Luz Jiménez, letter to Jean Charlot, March 2, 1942.

51. Villanueva Hernández, interview.

52. Luz Jiménez, letter to Jean Charlot, n.d., but clear from context that it was sent in 1942.

53. *Luz Jiménez: Símbolo de un pueblo milenario 1897–1965* (Mexico City: Instituto Nacional de Bellas Artes y Literatura, 2000), 161.

54. Luz Jiménez, letter to Jefe de Departamento de Maestros Rurales, Secretaria de Educación Pública, May 20, 1936.

55. Luz Jiménez, letter to Jefe de Departamento de Maestros Rurales, Secretaria de Educación Pública, August 1, 1936.

56. Joaquin Jara Díaz (Jefe del Departamento de Eseñanza Primaria y Normal), letter to Luz Jiménez, May 20, 1936.

57. McDonough, *The Learned Ones*, 134.

58. Luz kept receipts for much of the scholarly work she was paid to do, and much of this has been preserved in her family archive. No records of royalty payments are included in this archive.

59. Luz Jiménez, letter to Jean Charlot, October 11, 1942.

60. Luz Jiménez, letter to Jean Charlot, August 1, 1942.

61. Gleaned from the archive of letters from Luz Jiménez to Jean Charlot held at the University of Hawaii's Charlot Collection.

62. Luz Jiménez, letter to Jean Charlot, November 11, 1942.

63. Nicolas Cano, letter, July 11, 1942.

64. Luz Jiménez, letter to Jean Charlot, April 20, 1948.

65. Kelly McDonough explores this topic in much greater detail in *The Learned Ones*.

66. Villanueva Hérnandez, interview.

67. Ibid.

68. Ibid.

69. Jesús Villanueva Hérnandez, "Doña Luz: Inspiration and Image of a National Culture," *Voices of Mexico* 41 (1997): 19–24, 23.

70. Susie S. Porter, *Working Women in Mexico City: Public Discourses and Material Conditions, 1879–1931,* (Tucson: University of Arizona Press, 2003), xiii.

71. Evidenced by correspondence and records held in the Fondo Documental y fotográfico Luz Jiménez.

72. Luz Jiménez, letter to Jean Charlot, January 13, 1962.

73. According to Villanueva Hernández and my own searches, footage from this interview no longer exists.

74. Villanueva Hérnandez, interview.

75. Concepción (Concha) Hernández, letter to Jean Charlot, February 13, 1965.

76. Luz Jiménez, letter to Jean Charlot, May 29, 1963.

77. Luz Jiménez, letter to Jean Charlot, February 13, 1965.

78.   "Atropellada Pareció la que fuera modelo de Rivera, Orozco, y Siqueiros," *El Excélsior*, January 25, 1965.

79.   "Luz: Her Legend," *Mexico This Month* (March 10, 1965), 12–13. No author attribution but Jean Charlot credits Anita Brenner in Charlot, "Jean Charlot and Luz Jiménez," no page number.

CONCLUSION

1.   Temporary exhibit at the Museo Nacional de Antropologia, *La flor en la cultura mexicana* (2018).

2.   Jonathan Watts, "Mexico City's Water Crisis—From Source to Sewer," *Guardian*, November 12, 2015, http://www.theguardian.com/cities/2015/nov/12/mexico-city-water-crisis-source-sewer.

3.   Diego Cevallos, "Mazahuas Choose Jail over Going without Water," Inter Press Service, December 30, 2006, http://www.ipsnews.net/2006/12/mexico-mazahuas-choose-jail-over-going-without-water/. Teresa Montaño, "Protesta de mazahuas deja sin agua a seis millones," *El Universal*, December 14, 2006, http://archivo.eluniversal.com.mx/primera/28115.html.

4.   Patrick Wolfe, *Traces of History: Elementary Structures of Race* (London: Verso Books, 2016), 10.

5.   Jean M. O'Brien, *Firsting and Lasting: Writing Indians out of Existence in New England* (Minneapolis: University of Minnesota Press, 2010), xxii.

6.   Constitución Política de los Estados Unidos Mexicanos, Secretaría de Gobernación, http://www.ordenjuridico.gob.mx/Constitucion/articulos.php.

7.   Charles R. Hale, *Más que un indio: Racial Ambivalence and Neoliberal Multiculturalism in Guatemala* (Santa Fe, N.Mex.: School of American Research Press, 2006), 34.

8.   Shannon Speed, Native American and Indigenous Studies Association presentation, Los Angeles, May 2018.

BIBLIOGRAPHY

Anderson, Benedict. *Imagined Communities: Reflections on the Origin and Spread of Nationalism*. 2nd ed. New York: Verso Books, 2006.

Bannister, Jeffrey M., and Stephanie G. Widdifield. "The Debut of 'Modern Water' in Early 20th Centruy Mexico City: The Xochimilco Potable Waterworks." *Journal of Historical Geography* 46 (2014): 36–52.

Barthes, Roland. "The Face of Garbo." In *Film Theory and Criticism: Introductory Readings*, edited by Leo Braudy and Marshall Cohen, 471–73. New York: Oxford University Press, 2009.

Bazin, André. "The Evolution of the Language of Cinema." In *Film Theory and Criticism: Introductory Readings*, edited by Leo Braudy and Marshall Cohen, 41–53. New York: Oxford University Press, 2009.

Berger, Dina. *The Development of Mexico's Tourism Industry: Pyramids by Day, Martinis by Night*. New York: Palgrave Macmillan, 2006.

Blum, Ann. *Domestic Economies: Family, Work, and Welfare in Mexico City, 1884–1943*. Lincoln: University of Nebraska Press, 2009.

Boardman, Andrea. *Destination México: "A Foreign Land a Step Away"; U.S. Tourism to Mexico, 1880s to 1950s*. Dallas, Tex.: DeGoyler Library, Southern Methodist University, 2001.

Bueno, Christina. "Excavating Identity: Archaeology and Nation in Mexico, 1876–1911." PhD diss., University of California Davis, 2004.

Bunten, Alexis Celeste. "Indigenous Tourism: The Paradox of Gaze and Resistance." *La ricera folklorica: Indigenous Tourism, Performance, and Cross-Cultural Understanding in the Pacific*, no. 61 (2010): 51–59.

Brenner, Anita. *Avant-Garde Art and Artists in Mexico: Anita Brenner's Journals of the Roaring Twenties*, edited by Susannah Joel Glusker. Austin: University of Texas Press, 2010.

Camayd-Freixas, Erik, and José Eduardo González, eds. *Primitivism and Identity in Latin America: Essays on Art, Literature, and Culture*. 2nd ed. Tucson: University of Arizona Press, 2000.

Cameron, Ardis, ed. *Looking for America: The Visual Production of Nation and People*. Malden, Mass.: Blackwell, 2005.

Casanova, Rosa, Alberto del Castillo Troncoso, Rebeca Monroy Nasr, and Alfonso Morales. *Imaginarios y fotografía en México, 1839–1970*. Madrid: Lunwerg Editores, 2005.

Castellanos, M. Bianet. Introduction to "Settler Colonialism in Latin America." Special issue, *American Quarterly* 69, no. 4 (December 2017): 777–81.

Coffey, Mary K. *How a Revolutionary Art Became Official Culture: Murals, Museums, and the Mexican State*. Durham, N.C.: Duke University Press, 2012.

Dawson, Alexander. *Indian and Nation in Revolutionary Mexico*. Tucson: University of Arizona Press, 2004.

Deloria, Philip J. *Indians in Unexpected Places*. Lawrence: University of Kansas, 2004.

Deloria, Philip J. *Playing Indian*. New Haven, Conn: Yale University Press, 1998.

de los Reyes, Auerelio. *Manuel Gamio y el cine*. Mexico City: Universidad Nacional Autónoma de México, Instituto de Investigaciones Estéticas, 1991.

Desmond, Jane. *Staging Tourism: Bodies on Display from Waikiki to Sea World*. Chicago: University of Chicago Press, 1999.

Dixon, Seth. "Mexico City's Indios Verdes: Exploring Cultural Processes Using Public Memorials." *Journal of Geography* 109, no. 2 (2010): 54–60.

Fernandez Poncela, Anna M., and Lilia Venegas Aguilera. *La Flor Más Bella del Ejido*. Mexico City: INAH, 2002.

Fuentes, Alma Lilia Roura. *Olor a tierra en los muros*. Mexico City: Instituto Nacional de Bellas Artes y Literatura, 2012.

Fullerton, John. "Creating an Audience for the Cinématographe: Two Lumière Agents in Mexico, 1896." *Film History* 20, no. 1 (2008): 95–114.

Gamio, Manuel. *Forjando Patria: Pro-Nacionalismo*. Translated by Fernando Armstrong-Fumero. Boulder: University Press of Colorado, 2010.

Glusker, Susannah Joel, ed. *Avant-Garde Art and Artists in Mexico: Anita Brenner's Journals of the Roaring Twenties*. Austin: University of Texas Press, 2010.

Gunning, Tom. "An Aesthetic of Astonishment: Early Film and the (In)credulous Spectator." In *Film Theory and Criticism: Introductory Readings*, edited by Leo Braudy and Marshall Cohen, 736–50. London: Oxford University Press, 2009.

Hale, Charles R. *Más que un indio: Racial Ambivalence and Neoliberal Multiculturalism in Guatemala*. Santa Fe, N.Mex.: School of American Research Press, 2006.

Hall, Linda B. *Dolores del Río: Beauty in Light and Shade*. Stanford, Calif.: Stanford University Press, 2013.

Hershfield, Joanne. *Imagining la chica moderna: Women, Nation, and Visual Culture in Mexico, 1917–1936*. Durham, N.C.: Duke University Press, 2008.

Hershfield, Joanne. *Mexican Cinema/Mexican Woman, 1940–1950.* Tucson: University of Arizona Press, 1996.

Hobsbawm, Eric, and Terence Ranger, eds. *The Invention of Tradition.* Canto Classics. Cambridge: Cambridge University Press, 1983.

hooks, bell. *We Real Cool: Black Men and Masculinity.* New York: Routledge, 2004.

Jackson, Shona N. *Creole Indigeneity: Between Myth and Nation in the Caribbean.* Minneapolis: University of Minnesota Press, 2012.

Jolly, Jennifer. *Creating Pátzcuaro, Creating Mexico: Art, Tourism, and Nation Building under Lázaro Cárdenas.* Austin: University of Texas Press, 2018.

Joseph, Gilbert, Ann Rubenstein, and Eric Zolov, eds. *Fragments of a Golden Age: The Politics of Culture in Mexico Since 1940.* Durham, N.C.: Duke University Press, 2001.

Kahaleole Hall, Lisa. "Navigating Our Own 'Sea of Islands': Remapping a Theoretical Space for Hawaiian Women and Indigenous Feminism." *Wicazo Sa Review* 24, no. 2 (2009): 15–28.

Karttunen, Frances. *Between Worlds: Interpreters, Guides, and Survivors.* New Brunswick, N.J.: Rutgers University Press, 1996.

Kauanui, J. Kēhaulani. "'A Structure, Not an Event': Settler Colonialism and Enduring Indigeneity," *Forum: Emergent Critical Analytics for Alternative Humanities* 5.1 (Spring 2016).

Kelly, Larissa. "Waking the Gods: Archaeology and State Power in Porfirian Mexico." PhD diss., University of California, Berkeley, 2011.

Kiddle, Amelia M. "Cabaretistas and Indias Bonitas: Gender and Representations of Mexico in the Americas during the Cárdenas Era." *Journal of Latin American Studies* 42, no. 2 (2010): 263–91.

López, Rick. *Crafting Mexico: Intellectuals, Artisans, and the State after the Revolution.* Durham, N.C.: Duke University Press, 2010.

McDonough, Kelly S. *The Learned Ones: Nahua Intellectuals in Postconquest Mexico.* Tucson: University of Arizona Press, 2014.

Morgensen, Scott. *The Spaces between Us: Queer Settler Colonialism and Indigenous Decolonization.* Minneapolis: University of Minnesota Press, 2011.

Moreno Figueroa, Mónica G. and Megan Rivers-Moore. "Beauty, Race, and Feminist Theory in Latin America and the Caribbean." *Feminist Theory* 14, no. 2 (2013): 131–36.

Mraz, John. *Looking for Mexico: Modern Visual Culture and National Identity.* Durham, N.C.: Duke University Press, 2009.

Mulvey, Laura. "Visual Pleasure and Narrative Cinema." In *Film Theory and Criticism: Introductory Readings,* edited by Leo Braudy and Marshall Cohen, 711–22. New York: Oxford University Press, 2009.

Mundy, Barbara E. *Death of Aztec Tenochtitlan, the Life of Mexico City.* Austin: University of Texas Press, 2015.

Nakano Glenn, Evelyn. "Settler Colonialism as Structure: A Framework for Comparative Studies of U.S. Race and Gender Formation." *Sociology of Race and Ethnicity* 1, no. 1 (2015): 52–72.

Nash, Jennifer C. *The Black Body in Ecstasy: Reading Race, Reading Pornography.* Durham, N.C.: Duke University Press, 2014.

Nelson, Diane. *A Finger in the Wound: Body Politics in Quincentennial Guatemala.* Berkeley: University of California Press, 1999.

Noble, Andrea. *Mexican National Cinema.* London: Routledge, 2005.

Nora, Pierre. "Between Memory and History: Les lieux de mémoire." *Representations,* no. 26 (1989): 17–24.

O'Brien, Jean M. *Firsting and Lasting: Writing Indians out of Existence in New England.* Minneapolis: University of Minnesota Press, 2010.

Olcott, Jocelyn H., Mary Kay Vaughn, and Gabriela Cano, eds. *Sex in Revolution: Gender, Politics, and Power in Modern Mexico.* Durham, N.C.: Duke University Press, 2006.

Ortiz, Alejandro. "Xochimilco y sus mujeres." In *Mujeres de Xochimilco,* edited by Estafania Chávez Barragán and Carol de Swan, 21–30. Mexico City: Gobierno del Distrito Federal, Delegación Xochimilco, 2000.

Pérez Montfort, Ricardo. *Estampas de nacionalismo popular mexicano: Diez ensayos sobre cultural popular y nacionalismo.* 2nd ed. Mexico City: Centro de Investigacionces y Estudios Superiores en Antropología Social, 2003.

Poole, Deborah. "An Image of 'Our Indian': Type Photographs and Racial Sentiments in Oaxaca, 1920–1940." *Hispanic American Historical Review* 84, no. 1 (2004): 37–82.

Poole, Deborah. *Vision, Race, and Modernity: A Visual Economy of the Andean Image World.* Princeton, N.J.: Princeton University Press, 1995.

Porter, Susie S. *Working Women in Mexico City: Public Discourses and Material Conditions, 1879–1931.* Tucson: University of Arizona Press, 2003.

Pratt, Mary Louise. *Imperial Eyes: Travel Writing and Transculturation.* 2nd ed. New York: Routledge, 2007.

Quezada, Noemí. *Amor y magia amorosa entre los Aztecas.* 3rd ed. Mexico City: Universidad Nacional Autónoma de México, 1996.

Robles Berlanga, Rosario. *Mujeres de Xochimilco.* Mexico City: Gobierno del Distrito Federal, 2000.

Rubenstein, Ann. "Theaters of Masculinity." In *Masculinity and Sexuality in Modern Mexico,* edited by Víctor M. Macías-González and Ann Rubenstein, 132–56. Albuquerque: University of New Mexico Press, 2012.

Ruiz, Jason. *Americans in the Treasure House: Travel to Porfirian Mexico and the Cultural Politics of Empire.* Austin: University of Texas Press, 2014.

Rustomji-Kerns, Roshni. "Mirrha-Catarina de San Juan: From India to New Spain." *Amerasia Journal* 28, no. 2 (2002): 29–36.

Said, Edward. *Orientalism.* New York: Vintage Books, 1979.

Salazkina, Masha. *In Excess: Sergei Eisenstein's Mexico.* Chicago: University of Chicago Press, 2009.

Saldaña-Portillo, María Josefina. *Indian Given: Racial Geographies across Mexico and the United States.* Durham, N.C.: Duke University Press, 2016.

Sluis, Ageeth. *Deco Body, Deco City: Female Spectacle and Modernity in Mexico City, 1900–1939.* Lincoln: University of Nebraska Press, 2016.

Sluis, Ageeth. "Projecting Pornography and Mapping Modernity in Mexico City." *Journal of Urban History* 38, no. 3 (2012): 467–87.

Spears-Rico, Gabriela. "Consuming the Native Other: Mestiza/o Melancholia and the Performance of Indigeneity in Michoacán." PhD diss., University of California, Berkeley, 2015.

Speed, Shannon. "Structures of Settler Capitalism in Abya Yala." *American Quarterly* 69, no. 4 (2017): 783–90.

Tenorio Trillo, Mauricio. *Mexico at the World's Fairs: Crafting a Modern Nation.* Berkeley: University of California Press, 1996.

Terrones López, María Eugenia. *A la orilla del agua: Política, urbanización y medio ambiente; Historia de Xochimilco en el siglo XX.* Mexico City: Instituto Mora, 2004.

Tuñón, Julia. "Femininity, 'Indigenismo,' and Nation: Film Representation by Emilio 'El Indio' Fernández." In *Sex in Revolution: Gender, Politics, and Power in Modern Mexico,* edited by Jocelyn Olcott, Mary Kay Vaughn, and Gabriela Cano, 81–96. Durham, N.C.: Duke University Press, 2006.

Vanderwood, Paul. "Betterment for Whom? The Reform Period, 1855–75." In *The Oxford History of Mexico,* edited by William Beezley and Michael C. Meyer, 349–72. New York: Oxford University Press, 2010.

Vaughn, Mary Kay, and Stephen Lewis, eds. *The Eagle and the Virgin: Nation and Cultural Revolution in Mexico, 1920–1940.* Durham, N.C.: Duke University Press, 2006.

Vasconcelos, José. *La raza cósmica: Misión de la raza iberoamericana; Notas de viajes a la América de Sur.* Madrid: Agencia Mundial de Librería, 1925.

Villalba, Angela. *Mexican Calendar Girls.* San Francisco: Chronicle Books, 2006.

Villanueva Hérnandez, Jesús. "Doña Luz: Inspiration and Image of a National Culture," *Voices of Mexico* 41 (1997): 19–24.

Villanueva Hérnandez, Jesús. "Tecualnezyolehua: La Que Sublima Cosas Bellas a la Gente." In *Luz Jiménez, símbolo de un pueblo milenario 1897–1965,* 133–44. Mexico City: Instituto Nacional de Bellas Artes y Literatura, 2000.

Vitz, Matthew. *A City on a Lake: Urban Political Ecology and the Growth of Mexico City.* Durham, N.C.: Duke University Press, 2018.

Wolfe, Patrick. *Traces of History: Elementary Structures of Race.* London: Verso Books, 2016.

Wolfe, Patrick. "Settler Colonialism and the Elimination of the Native." *Journal of Genocide Research* 8, no. 4 (December 2006): 387–409.

Zavala, Adriana. *Becoming Modern, Becoming Tradition: Women, Gender, and Representation in Mexican Art.* University Park: Pennsylvania State University Press, 2010.

INDEX

Note: Page references in *italics* refer to illustrative matter.

agricultural pageantry, 65, 67. *See also* chinampas; La Flor Más Bella del Ejido pageant

Alemán, Miguel, 73

Allá en el rancho grande (film), 87

Alma Tehuana (Demetrio), 147

Alonso, Leonor, 68

anthropology, 6–7, 33. *See also* Gamio, Manuel; Museo Nacional de Antropología

Arriaga, José P., 40

Asociación Mexicana de Turismo, *106*, 107

assimilation, 6–10, 15, 25, 34, 48, 121, 140, 154n20. *See also* Indigenous erasure; settler colonialism

El automóvil gris (film), 82

Avila de la Canal, Ramón, 126

Azarte, Aurora, 31–32

Aztec civilization, 154n9, 154n12

Aztec nationalism, 5–7, 10, 15–16, 31, 34, 35, 51–53, 148–49. *See also* Indigenous authenticity; Indigenous erasure

Barlow, Robert, 138, 139

beauty pageants. *See* La Flor Más Bella del Ejido pageant; India Bonita pageant; Indigenous femininity; Miss Universe pageant (2010)

Bibiana Uribe, María: authenticity of, 33, 43–47; as pageant winner, 34–35; portraits and recognition of, 36–43; sexuality of, 35–36, 150

Blackwell, Maylei, 17

Brehme, Hugo, 11, 100

Brenner, Anita, 129, 138–39, 144, 170n10

Bustamante, Adolfo Fernández de, 84–85

Cajigal, Vicente Estrada, 77

Calderón, Felipe, 4

Camacho, Manuel Ávila, 110

Cameron, Ardis, 14

La campesina (film), 92–97, 149–50. *See also* cine folclórico

campesina trope, 65, 67–72

Campillo, Anita, 88

Campos, Rubén M., 70

camposcape, 14, 94–95, 156n51

Canal de la Viga, Mexico City, 51–52

Cárdenas, Lázaro, 8, 67, 72, 87, 91, 103–5

Carpio Pavón, Itzel, 76

Carranza, Venustiano, 12, 125

Castellanos, Bianet, 157n60

Castillo, Gudelia, 29

Charlot, Jean, 128–29, 130, 136, 170n3

Chavero, Alfredo, 154n12

chicas modernas, 55. See also *india bonita* trope

chinampas: agricultural production in, 75, 104; destruction of, 110, 117, 119; as idyllic, 27, 99, 101

chinas poblanas trope, 12, *108*; in festivals and pageants, 55–58, 60–61, 65–68, 74; in film, 78, 87, 90. See also *india bonita* trope

cine folclórico, 21, 97–98, 151; by anthropologist Gamio, 80–81; *La campesina* (film), 92–97, 149–50; *La india bonita* (film), 77, 88–92; *María Candelaria*, 21–22, 111–20, 168n27; national industry of, 91; on nationhood, 78–79; "playing Indian" on, 81–82, 92; *Que viva México!*, 21, 82–87; viewing experience of, 79–80, 165n10, 165n19

clothing as Indigenous marker. See *traje*

Coffey, Mary, 131

comedia ranchera film genre, 87

Condesa (community), 134

Conesa, María, 38, *39*, 40, 82

Cultural Revolution (1920–1946), 4, 5, 24, 50, 84, 153n5, 158n13

Dalevuelta, Jacobo: as name, 36, 161n10; on negative Indigenous behaviors, 59; on pageant winner, 33, 34; on Viernes de Dolores festival, 52, 54, 61–63. See also *El Universal* and *El Universal Ilustrado*

Dawson, Alexander, 7, 154n20

DDF (Departamento del Distrito Federal), 62, 65, 102–3

Deloria, Philip, 13, 17, 18, 164n4

del Río, Dolores, 111–17, 145

Día del Ejido festival, 67

Díaz, Ernestina, 66–67

Díaz, Joaquin Jara, 138

Díaz, Porfirio. *See* Porfiriato

Díaz de Léon, Francisco, 126

Dirección General de Acción Cívica (DGAC), 65–66, 73–74

disease, 24, 51

displacement, 44, 45, 125, 137, 161n9. *See also* migration and women's work

education, 8, 37, 72, 124–25, 137, 155n28

Eisenstein, Sergei, 21, *85*. See also *Que viva México!* (film)

Enciso, Jorge, 33

En la hacienda (film), 81–82, *83*

Estrella, Natalia, 26–27

Excélsior, 44–47, 142, 144

femininity. *See* Indigenous femininity

Fernández, Andres, 37

Fernández, Emilio "El Indio," 113, 169n36. See also *María Candelaria* (film)

Fernández Urbina, José María, 122, *123*, 134

Fiesta de Amapolas, 66

Fiesta de Flores, 56–60. *See also* Viernes de Dolores festival

Fiestas de Chalma (film), 81, 130

Las Fiestas del Viernes de Dolores. *See* Viernes de Dolores festival

Figueroa, Gabriel, 116

filmmaking, 11–12, 100, 109. See also *cine folclórico*; *María Candelaria* (film)

Fischer, Paul, 100

Flores, Damián, 110–11

La Flor Más Bella del Ejido pageant, 20–21, 50, 66–75, 120, 125, 161n12, 161n16. *See also* Viernes de Dolores festival

Folkways, 135

El fuente de los cántaros (statue), 122, *123*, *134*

Gamio, Manuel, 7, 9, 20, 33–35, 46, 80–81, 130

García, Concepción, 29–30

Garduño, Emma, 26

Gauguin, Paul, 126

Glusker, Susannah, 144

González, Carlos, 61

González Carrasco, Aurelio, 33, 36

Gott, Richard, 16, 157n60

Guerrero, Ignacia, 38

Guzmán, Amada, 38

Henle, Fritz, 99

Hérnandez, Domitila, 31

Hernández, Petra, 68, 69, 70

Herrán, Saturnino, 100

Hershfield, Joanne, 116

Hispanismo, 62

Hobsbawm, Eric, 73
Hollywood films, 82, 88–89. See also *cine folclórico*
hooks, bell, 75
Horcasitas, Fernando, 125, 138
Hunt, Ernest M., 109

El Imparcial, 51
La india bonita (film), 77, 88–91. See also *cine folclórico*
India Bonita pageant: contest winner of, 34–36; first contest of, 24–34; on Indigenous authenticity, 31–32, 35, 44–47; recognition and prizes for, 29–30, 36–44. See also *El Universal* and *El Universal Ilustrado*
India Bonita Panameña, 77, 91
india bonita trope, 12–15, 57–58, 78–79, 105–9, 120–21. See also *cine folclórico*; La Flor Más Bella del Ejido pageant; India Bonita pageant
Indian, as term, 5
"Indian Problem," 5–10, 25, 124, 148. *See also* Indigenous erasure
Indigenous authenticity: beauty pageants on, 20–21, 31–32, 35–36, 44–47, 50, 56–60, 66–76; *cine folclórico* and, 82; Dawson on, 154n20; development of, 7–9, 14–15, 18–19; Museo Nacional and, 62–63, 69, 146–47. *See also* Aztec nationalism; Mestizaje; *Mexicanidad*; purity, as concept; *traje*
Indigenous dress. See *traje*
Indigenous erasure: beauty pageants and, 3–4; in *cine folclórico*, 87–98; *india bonita* and, 12–15, 30; of Jiménez, 122–24, 133–34, 144–45; from Mexican constitution, 5; museum exhibit and, 146–48; through settler colonialism, 15–20, 111; vanishing Indian trope, 42, 110, 133, 135, by Vasconcelos, 8. *See also* assimilation; Aztec nationalism; Indigenous authenticity; Mestizaje
Indigenous femininity: in *cine folclórico*, 94–95; elevation and exploitation of, 3–4, 9–10; Fiesta de Flores and, 56–59; ideal of, 3–4, 9–10; *india bonita* trope on, 12–15, 24–26, 31–32. *See also* India Bonita pageant; Jiménez, Luz; sexuality

Indigenous masculinity, 59, 69
Indios Verdes (statues), 51, 72–73, 75
El Informador, 42
Ixtacalco (community), 43

Jackson, Shona, 16
Jamaica (community), 68
Jiménez, Concha, 127, 128, 134–37, 140, 143
Jiménez, Luz, 144–45; as cultural teacher, 128–29, 138–39; death of, 143–44; impoverishment and work by, 135–42, 171n45; modeling work by, 86, 125–28, 130–34, 171n23, 171n45; as mother, 134–35, 137; personal life of, 122–25, 161n9, 170n3, 170n10
Jiménez, Petra, 38
Jiménez Rueda, Julio, 53–54
Jolly, Jennifer, 19
Juarez, Benito, 6

Kahlo, Frida, 99, 100, 101, 117, 127, 145
Karttunen, Frances, 124
Kauanui, J. Kēhaulani, 17
Kubli, Luciano, 59, 69, 75

land-grant laws, 7–8
Leal, Fernando, 126, 131–32, 150
Lerdo de Tejada, Miguel, 44
Lombardo Toledano, Vicente, 60
Lopez, Floridalma Boj, 17
López, Rick, 8, 11, 43, 155n40
Loyo, Alicia, 63
Loyo, Silvia, 59, 63
Lozano, Manuel Rodríguez, 140–41

Machada, Xavier, 146–47
Madero, Francisco, 51–52
Maguard, Adolfo Best, 84
María Candelaria (film), 21–22, 111–20, 168n27, 169n37
masculinity. *See* Indigenous masculinity
Maximiliano (emperor), 5–6
Mayan culture and women, 3–4
Mayer, Franz, 100
McDonough, Kelly, 8, 124
M. de Fernández, Esperanza, 37

media technology, emergence and innovations in, 10–12, 80, 81, 167n58. *See also cine folclórico*

Memorias de un Mexicano (film), 43

Mestizaje, 4, 8–10, 16, 115, 133, 135, 148–49. *See also* Indigenous authenticity

"Mexicana" (musical revue), 91

Mexicana Más Bella contest, 30

Mexicanidad, 4, 21, 54, 58, 67, 74–75. *See also* Indigenous authenticity; Mestizaje

México a través de los siglos, 6

Mexico This Month (publication), 144

migration and women's work, 28, 158n13. *See also* displacement

Milpa Alta, 124–25, 129–30

Miss Universe pageant (2010), 3–4, 17

Moctezuma. *See* Aztec nationalism

Modotti, Tina, 86, 122, 135

Morreno, Matiana, 27

Mujeres que trabajan (television show), 142

Mulvey, Laura, 91

murals, 49–50, 55, 76, 131–32, 171n23

Museo Nacional de Antropología, 62–63, 69, 139, 146–47. *See also* anthropology

El Nacional, 110–11

Nahua culture and women, 10, 33, 91, 128–29, 134–35, 138–39, 145

Nahuatl language, 6, 35, 44, 125, 154n9, 155n34. *See also* Aztec nationalism

national cinema, 87–92. See also *cine folclórico*

Navarette, Ximena, 3–4

Newman, Stanley, 139

New York Times, 42, 91

nudity, 130–34, 171n36

Nuestra Belleza de México contest, 4

Obregón, Álvaro, 38, 56, 102

Obrera Simpática pageant, 54

O'Brien, Jean, 14, 17, 149

O'Higgins, Pablo, 128, 130

Orozco, José Clemente, 22, 122, 131, *132*, 142, 144

Orquesta Típica del Centenario, 44

Ortega, Carlos M., 33

Palato, Eleuteria, 32

Palavicini, Félix, 12, 38

Palma, María, 70–72

Panama City, Panama, 77

Paseo de la Reforma, Mexico City, 51

patrias chicas, 19

Pérez Taylor, Rafael, 33, 37, 38

Peru, 126

photography, 10–12, 28–29, 100

La Pintura al Aire Libre de Chimalistac, 125–26

La población del valle de Teotihuacán (film), 80

Poole, Deborah, 18, 19

Porfiriato, 5, 6, 51, 60, 101, 124–25

pornographic films, 92–97, 149–50, 167n59, 167n64. See also *cine folclórico*

Porter, Susie, 158n13

Posada, José Guadalupe, 100

Puig Casauranc, José Manuel, 8, 25–26, 103

purity, as concept, 100, 109–11, 149. *See also* Indigenous authenticity

Quetzalcóatl (film), 81

Que viva México! (film), 21, 82–87

Quielva, Virginia, 31

Rabasa, Emilio, 25

racial and ethnic categorization, 5, 8, 14, 19, 31

Ramírez de Aguilar, Fernando. *See* Dalevuelta, Jacobo

Rangel, Nicolas, 60

Ranger, Terrence, 73

la raza cósmica, as concept, 8, 79

Revista de Revistas, 42, 52

revolutionary violence, 5, 101–2, 125, 158n13

Rivera, Diego: on del Río, 115; influence of, 49, 56, 84, 86; Jiménez and, 122, 127–28, 137; works by, 49, 55, 127, 135, 171n23; Xochimilco and, 100

Rivera Marín, Guadalupe, 127

Romero, Evangelina, 120

Rubio, Dario, 60

Sabogal, José, 126

Saldaña-Portillo, María Josefina, 4, 7–8, 16, 17
San Antonio Abad (community), 43
Sánchez Valenzuela, Elena, 82, *83*
Santa (film), 87, 167n58
Santa Anita Zacatlamanco (community), 43, 50–51, 72–73, 75, 150, 160n59
settler colonialism, 15–20, 34, 111, 129, 149, 156n57. *See also* assimilation
sexuality, 35–36, 149–50, 155n33, 159n42. *See also* Indigenous femininity
sexual violence, 93–97, 125, 131, 150, 152, 165n10, 171n39
Sierra, Justo, 8
Siqueiros, David Alfaro, 84
Sluis, Ageeth, 14, 30, 79, 156n51
Solórzano, Guadalupe, 142
Spears-Rico, Gabriela, 16, 19, 121
Speed, Shannon, 14, 16, 17, 151, 156n57, 157n60

Teatro Colón, 37–38, 40
Tehauna women, 10, 12, 56–57, 147, 155n33, 155n35
Tlahuac (community), 102
Tlahuicole (film), 81
Toor, Frances, 130, 135, 138
Toscano, Silvio, 43
tourism, 18, 101, 102–8, 119, 121
traditional, as term, 18
"traditional zone" protection laws, 105
traje, 10, 31–32, 35, 40, 44–45, 49, 57, 62–63, 146–48. *See also* Indigenous authenticity

United States, 8, 14, 18, 25, 75, 103–4
El Universal and *El Universal Ilustrado*, 12, 54, 57, 84, 85, 155n46. *See also* India Bonita pageant
Universidad de las Américas, 143, 144
Urrieta, Luis, Jr., 17
Urzais, Matilde, 63, *64*

vanishing Indian trope, 42, 110, 133, 135
Vasconcelos, José, 8, 11, 49, 130, 146
"La Venecia Mexicana." *See* Xochimilco
Viernes de Dolores festival, 51–65. *See also* La Flor Más Bella del Ejido pageant

Viernes de la Primavera festival, 51–53
Villanueva Hernández, Jesús, 124, 126, 130, 133, 137, 139–40
Villista movement, 101
violence. *See* revolutionary violence; sexual violence
visual economy, 10–12, 18, 155n40, 159n42
Vitz, Matthew, 101
viuda de Bandala, Carmen F., 31
Viveros, Guadalupe, 27
Vollrath, Ernesto, 81–82

Waite, C. B., 100
water access, 21–22, 99–100, 101–2, 148. *See also* chinampas
Weston, Edward, 122, 130–31, 171n39
Whorf, Benjamin Lee, 130, 138
Wolfe, Patrick, 15, 16, 17, 149

Xochimilco, 21–22, 120–21; pageant in, 73, 76; purity and authenticity of, 27, 99–101, 105–11; tourism in, 102–8, 119, 150; warfare in, 101–2. See also *María Candelaria* (film)

Zapatista movement, 101, 125
Zavala, Adriana, 13, 124, 155n35, 159n42

ABOUT THE AUTHOR

NATASHA VARNER (PhD) is a writer and historian whose work focuses on race, identity, and settler colonialism in Mexico and the United States. She is the recipient of the 2017 Lewis Hanke postdoctoral research award presented by the Conference on Latin American History. In addition to traditional academic pursuits, she is a public scholar who has written for Public Radio International and Jacobin, among other outlets.